AFRICA IN WORLD POLITICS

Also by Ralph I. Onwuka

AFRICA AND THE NEW INTERNATIONAL ECONOMIC ORDER (*with O. Aluko*)
AFRICAN DEVELOPMENT (*with O. Abegunrin and D. Ghista*)
DEVELOPMENT AND INTEGRATION IN WEST AFRICA
THE FUTURE OF REGIONALISM IN AFRICA (*with A. Sesay*)

Also by Timothy M. Shaw

AFRICA PROJECTED (*editor with Olajide Aluko*)
CONFRONTATION AND LIBERATION IN SOUTHERN AFRICA (*co-editor*)
COPING WITH AFRICA'S FOOD CRISIS (*co-editor*)
CORPORATISM IN AFRICA (*co-editor*)
NEWLY INDUSTRIALIZING COUNTRIES AND THE POLITICAL ECONOMY OF SOUTH-SOUTH RELATIONS (*editor with Jerker Carlsson*)
NIGERIAN FOREIGN POLICY (*editor with Olajide Aluko*)
PEACE, DEVELOPMENT AND SECURITY IN THE CARIBBEAN
POLITICAL ECONOMY OF AFRICAN FOREIGN POLICY (*co-editor*)
TOWARDS A POLITICAL ECONOMY OF AFRICA

AFRICA IN WORLD POLITICS:

Into the 1990s

Edited by
Ralph I. Onwuka
Professor of Political Science, Imo State University, Okigwe, Nigeria
and
Timothy M. Shaw
Professor of Political Science
Director of International Development Studies
Dalhousie University, Canada

UNIVERSITY OF CONNECTICUT
AT STAMFORD - LIBRARY
SCOFIELDTOWN ROAD
STAMFORD, CONN. 06903

St. Martin's Press
New York

DT
353
A4
1989

© Ralph I. Onwuka and Timothy M. Shaw 1989

All rights reserved. For information, write:
Scholarly and Reference Division,
St. Martin's Press, Inc., 175 Fifth Avenue, New York, NY 10010

First published in the United States of America in 1989

Printed in Hong Kong

Library of Congress Cataloging-in-Publication Data
Africa in world politics: into the 1990s/ edited by Ralph I. Onwuka and Timothy M. Shaw.
p. cm.
Includes index.
Contents: Introduction: marginalisation, differentiation, and redefinition/ Timothy M. Shaw – The non-aligned movement and the new international division of labour/ Timothy M. Shaw – The Organisation of African Unity in world politics/ K. Mathews – Beyond Lomé III: prospects for symmetrical EurAfrican relations/ Ralph I. Onwuka – CMEA-African economic relations/ Ralph I. Onwuka – The revival of regionalism: cure for crisis or prescription for conflict? / Timothy M. Shaw – ECOWAS: towards autonomy or neo-colonialism?/ S.K.B. Asante – Foreign military intervention in Africa / Ladun Anise – France's Africa/ Emeka Nwokedi – The Angolan puzzle/ Kenneth W. Grundy – Conclusion: the political economy of Africa in the world system, 1960–85/ Timothy M. Shaw.
ISBN 0–312–02769–9: $45.00 (est.)
1. Africa, Sub-Saharan–Foreign relations–1960– 2. Africa. Sub-Saharan–Politics and government–1960– 3. World politics–1945– 4. Africa, Sub-Saharan–Economic conditions–1960– I. Onwuka, Ralph I. II. Shaw, Timothy M.
DT353.A4 1989
320.967–dc19 88–33332
CIP

Contents

Lists of Tables and Figures

Tables

Figures

List of Abbreviations

ACP	African, Caribbean and Pacific (states associated with the EEC)
APPER	Africa's Priority Programme for Economic Recovery
BHN	Basic Human Needs
ECA	(UN) Economic Commission for Africa
ECOWAS	Economic Community of West African Studies
EEC	European Economic Community
IBRD	International Bank for Reconstruction and Development (World Bank)
IMF	International Monetary Fund
LDCs	Less Developed Countries
LLDCs	Least Developed Countries
LPA	Lagos Plan of Action
MPLA	Popular Movement for the Liberation of Angola
NAM	Non-Aligned Movement
NICs	Newly Industrialising Countries
NIDL	New International Division of Labour
NIEO	New International Economic Order
OAU	Organisation of African Unity
OECD	Organisation for Economic Co-operation and Development
SADCC	Southern African Development Co-ordination Conference
SADF	South African Defence Forces
SWAPO	South West African Peoples' Organisation
US	United States of America

Notes on the Contributors

Ladun Anise is Associate Professor of Political Science at the University of Pittsburgh. He has taught at the University of Ife and contributed articles to *Black World* and *Issue*.

S. K. B. Asante is Professor of Political Science at the UN Institute for Namibia in Lusaka. He previously lectured at the Universities of Florida, Ghana and Calabar. He is author of *The Political Economy of Regionalism in Africa: a decade of ECOWAS* and of essays in Adedeji & Shaw (eds) *Economic Crisis in Africa*, Mazzeo (ed.) *African Regional Organizations*, Sesay (ed.) *Africa and Europe*, *Afrika Spectrum*, *African Affairs*, *Development and Cooperation*, and *Third World Quarterly*.

Kenneth W. Grundy is Professor of Political Science at Case Western Reserve University in Cleveland, Ohio. He is author of *Confrontation and Accommodation in Southern Africa, Guerilla Struggle in Africa*, *The Militarization of South African Politics, Soldiers Without Politics* and articles in, among others, *International Studies Quarterly*, *Issue* and the *Journal of Strategic Studies*.

K. Mathews is Senior Lecturer in Political Science at the University of Nigeria, Nsukka. He previously taught at the University of Dar es Salaam. Dr Mathews is co-editor of *Foreign Policy of Tanzania, 1961–1981* and has contributed to *Africa Quarterly* and Mazzeo (ed.) *African Regional Organisations*.

Emeka Nwokedi is a Senior Lecturer in International Relations at Obafemi Awolowo University in Ife where he specialises in Franco-African relations. His essays have appeared in Olusanya and Akindele (eds) *Nigeria's External Relations*, *African Affairs* and *World Today*.

Ralph I. Onwuka, formerly Professor of International Relations at Obafemi Awolowo University, where he served as Head of Department and Editor of the *Nigerian Journal of International Studies* and *Quarterly Journal of Administration*, is now Professor of

Political Science at Imo State University and is author of *Development and Integration in West Africa: the case of ECOWAS* and co-editor of *The Future of Regionalism in Africa* (Macmillan, 1985).

Timothy M. Shaw is Professor of Political Science and Director of the Centre for African Studies at Dalhousie University in Nova Scotia. He has taught at Makerere University, University of Zambia and University of Ife and is author of *Towards a Political Economy for Africa: the dialectics of dependence* (Macmillan, 1985).

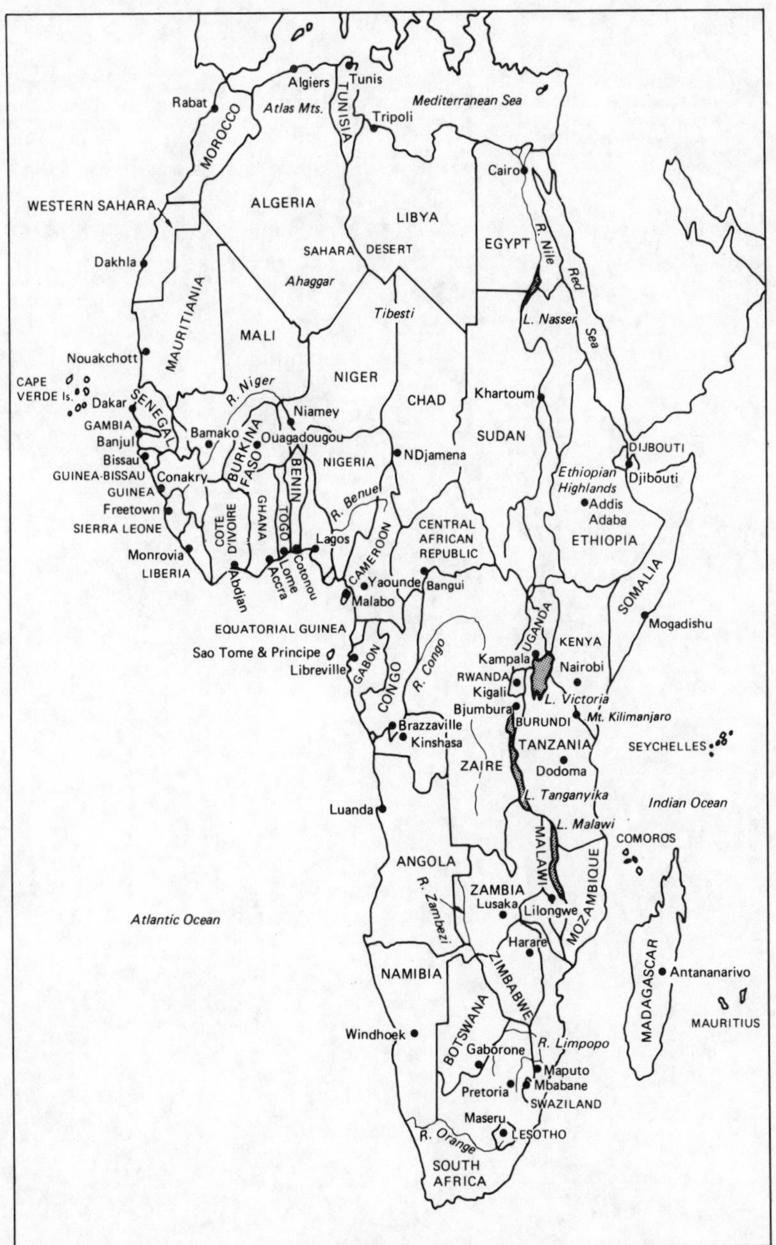

FIGURE 1 *Africa in Peters' projection*

SOURCE From the *South Atlas*, designed by Dr Arno Peters, and published by South Publications Ltd, with the kind permission of South Publications Ltd, Lasa.

Introduction: Marginalisation, Differentiation and Redefinition

Timothy M. Shaw

'There must be a devil somewhere in Africa.'

Julius K. Nyerere[1]

'Developing countries will continue to face domestic and external constraints that will severely restrict the range of options and the authority of their foreign policies.'

John J. Stremlau[2]

'Africa has no future.'

V. S. Naipaul[3]

The momentum and direction of development in Africa since independence has been largely a function of its position in the world system, a system that is dynamic, with particularly profound changes since the early 1970s. Yet Africa's incorporation has never been singular in incidence or implication. Rather, the diverse results and prospects of Africa's dependence are still being realised and evaluated even as they are in flux. The relationship of particular African classes and countries to extra-continental interests and institutions is complex and variable. This collection seeks to capture some of this complexity and variance in the increasingly contradictory interactions between social forces situated within Africa and others located outside the continent.

Most African states regained their formal independence more than 25 years ago. Given the disappointment and disillusionment of this first era of independence, they are concerned that the remaining decade of this century should not be equally difficult. Hence the appearance of 'new' African studies and concepts in the late 1980s: from self-reliance to reform. Africa's current leaders — a mixed group of first-generation nationalists, second-generation politicians and third-generation soldiers — are re-evaluating their place in the global political economy for two main reasons. First, the fruits of independence have been minimal (see Table 1); and second, the world system has been through a metamorphosis since the 1970s (see chapters 1 and 3). African academics and diplomats have responded in the 1980s by developing new approaches to analysis and *praxis*.

Some African countries and classes have benefited more than others from political liberation and economic change. A few have grown rich; but most have either stayed where they were in 1945 or 1960 or even regressed. Hence the new variability and complexity in African international relations leading to (1) alternative development strategies for statesmen, particularly post-drought and post-debt; and (2) alternative modes of analysis among scholars: the new African strategies and studies. This collection of essays is intended to explore some aspects of Africa's recent 'loss of innocence'.[4]

There is, inevitably, resistance to new policies and perspectives as well as persistent advocacy of them, from radicals as well as reactionaries. The old and the new have coexisted in Africa; this is particularly so in the present period. However, the old strategies and approaches — non-alignment, integration, modernisation — not only failed over the last 20 years, but are increasingly inappropriate for the transformed world of the next ten years, hopefully of reform and revival (see chapters 5 and 6). Old, ineffective solutions are being replaced by or juxtaposed with new, innovative suggestions — devaluation, privatisation and self-reliance — but the range of cases and issues that these are meant to address has grown meanwhile. There is a new strand of revisionism if not scepticism being revealed in response to the persistence of old problems and the appearance of new ones. However, there is sufficient evidence on the continent of (1) renewed growth in a few countries and classes; and (2) worrisome projections for the future[5] (see Table 2) that conservatism (even of a nationalist or socialist persuasion) is gradually giving ground to revisionism, caution to reconsideration at national, regional (see chapters 5 and 6) and continental levels (see chapter 2).

The next decade in the practice and analysis of African international relations promises to be exciting. The world of the 1990s is quite different from that of the 1960s, even the 1970s: it has moved from parastatals to privatisation and from stagnation to expansion. If African leaders can assimilate new global dynamics and respond in imaginative ways to contemporary problems and likely projections, then African international relations may be transformed.[6] These

TABLE 1 *Sub-Saharan Africa and the World: Basic Data*

Countries	*Population (millions) mid–1979*	*GNP per capita average annual growth rate (percent) 1960–70*	*1970–79*	*Per capita growth 1970–79 (percent) Agriculture*	*Volume of exports*	*Adult literacy rate (percent) 1976*	*Life expectancy at birth (years) 1979*	*Death rate of children aged 1–4 (per thousand) 1979*
Sub-Saharan Africa	343.9	1.3	0.8	–0.9	–3.5	28	47	25
Low-income	187.1	1.6	–0.3	–1.1	–4.5	26	46	27
Nigeria	82.6	0.1	4.2	–2.8	–2.8	n.a.	49	22
Other middle-income	74.2	1.9	–0.5	–0.4	–3.5	34	50	22
South Asia[a]	890.5	1.5	1.5	0.0	0.6	36	52	15
All developing	3 245.2	3.5	2.7[b]	0.1	–1.5	57	58	11
Low-income	2 260.2	1.8	1.6[b]	0.1	–3.1	50	57	11
Middle-income	985.0	3.9	2.8[b]	0.6	1.9	72	61	10
All industrialised	671.2	4.1	2.5[b]	0.2	5.2	99	74	1

a. Bhutan, Bangladesh, Nepal, Burma, India, Sri Lanka and Pakistan.
b. 1970–80.
SOURCE World Bank *Toward Sustained Development in Sub-Saharan Africa 3.*

TABLE 2 *Population and GNP Per Capita, 1980, and Growth Rates, 1965–86*

Country group	*1980 GNP (billions of dollars)*	*1980 population (millions)*	*1980 GNP per capita (dollars)*	*Average annual growth of GNP per capita (percent)*						
				1965–73	*1973–80*	*1982*	*1983*	*1984*	*1985*[a]	*1986*[a]
Developing countries	2 078	3 123	670	4.0	3.1	–0.7	0.1	3.1	2.7	2.5
Low-income countries	565	2 118	270	2.9	2.6	3.5	5.9	6.9	7.0	4.3
Middle-income countries	1 513	1 005	1 500	4.6	3.1	–2.4	– 2.5	1.1	0.5	1.4
Oil exporters	506	405	1 250	4.7	3.1	–3.6	–4.5	0.0	–0.2	–3.2
Exporters of manufactures	946	1 886	500	4.8	4.0	2.1	3.3	6.2	6.1	5.4
Highly indebted countries	868	492	1 770	4.4	2.8	–4.6	–5.9	–0.3	0.6	0.5
Sub-Saharan Africa[b]	182	331	550	3.4	0.5	–4.3	–4.9	–4.8	–0.2	–2.3
High-income oil exporters	223	16	14 400	3.9	5.7	–6.7	–14.3	–2.4	–8.6	–1.0
Industrial market economies	7 613	716	10 630	3.7	2.1	–1.3	1.6	4.1	2.4	1.9

a. Preliminary.
b. Excludes South Africa.
SOURCE *World Development Report 1987*, 171.

leaders need to be especially aware, however, that the content of seeming continuities, such as bipolarity and EurAfrica, have changed in recent times even if the labels have remained unchanged (see chapters 3, 4 and 7): to multipolarity and to new South-South connections, notably with the NICs (see Figure 2).

For the study of international relations in Africa to remain relevant to the continent's crises and to comparative analyses, it needs more than ever to treat 'economics' as 'high' politics. This also means noticing and incorporating seemingly disparate materials into its purview, such as contemporary analyses of the environment, informal sector and gender: democratic development which is self-sustaining. Three particular genres need to be embraced to ensure relevance and comprehensiveness: first, the impressive if controversial series of official interstate reports, notably from the OAU/ECA and IBRD: from *Lagos Plan of Action* and *Africa's Priority Programme for Economic Recovery* to the Bank's growing set of studies, most recently the fourth on *Financing Adjustment with Growth in Sub-Saharan Africa*[7]; second, a set of volumes on Africa's decline and difficulties, such as Richard Sandbrook's *The Politics of Africa's Economic Stagnation* and John Ravenhill's *Africa in Economic Crisis* as well as Preston King's *An African Winter*[8]; and third, the rejuvenation of regionalist analyses both continental, like the collection on *The Future of Regionalism in Africa* edited by Ralph Onwuka and Amadu Sesay, and Southern African, most notably Joseph Hanlon *Beggar Your Neighbours* and Phyllis Johnson and David Martin's coedited *Destructive Engagement*.[9] If such novel materials are included in the mainstream then African foreign policy and international relations will remain vibrant and relevant. If they are excluded as being outside the realm of diplomacy and security in the latters' old-fashioned format then the field will be endangered. Happily, they are incorporated throughout the present collection of original chapters, and are reflected in Figure 1, Peters' projection of the continent.

Two recent collections give particular pause for thought; they have appeared since the literature overview presented in the conclusion: Stephen Wright and Janice N. Brownfoot (eds) *Africa in World Politics: Changing Perspectives*[10] and the special issue on 'International Affairs in Africa' in *The Annals of the American Academy of Social and Political Science* (489, January 1987: 9–163). These cover and combine both orthodox issues — comparative foreign policies, conflicts in Northern and Southern Africa, the OAU — and the new agenda — notably debt and the IMF in the former and gender and distinctive definitions of security in the latter.[11]

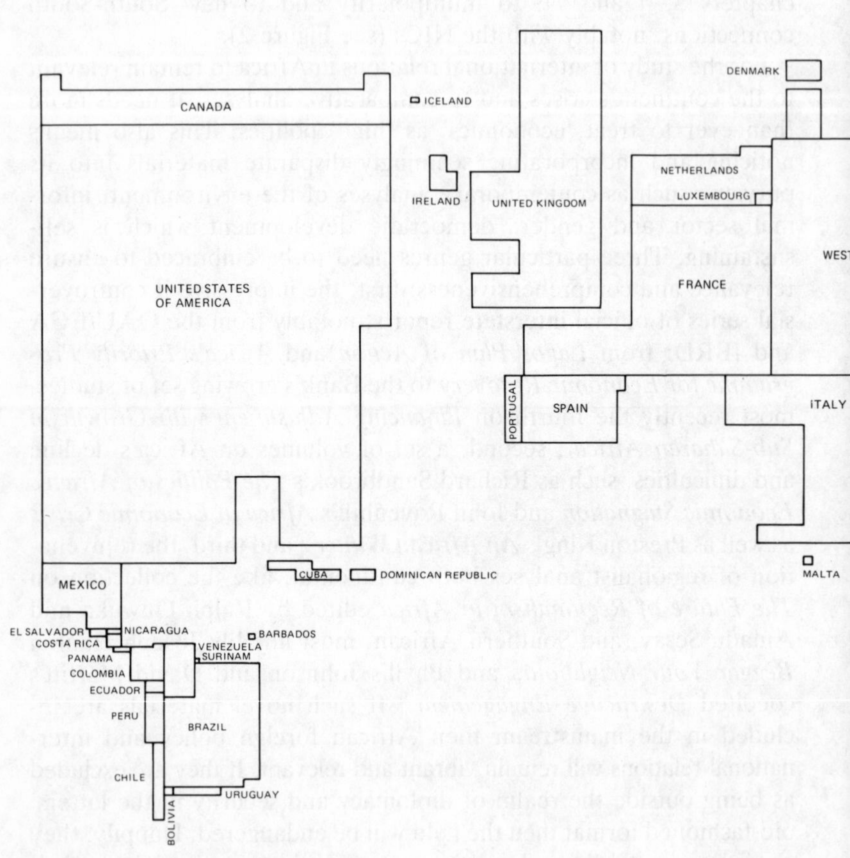

FIGURE 2 *Africa in a world of industrial powers*
SOURCE: Michael Kidron & Ronald Segal *New State of the World Atlas* (London: Pan, 1984) #15

If African scholars and statespersons have difficulty in accepting and treating such hard issues then extra-continental institutions will come to set the agenda for them. This tendency towards defeatism or escapism is already apparent in the economic area where the Bank

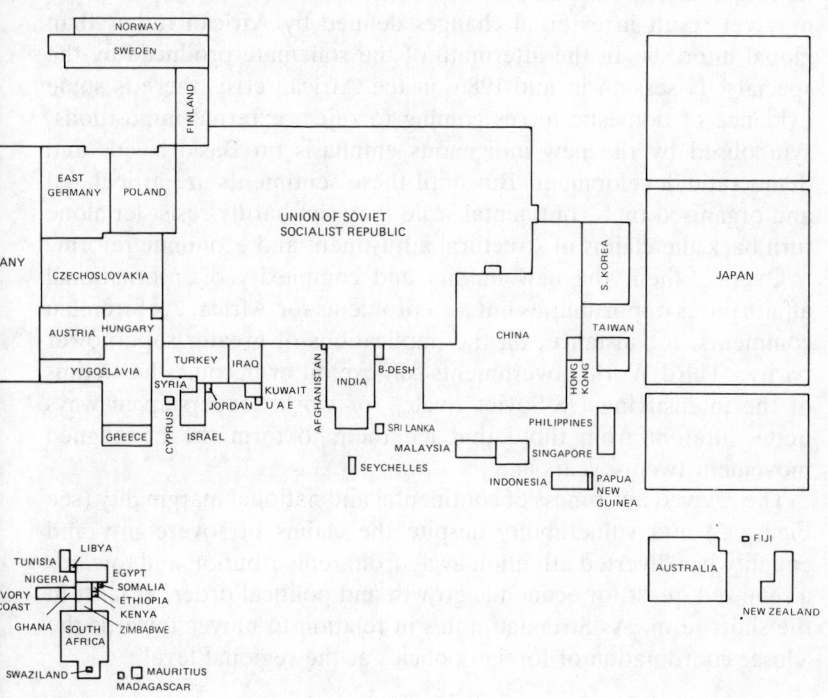

and Fund have abrogated to themselves *de facto* authority over 'structural adjustment': economic reforms to treat sluggish growth, exchange rates, increasing indebtedness and so on. To be sure, some African leaders and organisations have attempted to respond in a creative and coherent manner, notably the ECA with the *Lagos Plan of Action* and its successors, but the continent as a whole has been subjected to further divide and rule of a rather familiar kind, albeit on less familiar questions. Unless indigenous interests articulate an alternative set of responses to the crisis then external forces will fill the void; at least until it is apparent that the new orthodoxy is no more efficacious than the old, in which case internal contradictions may yet result in external changes defined by African rather than global interests. In the aftermath of the stalemate produced by the special UN session in mid-1986 on the African crisis there is some evidence of domestic forces coming to reject external impositions, symbolised by the new indigenous emphasis on Basic Needs and democratic development. But until these sentiments are articulated and organised on a continental scale they can hardly resist let alone turn back the claims of structural adjustment and economic reform.

Overall, then, the new fluidity and complexity of international affairs poses opportunities but also problems for Africa. As Stremlau comments, for instance, on the implications of greater superpower parity: 'Third World governments can exploit or become the victims of the intensifying US-Soviet rivalry for world leadership in ways quite different from those that led them to form the nonaligned movement twenty years ago'.[12]

The revived awareness of continental and national marginality (see Figure 2) and vulnerability despite the claims of sovereignty and equality has diverted attention away from redistribution and towards a renewed quest for economic growth and political order, at least in the short-term. As Stremlau notes in relation to moves towards the 'closer coordination of foreign policies at the regional level':

> Ironically, progress toward improved collective security, closer regional economic cooperation, and greater social justice in the Third World may eventually result more from policies that reflect shared fears of growing instability and the risk of foreign intervention than from the long-held common aspirations for a new and more equitable international order.[13]

The dialectics of interclass relations as well as interstate relations will continue to exert a powerful pull on African international affairs in the post- as in the pre-colonial period.[14] African leaders in particular as well as African peoples in general have reason to be concerned about extra-continental intentions, whether the threat of foreign intervention is structural and economic or strategic and military; from food aid and structural adjustment to common security (see chapters 7 to 9). For one element displays great continuity: the world system today is just as threatening to Africa as it ever was — *plus ça change*!

NOTES

1. *The Reporter*, 18 November 1966, 11.
2. John J. Stremlau, 'The foreign policies of developing countries in the 1980s', *Journal of International Affairs*, 34, 1 (Spring/Summer 1980) 161.
3. V.S. Naipaul, *New York Times Book Review*, 15 May 1979, 36.
4. See Cranford Pratt, 'Foreign policy issues and the emergence of socialism in Tanzania, 1961–68', *International Journal* 30, 3 (Summer 1975) 448.
5. See *inter alia* Timothy M. Shaw (ed.) *Alternative Futures for Africa* (Boulder: Westview, 1982) and, with Olajide Aluko (eds), *Africa Projected: from recession to renaissance by the year 2000*? (London: Macmillan, 1985).
6. For evaluations of this possibility, see Timothy M. Shaw, 'Foreign policy, political economy and the future: reflections on Africa in the world system', *African Affairs* 79, 315 (April 1980) 260–8, and 'Africa' in Werner Feld and Gavin Boyd (eds) *Comparative Regional Systems* (Elmsford, New York, and Oxford: Pergamon, 1980) 355–97.
7. See OAU *Lagos Plan of Action for the Economic Development of Africa, 1980–2000* (Geneva: International Institute for Labour Studies, 1981) and *Africa's Priority Programme for Economic Recovery, 1986–1990* (Addis Ababa, 1985); and IBRD *Accelerated Development in Sub-Saharan Africa: an agenda for action* (1981), *Sub-Saharan Africa: progress report on development prospects and programs* (1983), *Toward Sustained Development in Sub-Saharan Africa: a joint program of action* (1984), and *Financing Adjustment with Growth in Sub-Saharan Africa, 1986–90* (1986).
8. Richard Sandbrook *The Politics of Africa's Economic Stagnation* (Cambridge: Cambridge University Press, 1985); John Ravenhill (ed.) *Africa in Economic Crisis* (London: Macmillan, 1986); and Preston King *An African Winter* (Harmondsworth: Penguin, 1986). See also Robert J. Berg and Jennifer Seymour Whitaker (eds) *Strategies for African Development* (Berkeley: University of California Press, 1986 for CFR and ODC).
9. Respectively (London: Macmillan, 1985), (London: James Currey, 1986) and (Harare: Zimbabwe Publishing House, 1986).
10. (London: Macmillan, 1987).
11. See also introductions to Naomi Chazan and Timothy M. Shaw (eds) *Coping with Africa's Food Crisis* (Boulder: Lynne Rienner, 1988) 1–37, Julius E. Nyang'oro and Timothy M. Shaw (eds) *Corporatism in Africa* (Boulder: Westview, 1988) 1–19; and Jerker Carlsson and Timothy M. Shaw (eds) *Newly Industrialising Countries and the Political Economy of South-South Relations* (London: Macmillan, 1988) 1–22.
12. Stremlau, 'The foreign policies of developing countries in the 1980s', 174.
13. *Ibid*, 178. Cf. the rather orthodox texts from within and about Africa: Olatunde J. B. Ojo *et al.*, *African International Relations* (London:

Longman, 1985) and Gerald J.Bender *et al*. (eds) *African Crisis Areas and US Foreign Policy* (Berkeley: University of California Press, 1985).

14. See Timothy M. Shaw, 'The actors in African international politics', in Timothy M. Shaw and Kenneth A. Heard (eds), *The Politics of Africa: dependence and development* (London: Longman, and New York: Africana, 1979), 357–96.

1 The Non-Aligned Movement and the New International Division of Labour[1]

Timothy M. Shaw

The purpose of common security applies with great force to Third World countries . . . They too must find political and economic security through a commitment to joint survival . . .
In the Third World, as in all our countries, security requires economic progress as well as freedom from military fear.[2]

The Heads of State . . . expressed grave concern that since . . . 1983, the world economic crisis has continued to escalate, characterised inter alia by the accentuation of structural imbalances and inequities resulting from the inadequacy of the present international division of labour for the balanced and equitable development of the world economy as well as in the breakdown of the international payments system. The widening gap between the developed and developing countries and the persistence of the unjust and inequitable international economic system constitute a major impediment to the development process of non-aligned and other developing countries and poses a serious threat to international peace and security. In this regard, they reiterated the commitment of the Movement to continue to work for a restructuring of the international economic system with a view to establishing the New International Economic Order based on justice, equity, equality and mutual benefit.[3]

The 'new international order' is, at one and the same time, a program and an analysis. It is a programme of social transformation; it is an analysis of why such social transformation is possible or even probable . . . The very discussion is part of the *kairos* (crisis/change) . . . It is an attempt to keep us all operating within the temporality of conjuncture, when an understanding of the temporality of the *longue durée* will make it clear that we are participating in the *kairos*. This attempt will not succeed.[4]

A sense of *kairos* — common crisis? — is apparent in the dialectic between the reality projected by the New International Division of Labour (NIDL) and the ideology expressed in demands for a New International Economic Order (NIEO). This mood is particularly apparent in Africa which is increasingly marginal and vulnerable in the emerging post-industrial global economy. Ironically, the Non-Aligned Movement (NAM) which 25 years after its establishment calls for the latter is increasingly divided and diverted by the imperatives of the former. Hence its political divergence as reflections of economic differentiation. Thus any analysis of the Movement in the contemporary global context a quarter century after its founding requires the adoption of a political economy perspective: how to explain the contradictions within and around NAM? Will NIDL forever remain essentially unaffected by claims for a NIEO? Will the imperative of interdependence continue to be undiminished by the incidence of dependence? Will conjuncture or contradiction prevail in international affairs until the end of the present century? And do either NIEO or NIDL provide promising prospects for the impoverished and endangered continent of Africa?

One indicator as well as factor in the continuing struggle to redefine the world political economy is the proliferation of reports and debates about the current crisis. Following in the tradition of the late-1960s Pearson Commission on International Development are the Brandt and Palme 'Independent Commissions' on Development and Disarmament, respectively.[5] Yet as consensual, reflective and bourgeois instruments these can at best describe and prescribe; they cannot really criticise or blame. Hence the articulation of new internationalist concepts: 'mutuality of interest' and 'common security', respectively. These formulations influence perspective and discourse but they can hardly be implemented as they are neither operational nor socially-rooted. Nevertheless, they do point towards a more rational and sustainable, albeit idealistic, way to organise the global system. Yet unless they come to represent transnational constituencies their proposals are likely to remain stillborn. Their long-term aspirations are compatible with those of the NAM, yet its short-term goals are more immediate and explicit: a NIEO rather than mutuality; redistribution rather than commonality.

Unhappily, common security is likely to remain elusive while the bases for it in the global economy — common prosperity — are so elusive.[6] Hence the imperative of a NIEO not only for Third World, especially African, development but also for the South's security, as indicated in Olaf Palme's opening quotation. Until most of the social correlates of war are removed or contained, common security will remain a dream. As PM Robert Mugabe indicated in an evocative phrase at the mid-1986 NAM summit in Southern Africa: common 'mental liberation' is a prerequisite for both security and development.[7] And such liberation may be threatening to some established interests in Third as well as First and Second Worlds.

So although a sense of *kairos*, as conceived in the third opening quotation from Wallerstein, is apparent in the regular demand by the NAM for a NIEO, its members cannot easily escape from their collective inheritance of dependence and incorporation. For the contradictions and crises into which the ruling classes of member states have been plunged cannot be resolved without fundamental structural transformation: transformation within both national and international political economies.

NON-ALIGNMENT AS IDEOLOGY AND DIPLOMACY

In the absence of such interrelated fundamental changes, the NIEO becomes an ideological construct, designed to salvage residual dignity and development for a few countries and classes in the Third World. If the Non-Aligned call for a NIEO is not merely an exercise in frustration, it must constitute an attempt to devise an ideology to legitimise and protect the interests of the new indigenous ruling classes, as indicated in the second opening quotation.

To conceive of the NIEO demand and debate as an ideological construct is to deny neither their seriousness nor their prospects of success. Rather, it is to recognise the inherent futility of the NAM calling for a fundamental and fast restructuring of the global capitalist system, which has evolved over several centuries and continues to evolve under pressures more salient than those generated by this Movement. Changes in the international division of labour, in the prices and supplies of essential factors of production, and in particular relations of production in different parts of the world system have more impact on prospects for development than endless resolutions at Non-Aligned and United Nations conferences.

Moreover, some elements among the Non-Aligned are themselves both ambivalent and nonchalant about the Movement's declarations, because various classes and countries within it have variable chances for growth. This is due to the fact that some factions within Third World bourgeoisies and some economies within the Less Developed Countries (LDCs) are better able than others to take advantage of the continuing evolution of the world system. In addition to this, the apparent cohesion of the Non-Aligned coalition remains intact, because occasional efforts by major forces within the advanced industrialised states of the OECD — for example, the Trilateral Commission — to 'peel off' particular leaders and countries from the ranks of the Non-Aligned are less important than continuing historical trends within the international division of labour. To be sure, such efforts do yield some results; but the essential cause both of tensions within the Non-Aligned and of collaboration between First and Third World toward a NIEO is the structural position of major classes and countries in the world system of the 20th century. In short, substructural relations determine outcomes rather than superstructural manifestations, appearances and assertions to the contrary notwithstanding.

The Movement will continue to change as dominant interests within it rise and fall; hence the relevance of the relationship between its past characteristics and likely trends in its further evolution over the next 15 years. To this extent, the eighth summit in Harare constituted a symbolic turning point: the first NAM meeting since the failure of OPEC and the appearance of major development difficulties in Africa. The last time the Movement met in Sub-Saharan Africa — neighbouring Lusaka in 1970 — it was preoccupied politically by Rhodesia; 15 years later it focused on the liberation of South Africa and Namibia — special appeals on both, a package of proposals for the Front Line States, and a solidarity fund for the region. But its Africa declaration also included the contemporary legacies of drought and debt: the unfavourable 'Fourth World' position of the continent in the new global division of labour.

The NIEO, as a complete package of reforms is, then, likely to remain elusive but some issues on its agenda will be recognised and resolved whenever they are of salience to major interests in the North and/or the South. This chapter thus proceeds from an overview of central changes (and contradictions) in the contemporary world system — NIDL — to a history of the evolution of the NAM as its perceptions of and location in the system have developed.

The major theme presented here is that, because of the continual inter-action between Movement and system (and, of course interaction among and between central forces within both Movement and system), neither can be understood out of historical context.[8] In short, the Non-Aligned states are both products of, and now actors within, the global capitalist economy; so their design of and demand for a NIEO are historically conditioned. Hence the initial focus on NIEO as ideology: an idealist, mystifying, and ambivalent response by the ruling classes of the global periphery to their unsatisfactory inheritance and uncomfortably dependent situation. The elements of idealism and ambivalence increase as changes in the world system become more apparent: the uneven incidence of recession, inflation and protectionism between both countries and classes.

As we approach the last decade of the 20th century, we are, then, as Immanuel Wallerstein indicates, 'at the beginning of one of those periodic downturns, or contradictions, or crises that the capitalist world economy has known with regularity since its origins in Europe in the sixteenth century'.[9] This contemporary crisis, which commenced in the mid-1970s with the ending of the post-war Bretton Woods system and the beginning of an era of unstable oil prices has three major features:

(1) US hegemony is over and a period of inter-Western rivalries — involving both countries and corporations — has begun;
(2) The unity of the Socialist Commonwealth is also over and a period of intense Sino-Soviet rivalry, as well as fragmentation in Eastern Europe, is in process;
(3) Although most Third World countries continue to be very marginal in the world system, a few — those Newly Industrialising Countries (NICs) at the semi-periphery — are increasingly important to international production and exchange.

These three factors are, of course, interrelated; major states, capitalist and socialist alike, are engaged in competition for the scarce resources and markets of the minority of Third World countries with expanding economies. Together, they could constitute an historic conjuncture[10] — a turning-point in the world system. And it is with such a situation that the NAM has now to deal in its quest for order and justice for the majority of countries and peoples.

If the Movement of Non-Aligned states was declared pregnant in 1955 at Bandung, it was born in the era of the early 1960s, at Belgrade in 1961. The 1970s were a difficult decade for it as development became ever more elusive. And by the mid-1980s it had begun to appear quite middle-aged, established, pragmatic, even defensive. Its first decade had been characterised by optimism — decolonisation, development and *détente* were both possible and probable — but its second decade was characterised by greater pessimism (realism?) — decolonisation, development and *détente* were problematic and generated ironies rather than irreversible advances.The Movement recorded continued progress towards political decolonisation in the 1960s — in many ways its golden age — but by the early 1970s it had begun to appreciate its lack of power to force economic decolonisation or strategic *détente*. Indeed, the prospects for its second 20 years are, if anything, gloomier in this regard than for the previous ten or twenty: Southern Africa may come under majority rule by the year 2000, but dependence and underdevelopment are likely to be not only perpetuated but also intensified. Hence the growing concern of Non-Aligned leaders in New Delhi as the 1980s opened:

> Reviewing developments in the international economic situation since the Havana Summit, the Ministers noted with grave concern that while, on the one hand, the acute problems facing the developing countries had been aggravated and increased as a result of the pursuance of policies contrary or unfavourable to their interests by the developed countries; on the other hand, there had been no substantial progress in resolving the stalemate in international negotiations for the restructuring of international economic relations.[11]

Nevertheless, the NAM is caught in the web of its own contradictions and can hardly opt out of the halting process of so-called 'global negotiations' as advanced by Brandt and Palme.

Indeed, the heady optimism of the 1960s and the new cautiousness of the 1970s were reflective not only of shifts in the world system but also of a growing self-consciousness among Non-Aligned leaders: their position as the ruling class at the periphery remains tenuous, hence, the imperative of external association and support. Unless this leadership is willing and able to opt out of such global networks — even though its place in them is marginal — it has few options other than to hang in there and hope that a NIEO will somehow, someday materialise.[12] Meanwhile, the Movement itself has little choice but to revise its ideological position to incorporate contemporary demands and concepts from both external associates and internal constituents: how can it extract common security out of common crisis?

In short, Non-Alignment can be seen increasingly as an ideological construct — a form of collective 'defensive radicalism'.[13] This chapter provides a critical overview of the intellectual history of the Movement in terms of the current conjuncture and the contradictions surrounding Non-Aligned leaders especially following the new inequalities apparent since the mid-1970s.[14]

NON-ALIGNMENT AS A COLLECTIVE RESPONSE TO DECOLONISATION

The charter members of the NAM in the early 1960s were the first independent states of the post-war period, eager to maintain the momentum towards global decolonisation. Given that the central issues of the time were considered to be essentially political the Movement concentrated also on the decentralisation of the world power structure. However, a combination of successful *political* decolonisation and decentralisation (that is, *détente*) plus the elusiveness of *economic* decolonisation and decentralisation (that is, development) fostered a shift away from the political towards the economic in the second decade of the Movement's history. The perpetuation of some elements of colonialism and centralisation of world power along with the continued elusiveness of development generated a return to some original concerns of the 1960s as the 1980s opened: dominance, interference and exclusion. These retrieved concerns are now expressed as *self-reliance rather than decolonisation, NIEO rather than development*.

If Non-Alignment was a response at first to bipolarity, it is now a reaction to underdevelopment. The shift away from Cold War issues along an East-West axis towards rich-poor issues along a North-South axis is symbolic both of changes in the world system including the increase in Third World influence. This has resulted in a tendency towards South-South preferences: from global to South commissions. Continuing trends in international affairs are reflective of these interrelated transitions away from strategic and political questions and towards a new concentration on economic and social issues. These are representative of the impact of the processes of decolonisation and underdevelopment in the world system — the dialectical relationship between formal independence and actual dependence — and the continuation of inequalities.

Global politics have evolved in important ways for the Non-Aligned, away from a Eurocentric system and towards a complex hierarchy of myriad actors, both state and non-state. The rise, first, of non-European superpowers (presently the United States and the Soviet Union, and for the future, China and Japan); second, the multiplication of states (particularly in the Third World); third, the explosion of non-state actors (especially transnational, transgovernmental and intergovernmental ones at both regional and global levels); fourth, the appearance of new coalitions as well as axes amongst these; and fifth, the recognition of a range of new issues from gender to environment together constitute a major change in the superstructure, if not the substructure, of the world system.

Students of global superstructure may argue that these several shifts represent a trend towards decentralisation and democratisation as the number of small states and of non-state actors grows. However, a more radical approach would tend to examine continuing international inequalities and hierarchies despite the proliferation of actors, institutions and issues.[15] This latter approach sees a perpetuation of the trend towards concentration rather than to diffusion, looking in particular at modes and relations of production rather than at diplomacy or resolutions at the United Nations. To be sure, substructure and superstructure are related in both analysis and practice. Yet the different levels and modes of analysis and prescription associated with the two major approaches lead to divergent explanations and expectations. These affect different perceptions of the place of the Non-Aligned states in the world system as well as ideological definitions and defences of their place.

The alternative forms of analysis and advocacy represented by the orthodox and radical approaches respectively are reflected in the resolutions of the Non-Aligned summit. As suggested below, these two approaches are espoused by different factions in the Movement leading to a growing debate and division. For the present, however, I merely note that the former, orthodox, perspective welcomes *détente* but continues to emphasise politico-diplomatic issues of a superstructural variety whereas the latter, radical, perspective concentrates on (under) development as an aspect of political economy; that is, on substructure. These two differing emphases are reflected very clearly in the political and economic resolutions of the Eighth Summit Conference of the Non-Aligned in Harare.

A.W. Singham has captured the common thread of these two approaches to (political and economic) decolonisation by arguing that 'the Non-Aligned Movement has indeed come of age in the contemporary era. It is slowly transforming itself from being a social movement into a much more highly organised pressure group'.[16] This new concern with 'economics' and its impact on 'politics' have implications for strategy and ideology. It also has implications, as shall been seen later, for unity. Nevertheless, for now note is just taken of Singham's succinct summary of the Non-Aligned's transition:

> . . . the major thrust of the Non-Aligned Movement has been its demand for a new economic order which is broadly defined at the United Nations and gradually translated into a programme of action through UNCTAD and other international gatherings. The Non-Aligned Movement has developed into what can be broadly described as a trade union strategy in dealing with capitalist nations of the world. It has essentially advanced a trade union bargaining process onto a global level.[17]

This trade union-type activism on NIEO is a considerable step form its earlier role as an advocate of decolonisation and is reflective of its collective espousal of *dependencia* assumptions.

In the first decade (from Belgrade, 1961 to Lusaka, 1970), the Non-Aligned were mainly preoccupied by issues of political independence and East-West tension. They largely defined their international position in terms of 'positive' support for nationalist movements throughout the Third World and 'neutral' abstention from (any overt and long-term) association with either of the Cold War blocs. They were 'positively neutral'. They designated an activist role for themselves in terms of:

(1) Mediation and arbitration in specific inter-state disputes.
(2) 'Bridge-building' between the blocs.
(3) Presenting an alternative, a Third Force, for those bloc states opposing bloc membership.
(4) Active support for liberation movements and acting as their spokesman in international bodies.
(5) Criticism of countries violating peace, that is, acting as the conscience of the world, putting blame on those who deserve it.[18]

This concern for independence and impartiality, both as status and spirit, continues, although it is harder to define and maintain in a consensual manner in a more complex multipolar system. Moreover, it has come to be conceived in terms of political economy rather than legality alone, in an era when economic pressure is being increasingly seen to be as effective as the political or the strategic. Hence the growing focus on South-South connections as a counter-balance to any South-North negotiations: from Brandt to Nyerere Commissions.

This may be so, but it must be recognised that resistance to external forces requires more than declarations and solidarity: economic autonomy and resilience are prerequisites to enhanced 'independence'. But in the case of the Non-Aligned this is, always, a function of the degree of ideological cohesion and challenge displayed by the Movement.

Not only has the international environment changed over the last two decades but the composition of the Movement has also evolved. Because of the history and incidence of formal decolonisation the almost balanced 'Afro-Asian' complexion of Belgrade shifted dramatically by Lusaka when Africa had double the number of representatives compared with Asia. Moreover, given the large number of highly dependent and very poor, largely francophone, African states that were eligible for membership by 1970, the balance shifted away from a more radical and towards a more conservative or orthodox orientation. As Hveem and Willetts note in their empirical analysis of 'new' and 'old' members at Lusaka:

> . . . the Movement increasingly has been taking aligned countries into its ranks . . . there is a decreasing degree of Non-Alignment from the 'veterans' through the 'once before' to the 'newcomers'. Moreover, there is a considerable change of balance between East and West. Formerly those that were aligned were split between an Eastern and a Western alignment. Now the West predominates completely. The explanation seems to be that the Movement really has remained an 'open club'. It recruits new members willingly if they meet at least two criteria: that they are underdeveloped or developing countries, and that they are relatively small. The Movement has maximised membership at the expense of Non-Alignment.[19]

Using their four indicators — diplomatic association, military alignment, UN voting, trade with the communist bloc — Hveem and Willetts conclude that at Lusaka 'only four nations, Ghana, India, Nepal and Kuwait, are Non-Aligned on every one of the four indices'.[20] And, even given a very liberal interpretation of their data, less than half of the 64 invited states were 'objectively Non-Aligned'.

However, with the changed nature of the decolonisation process in the 1970s compared to that of the 1960s, the pro-Western composition of the Movement shifted once again by Colombo (1976) when up to 30 of the 86 members claimed to be 'socialist'. This shift to the left continued with the sixth summit in Havana, although the ideological complexion of the Movement is considerably more 'progressive' than members' actual political economies. By Harare, however, under pressure of political and economic 'privatisation' as well as strategic and ideological differentiation, the NAM had returned somewhat to its first principles of democracy, *détente* and development, seen most clearly in the 'Harare Appeal' to Presidents Reagan and Gorbachev.

The Non-Aligned Movement constitutes, then, both a continuing response to and an influence on the world system. In its first decade it was a reaction to, but also a constraint on, international bipolarity; in its second decade it has been a critical reaction to international inequality. As will be seen in the concluding section, in its current, third, decade, the Movement may react to a combination of inequality and intervention and seek to advance both the development and the integrity and democracy of its members against bloc politics; at least this appears to be the direction in which its ideological predispositions are pointed.

The Non-Aligned Movement has moved, then, from being as impartial and objective as possible during the Cold War era to being partial and insistent during the North-South debate. In the 1980s, given the prospects of multipolarity and bloc politics on the one hand, and uneven development and resource scarcities on the other hand, the NAM has become preoccupied with a combination of issues, particularly those to do with intervention, of both structural (economic) and crisis (political) varieties as reflected in both Brandt and Palme Commissions. Moreover, as differentiation increases within the Movement because of unequal exchange and uneven development, so will questions about development strategy and foreign policy come to affect its dynamics and diplomacy. And it is on these central issues that the tension between orthodox and radical states and analyses will continue to be acute, even after the passing of the crisis-ridden 1970s. Hence the welcome unity of purpose over apartheid in South Africa.

So ideological ambiguity and argument are unlikely to decline in the 1990s despite the growing threat to the Movement from revived forms of neo-colonialism — political pressure and economic exertion — characteristic of the trend towards neo-mercantilism. However, in the 1970s, especially the first half of the decade, it was assumed that economics were the panacea; hence the ideology of development in response to the reality of dependence.

NON-ALIGNMENT AS A COLLECTIVE RESPONSE TO DEPENDENCE

Faith in development among the Non-Aligned was short-lived as a collective ideology because insufficient resources were released by dominant classes, corporations and countries in the world system to effect significant change in the Third World before the mid-1970s; and shocks to the system from the mid-1970s onwards provided dramatic opportunities for a few Third World forces but retarded prospects for the majority. However, the pervasive sense of crisis that has characterised the world system for much of the last ten years has both affected and, in part, been caused by, the Non-Aligned states.[21] If 'political' nationalism and decolonisation produced the downfall of colonialism, then 'economic' nationalism and decolonisation have begun to threaten the continuation of capitalism, at least in its characteristic Keynesian post-war variety. In turn, the age of *détente* and (under) development has necessitated changes amongst the Non-Aligned. As Singham notes, 'the growing global economic crisis, especially the disparity between the rich and the poor nations, has dramatically changed the whole course of the Non-Aligned Movement'.[22]

According to the radical mode of analysis, partly reflected in the Harare Political Declaration, the series of interrelated crises which have disrupted the global economy since the second half of the 1970s is reflective of a set of contradictions in the world system:

> The Heads of State or Government noted with grave concern that the world continues to be confronted with increasingly difficult problems stemming from deep-rooted and interrelated contradictions in international economic relations. This deepening crisis is manifested in the drastic widening of the gap between developed and developing countries, many of which are unable to meet even the most basic needs of their people or realize their development priorities. Prospects for the establishment of the New International Economic Order based on justice and sovereign equality continue to diminish. The North-South dialogue is in a state of paralysis and international co-operation for economic and social development

through the multilateral process embodied in the United Nations system is threatened.[23]

This crisis can be seen to exist at two rather distinctive levels — the superstructural and substructural. The former consists of the diplomatic debates and political posturing that occur in a variety of fora and media. The latter consists of the economic relations and social structure that underlie the former. A fundamental question about both the Non-Aligned states and the NIEO debates is whether they seek change at the level of super- and/or sub-structure. Before the 1970s, the Movement was largely concerned with superstructural issues — decolonisation, diplomacy and *détente*. It only became concerned with substructure as it became clear that dependence affects development and that incorporation in the global economy largely determines one's place in the world system as a whole. In other words, the contradictions and debate at the level of substructure affected diplomacy and debate at the level of superstructure. There was not only a 'gap' between economic dependence and political independence: there was a tension or a contradiction between the two.

Given the growing awareness of this relationship between substructure and superstructure a central question arises about the NIEO issue: is it going to be treated and (possibly) resolved at the level of superstructure only — ideological and diplomatic agreement — or will it also lead to change in the global economy, the substructure? The Non-Aligned states (particularly the radical faction amongst them) increasingly demand change in substructure, recognising that this will inevitably affect superstructure. By contrast, the industrialised states advocate change at this level of superstructure only, hoping both that they can prevent diplomatic agreement from affecting economic exchange and that they can meanwhile re-establish their dominance throughout the global economy. There are constraints on the class-type struggle between 'bourgeois' and 'proletarian' states because of the simultaneous class conflict occuring within each of them and the continuing connections between bourgeois interests in North and South. In short, there are limits to the ideology of confrontation articulated by the Non-Aligned given the place of the Movement's countries and classes in the world system.[24]

If the 1960s was a relatively optimistic decade of effective decolonisation, then the 1970s was a rather pessimistic decade of disillusion. The crisis which started in the 1970s has been characterised by several interrelated features, the rank ordering of which varies between 'worlds' and over time. Moreover, these aspects are related to changes in the world system identified above:

(1) Continued underdevelopment in most of the Third World so that Basic Human Needs are being met decreasingly.
(2) Growing incidence of resource shortages and depletion affecting level and price of production in the First World.
(3) Impact of the mid-decade 'oil crisis' leading to financial disarray, especially debt.
(4) Threat of protectionism and unilateralism in the North.
(5) Increasing environmental vulnerability in the South, especially Africa, as underdevelopment and overpopulation erode ecological reserves.[25]
(6) Impending changes in the international division of labour with the emergence of a group of Newly Industrialising/Influential Countries (NICs) and of a Europe of the Twelve (EEC).[26]

Recognition, ranking, and treatment of these several components of the current crisis are a function of theoretical perspective as well as of national status, of mood as well as ideological orientation, and of region as well as race.[27] The orthodox, superstructural approach tends to deal with them as temporary, local difficulties, whereas the radical, structural approach treats them as inherent, long-term contradictions. The former believe that they are susceptible still to incremental decisions whereas the latter asserts that they are merely features of a structural condition that requires fundamental change. From a radical world system perspective, the crisis may represent an historic conjuncture, not a passing problem.

The orthodox prescription to overcome the crisis consists, then, of a routine response — negotiation and co-operation — whereas the radical reaction is the opposite — confrontation and conflict. The former represents the traditional reply from the old majority within the Non-Aligned group, while the latter reflects the reaction of the new minority. Tradition is still contained in some of the resolutions from the Colombo and subsequent conferences:

> The international trend is . . . favourable to peaceful coexistence . . . it is furthermore a fact of great importance that the world is becoming increasingly interdependent, a factor of crucial significance in shaping the world of the future. In an interdependent

world, the only alternative to international cooperation is international rivalry, tension and conflict, and the human aspiration towards a better world has inevitably to manifest itself through international cooperation. Consequently the trend is favourable to international cooperation in accordance with the Non-Aligned principle of peaceful coexistence.[28]

By contrast, a growing number of new states recognise the inevitability of conflict between rich and poor if the latter are to be free to develop. Their more radical perspective represents a more critical historical mode of analysis; one that sees incorporation and co-operation as the problem, not the solution; hence the emphasis on South-South relations as both insurance and preference lest South-North dialogue becomes pointless.[29] The ambiguities of the NIEO debates are, then, an aspect of the tensions within the Movement over how to respond to the current crisis.

Heightened awareness of the elusiveness of development and the pervasiveness of dependence generated something of a metamorphosis in the NAM in the 1970s. As consciousness grew of the gap between political independence and economic dependence, so determination increased to bridge it by realising a greater degree of economic control and autonomy. The demand for international development and democratisation — instead of dependence and domination — along with the parallel dependency discourse — produced the NIEO debate. The 1970 Lusaka Summit (of Heads of State) and the 1972 Algiers Summit (of Foreign Ministers) led to the Sixth and Seventh Special UN General Assemblies. The international agenda for the decade after the second half of the 1970s was dominated by this debate,[30] for as Ervin Laszlo suggests,

> the historical process which gave the majority of the world's population sovereign and equal status, but left them at the same time in a position of economic dependence, triggered a set of factors configuring the context for the emergence of the NIEO.[31]

But definitions, interpretations and expectations of NIEO vary within the NAM: hence the ambiguities of its ideology. And, although some states still retain faith in incrementalism, many have come to recognise the imperative of structural change. New structures in the global economy are essential if co-operation is to replace conflict once again and if development is to reduce dependence:

> The Heads of State . . . consider that collective self-reliance within the NIEO is an important and necessary step in the wider process arriving at the establishment of international co-operation which would be a concrete and genuine expression of interdependence within the global economy. International co-operation is nowadays an imperative necessity. It requires the effective participation of all in decision making and demands that those processes and relationships which lead to increasing inequality and greater imbalance are put to an end. In their strategy of international economic co-operation, concurrently with the intensification of the relations between themselves, it is desirable that the Non-Aligned countries diversify their economic relations with the other countries, developed capitalist as well as socialist, on the basis of the principles of respect for national sovereignty, of equality and of mutual benefit.[32]

If mutual and stable forms of political and economic co-operation are to be established then new values and structures have to be agreed on and constructed, otherwise 'interdependence' will continue to be a cover for dependence. It is for this reason that Non-Aligned Ministers declared in 1981 that they categorically rejected any attempt:

> . . . to impose, under the pretext of interdependence, a world economy which would once again leave no place for the developing countries as full partners in their own right. [They] were of the view that interdependence could only result from the establishment of the NIEO . . .[33]

A persistent theme in the orthodox school of states and scholars in both Third and First Worlds is that international conflict over the maldistribution of income and opportunity can be overcome not by continuing tension but rather by writing a new global contract based on mutuality of interest in common prosperity. The possibility of resolving differences in this manner is reminiscent of earlier attempts by international lawyers to design world governments or federations. It also reflects the awareness that some degree of change in the global economy may be essential for the advanced industrialised states, too, as resource shortages and environmental pollution increase. And it is a characteristic response of the rich to challenges of the poor — a superstructural rather than a substructural remedy. As Laszlo recognises himself, 'The establishment of the NIEO is not only historically appropriate; it is also universally expedient'.[34]

The Non-Aligned adopted aspects of this notion of a new international contract or order for two reasons. First, they saw it as a goal that would enhance their own unity and hence effectiveness. And second, they saw it as a means to put pressure on, and to blame, the rich. Moreover, if simultaneously they advanced their own national and collective self-reliance, then should the contract prove elusive, they could always retreat into their own 'world'.[35]

The advantages — both developmental and tactical — of adopting self-reliance, were reflected in the economic declaration from Colombo:

> The principle of self-reliance, thus seen in its individual and collective aspects, is not only compatible with the aims of the NIEO but is a highly important factor in the strengthening of the solidarity of Non-Aligned and other developing countries in their struggle to achieve economic emancipation.[36]

Finally, as already indicated, self-reliance may also be a response to the *Limits to Growth* debates and decisions in the North, as well as to a history of dependence. It consists of intellectual and political reactions which are mutually reinforcing: the dependence approach advocates disengagement because in the past integration has only produced underdevelopment, whilst the 'over-development' approach advocates disengagement because in the future integration might well be impossible given ecological preoccupations in the North:

> The growing acceptance of national and collective self-reliance as a development strategy represents a victory for scholars who, during the 1960s and 1970s, have championed what is termed 'dependency' theory.[37]

The intellectual as well as political ascendency of dependence was most delayed and subsequently realised in Africa: see Samir Amin and the *Lagos Plan of Action*, respectively.[38]

Although dependence and over-development perspectives disagree profoundly on the causes of self-reliance — no development and no growth, respectively — they have been able to reinforce Third World perceptions of the imperative of disengagement and restructuring. This solidarity has been achieved at a time when some elements in the North — corporations and commissions even if not nationalistic regimes — have begun to reconsider and to advocate interdependence based on Southern growth, rather than isolation based on ignoring Southern demands. But it may be rather late to revive such classical economic doctrines.

So the convergence of limited growth and self-reliance — the ideology of NIEO and global contract — is problematic now that the dominant interests in the world economy seek economic revival through Southern markets and activities. The pressure on the Third World to abandon self-reliance even before it is really tried is likely to grow, especially within the semi-periphery, as discussed below: the familiar package of liberalisation, devaluation and privatisation rather than regulation.

NON-ALIGNMENT AS A COLLECTIVE RESPONSE TO DIVERGENCIES

The Non-Aligned states, for reasons of faction (class elements within national and transnational bourgeoisies) and function (divergent national elements within the LDCs), have attempted to render compatible contract and confrontation, interdependence and self-reliance. This continuing quest for ideological as well as institutional order is reflected in the reinterpretation of notions of coexistence and *détente*. So economic as well as political coexistence is supported and *détente* is advocated by NAM as well as the Palme Commission for conflicts and areas outside the original narrow East-West nexus. And the Non-Aligned agenda continues to grow from colonialism and independence, race and conflict, disarmament and interference to Southern Africa, Palestine, the Indian Ocean and the media.[39] A particularly problematic question underlying many of these items and issues is how the Movement copes with a growing diversity of interest and ideology, endowments and expectations.

The elusiveness of economic decolonisation and development, let alone indigenous forms of democracy, has led not only to increasing concern amongst the Non-Aligned for a change in the global economy; it has also produced a profound re-evaluation of development policy in a growing number of members. The majority continue to demand a NIEO as proposed at the Lusaka and Algiers meetings, compatible with an essentially orthodox approach to development. By contrast, the new minority rejects any notion of externally-oriented growth, prefering instead to overcome underdevelopment by escaping from dependence. This radical approach and faction advocates self-reliance rather than incorporation, autonomy rather than integration. And this division has important implications for the cohesion and influence of the Movement and reflects the emergence of a group of new states following a non-capitalist path.[40] By contrast, a subsequent minority has in the 1980s espoused structural adjustment and policy reform with encouragement from the IBRD and IMF: peripheral capitalism for the late 20th-century.

The established consensus (and optimism) favouring a new global economic structure is expressed in the (premature?) Colombo political declaration:

> The Conference noted with satisfaction that the principles of peaceful coexistence advocated by the Non-Aligned Movement as the basis for international relations had won widespread recognition from the world community. The timely initiative taken by Non-Aligned countries has led to the decision of the world community to create a New International Economic Order based on equity and justice.[41]

And the economic declaration related the call for NIEO to the whole issue of development, a central focus — both ideological and instrumental — of the Movement:

> The Heads of State. . . . are firmly convinced that nothing short of a complete restructuring of international economic relations through the establishment of the New International Economic Order will place developing countries in a position to achieve an acceptable level of development.[42]

However, whilst the majority reinforced by Bank and Fund conditionalities still favour an outward-looking strategy, a growing and influential minority prefers an inward-looking direction. Approximately 25 members (that is, over a quarter) now favour self-reliance and some form of non-capitalist path because of the inadequate results — in both aggregate and distributional terms — of the established growth policy. And within this more radical grouping there is something of a distinction between those who favour collective self-reliance (as a revised form of regionalism) and those who seek national (or 'individual') self-reliance (as an aspect of non-capitalism or socialism). The former collective variety is considered to be an important part of the demand for a NIEO:

> The Heads of State . . . are of the firm belief that only a confident spirit of collective self-reliance on the part of the developing countries can guarantee the emergence of the New International Economic Order. Self-reliance implies a firm determination on the part of developing nations to secure their legitimate economic rights in international dealings through the use of their collective bargaining strength.[43]

However, as Singham cautions, self-reliance is not an easy strategy. And it is one that poses difficulties for the Movement itself between the old majority and the new minority; between more and less benign definitions of the ideology of development:

> In developing a trade union strategy, the Non-Aligned Movement has no doubt recognised the fact that within their union itself there are a number of contradictions . . . there are indeed divisions between the nations who attempt to negotiate collectively with the capitalist nations, just as there were contradictions within the working class when they negotiated with capital.[44]

This tension at the level of substructure is most acute between those states in the semi-periphery and those following a non-capitalist path, as is noted below. The (somewhat hopeless, and possibly misguided) attempt to forge a new consensus bridging the orthodox-radical, NIEO-self-reliance 'gap' is reflected in Singham's own idealistic yet representative (as well as ahistoric and non-empirical) juxtaposition:

> The present era of economic reconstruction is a transitional one when a variety of nations will choose between the old capitalist order and a new world economic order. The Non-Aligned Movement has entered a dramatic era in its history. It is calling for a new economic system.
>
> The Non-Aligned Movement, which began as a broad anticolonialist movement seeking world peace by exhorting the powers to avoid a nuclear holocaust, has become the advocate for a new

> political and economic order on a global level . . . Most of the Non-Aligned countries are experimenting with non-capitalist paths of development. The search for a NIEO, then, is simply a demand by the Non-Aligned nations to rectify the present imbalance that exists among states.[45]

The issue of appropriate development strategy and ideology is a central one confronting the Movement. It has become more acute since the mid-1970s, initially because of inequalities among members, and more recently because of 'inter-imperial' rivalries among OECD states as well as 'policy' rather than North-South dialogue between NAM members and the IBRD/IMF. Historically, Non-Aligned states have been differentiated according to whether their leaders were influential in the Movement; now they can be ranked according to economic position, potential and orientation.

Changes in the world system at the level of both super- and sub-structure have generated an intermediate stratum of states between the centre and the periphery — the semi-periphery.[46] This group of 'middle powers' has been variously characterised as the Newly Influential Countries (superstructural role) or the Newly Industrialising Countries (substructural position). The NICs are semi-peripheral in the sense that they are larger, more powerful, more industrialised and have more 'developmental' potential than most countries in the Third World. They have also generated a lively intellectual and political debate over their role in the world system.[47]

Orthodox scholars take confidence from the 'success' stories afforded by the NICs to defend the claims of established development theory that outward-looking growth is still possible. Their renewed faith in 'trickle-down' approaches has been joined by the growing interest taken in such states by global strategic planners who seek close ties with regionally influential actors. The 'Nixon-Brezhnev' doctrine has in turn been reinforced by the proposal of the Trilateral Commission to bring at least more OPEC or NIC states into the charmed circle of the OECD as well as by IBRD/IMF reference to such 'models'.

The new attention accorded the new affluence of the NICs has raised questions about their role in the Third World as well as about their espousal of established economic policies. The orthodox position on both questions is that the semi-periphery can lead the Group of 77 and apply classical growth strategies without generating divisiveness. The radical response, given the close association between centre and semi-periphery and given the different experience of orthodox development policies in most of the periphery, is that the NICs are becoming sub-imperial and will thus split the NAM and upset its unity.

Ali Mazrui is a defender of the former position, arguing that through 'counter-penetration' the NICs can advance common Third World interests.[48] He sees the semi-periphery as serving a positive, integrative function of benevolent leadership rather than one of sub-imperial domination. Mazrui's optimism in seeing counter-penetration by the NICs as advancing both development and the advent of 'mature interdependence' was not shared by more radical analysts even before the demise of OPEC. Instead, they see the rise of the semi-periphery as a stage in the evolution of the world system brought about by emerging contradictions both within and between countries. For them, the emergence of NICs is not a vindication of established development strategy but rather an indication of the continuing omnipotence of corporate and state interests in the centre.

For the semi-periphery has not emerged on its own but rather by invitation and by design: the rich need regional branches and bases in the more complex contemporary system. And because of the semi-periphery's structural position, it can hardly avoid the charges of sub-imperialism.[49] It may attempt to be beneficent regionally and to practice counter-penetration globally but its intermediary status prevents it from contributing unequivocally to the cohesion of the NAM. This is particularly so in the two salient areas of the contemporary period — bloc politics and political democracy — which are the focus of the concluding paragraphs.

The Non-Aligned states have sought independence and autonomy through political and economic decolonisation and development. But inequalities, both structural and behavioural, in the world system tend to perpetuate dependence and domination, especially in the periphery but also, albeit in modified form, in the semi-periphery. The ubiquity of underdevelopment has led the NAM as a group to oppose bloc politics; in practice, some members have been prepared to take advantage of them whilst a few seek to avoid them altogether by implementing a comprehensive self-reliant strategy. Nevertheless, the official ideology of the group remains that it has 'contributed significantly to the relaxation of tensions and the solution of international problems through peaceful means. It noted the contribution that the NAM had made towards preventing the division of the world into antagonistic blocs and spheres of influence'.[50]

As with the issue of 'interference', the group sees bloc politics as an 'external' rather than as a structural or transnational phenomenon, so avoiding any notion of apparently 'national' ruling classes being dependent or comprador. On the one hand, therefore, the real significance of or constraints on self-reliance are ignored. On the other hand, recognition of continued foreign threats is a healthy antidote to the naive assumption that the world system is becoming more benign or equal. Bloc politics becomes a convenient motif for the variety of challenges and forms of domination in the contemporary international system for the Movement as a whole, the removal of which all can agree to as the *sine qua non* of development and independence:

> Although colonialism as traditionally understood is coming to an end, the problem of imperialism continues and can be expected to continue for the foreseeable future under the guise of neo-colonialism and hegemonic relations. The Non-Aligned have to be alert against all forms of unequal relations and domination that constitute imperialism.
>
> The Conference noted also that the international trend is against power blocs and notions of international order based on balance of power and spheres of influence, all of which imply unequal relations between nations which could amount to domination. The Non-Aligned will continue to oppose the principle of polarisation around power centres as it is inconsistent with true independence and the democratisation of international relations, without which a satisfactory international order cannot be realised.[51]

The NAM's rejection of international and national inequalities is a crucial antidote at the level of ideology to its memberships' growing differentiation at the level of reality. As Fred Halliday has noted in his critical analysis of NAM after Delhi, it is now plagued by regional and political differences as well as by personality and economy distinctions. If NAM is maturing it is also diversifying and dissipating as the world political economy evolves. Halliday thus argues that its advocacy of NIEO is bound to be problematic:

> . . . an appeal to the richer states of the capitalist world, whose self-interest and power to pursue it do not lead them to accept any radical restructuring of the world market. The failure to launch a NIEO . . . reflects a structural reality of the world economy, not a failure of negotiating skill or a lack of diplomatic energy.

> . . . the countries of the South are themselves, in the main., part of the capitalist market, and so are both disposed to compete with each other and to seek closer integration with the richer economies of the developed world. This again is a matter of the working of the market, rather than of lack of political will. The 1970s have seen substantial economic change in the Third World, most vividly represented by OPEC and the NICs: but these changes have been brought about by breaking ranks with the rest of the world, not by collective efforts of the NAM states. A new international economic order has been created since 1973, but it is a new, more viciously competitive capitalist order, in which differentiation between Third World states has increased.[52]

Thus, the rejection of blocs and dominance at the level of ideology is essential not only for national development but also for collective cohesion. As noted already, the emergence of a semi-periphery may pose problems for the Movement. However, some nationalist scholars reject any notion of differentation *within* the Third World as being of consequence compared to that *between* First and Third World, Thus saving the Movement from further fragmentation.

Such scholars see the Third World as an historical and ideological rather than as a contemporary category. Ismail-Sabri Abdalla, for instance, rejects any idea that differentiation within the Non-Aligned is either important or increasing. Instead, he asserts that they still share a common experience of exploitation and subordination:

> The Third World is a historical phenomenon that is part and parcel of the process of emergence of the present world order . . . the differentiation process did not produce during the last fifteen years effects of such a magnitude that any group of 'developing nations' can stand outside the Third World . . . the 'gap' between the higher income group and the industrialised nations was still growing.[53]

So Abdalla is critical of any notion of Third World differentiation and fragmentation, arguing instead that a shared historical and existential experience will serve to reinforce cohesion and so support confrontation against the rich:

> dependence is with all its corollaries the basic common denominator of Third World countries and comprehensive decolonisation is the only path out of it. Features and specifications that distinguish

> countries or groups of countries in the Third World fall short of destroying the fundamental community of condition and goal.[54]

Abdalla rejects superstructural approaches, then, in favour of more critical substructural and historical analysis. But while the former's focus on some aspects of differentiation may be dismissed as threats to the Movement's cohesion, the latter's orientation towards self-reliance poses a new and more profound challenge to the Non-Aligned.

National self-reliance is, in many ways, a logical extension of the ideology of decolonisation, a strategy that reduces external association and domination. Yet precisely because of the history of Third World incorporation in the world system, and the dependence of much of its leadership on links with countries and corporations in the North, it has not been widely espoused. And its adoption by a growing faction within the group not only undermines solidarity at the level of tactics but also at the levels of ideology and political economy. So even if sub-imperialism can be regarded as a superficial problem, self-reliance cannot be so readily dismissed: it poses fundamental questions and dilemmas for the Non-Aligned.

The challenge of self-reliance as an effective response to dependence and underdevelopment is exacerbated if the goal of development is seen to be a transformation in political economy, not just political and/or economic decolonisation. In other words, if development is defined in terms not only of stability and growth but also in terms of satisfying the demands for autonomy, order, and equitable income distribution, then self-reliance is a powerful and persuasive response to an inheritance of non-participation and non-production. When broadly conceived, self-reliance is a strategy designed to secure development and autonomy and to overcome underdevelopment and dependence. The very salience of this strategy, especially its emphasis on democracy and participation, is a challenge to a NAM which includes not only least developed states but also some rather oppressive regimes.

THE FUTURE OF NON-ALIGNMENT: FROM DEPENDENCE TO DEMOCRACY

Ultimately, then, the interrelated concerns of the Non-Aligned for development and equality come together in the notion of a political economy of democracy at the interrelated national and international levels. National development and international redistribution not only improve the prospects of satisfying Basic Human Needs; they also serve to enhance the resistance of a country (and of its ruling class?) to external domination. At Colombo, the Movement declared that

> as a result of recent developments, the importance of ensuring the genuine and complete independence of states as distinct from merely formal sovereignty had been enhanced. The problem of unequal relations between states, often amounting to domination, continues to be a disturbing phenomenon even negating the hard won freedom of some states. Today, one of the principal tasks of the Non-Aligned remains the combating of unequal relations and domination. . . .[55]

The demand for greater levels of development and equality to resist domination also enhances the prospects for democracy in both national and international domains. Given the adoption of welfare measures in the colonial metropoles on the basis of external exploitation, it may be a prerequisite for the achievement of Basic Human Needs in the periphery: self-reliance, like Non-Alignment, may be an expression of self-interest. Singham comments from his world system perspective:

> That liberty, democracy, enjoyed by those living in the capitalist centre has been earned at the expense of those living in the colonies. The Non-Aligned Movement is suggesting not only that colonisation and capitalism brought economic benefits to the centre capitalist countries but also that colonisation was largely responsible for the evolution of democratic institutions in the centre itself.[56]

Given the nature and results of the incorporation, disengagement and self-reliance may be prerequisites, therefore, not only for development but also for democracy in the periphery. And, even if the North is jealous for its own growth and welfare, it can hardly be selfish about its democracy. Political as well as economic redistribution and democratisation may be a central feature and result of any New International (Economic) Order, a paradox of political economy:

> The demand for a NIEO is an equalitarian as well as a libertarian demand. Redistribution of the world's economic resources is likely

> to weaken oligarchic and repressive regimes. Increases in standards of living should result in greater demands for democratic rights by those enjoying newly won economic rights. The struggle against poverty is, indeed, the most significant democratic goal.[57]

In which case, proletarian peoples as well as proletarian countries may yet come to benefit from ambiguities in the ideology of Non-Alignment. And, as Wallerstein suggests, this struggle between democracy and underdevelopment will be most acute in the NICs in the NAM, with special relevance given their symbolic and strategic positions:

> The semi-peripheral states in the coming decades will be a battleground of two major transnational forces. One will be the multinational corporations who will be fighting for the survival of the essentials of the capitalist system: the probability of continued surplus appropriation on a world scale. The other will be a transnational alignment of socialist forces who will be seeking to undermine the capitalist world economy, not by 'developing' singly, but by forcing relatively drastic redistributions of world surplus and cutting the long-term present and potential organisational links between multinationals and certain strata internal to each semi-peripheral country, including such strata in the socialist semi-peripheral states.[58]

Hence the Non-Aligned conferences' recognition and rejection of 'external' interference: a fine ideological position but a highly difficult, even idealistic, policy, given the contemporary conjuncture, or the paradoxical nature of the *kairos*:

> At twenty-five today, rich in wisdom and moral strength, our Movement is better armed to meet these challenges (of disarmament and development) and to carry out its historical mission of seeking the establishment of a new, just and democratic world order . . . The Movement . . . remains the foremost movement of peace, understanding and equitable cooperation in the world as it enters the twenty-first century.[59]

Reflective of the mutual interest of North and South, especially Africa, in common and reconceptualised security, or the mutual reinforcement between Palme and South Commissions, the NAM in Harare 'emphasized the direct relationship between peace, disarmament and development'.[60] Certainly, the growing spectre of South

African destabilisation throughout Southern Africa renders such interconnections poignant and critical for both region and continent (see Chapter 9).

NOTES

1. This chapter was commissioned originally for Kofi Buenor Hadjor (ed) *New Perspectives in North-South Dialogue: essays in honour of Olaf Palme* (London: Third World Book Review, 1988).
2. Olaf Palme 'Introduction' to *Common Security: a programme for disarmament* (London: Pan, 1982) xi and xii.
3. 'Final Document: Economic Declaration Harare, September 1986', *Review of International Affairs* 37(875), 20 September 1986, para 1, 166.
4. Immanuel Wallerstein, *The Capitalist World-Economy* (Cambridge: Cambridge University Press, 1979) 269 and 282.
5. See *North-South: a programme for survival* (London: Pan, 1980) and *Common Crisis, North-South: cooperation for world recovery* (London: Pan, 1983).
6. *Common Security*, 175.
7. See 'Harare Statement: South-South cooperation — experiences and prospects' in Bernard Chidzero and Altaf Gauhar (eds) *Linking the South: the route to economic cooperation* (London: Third World Foundation, 1986) 304.
8. For an earlier attempt to situate the Non-Aligned Movement in the context of the world economy using contrasting orthodox and radical approaches to analysis, see Timothy M. Shaw 'The Political Economy of Non-Alignment: from Dependence to Self-Reliance', *International Studies* 19(3), July/September 1980, 475–502. For a related attempt to advance the sociology of knowledge about Non-Alignment in a more critical and historical direction, see A.W. Singham 'Non-Alignment — from Summit to Summit', *Man and Development* 1(3), October 1979, 1–40, and, with Shirley Hune, *Non-Alignment in an Age of Alignments* (London: Zed, 1986).
9. Wallerstein, *The Capitalist World-Economy*, 95.
10. On the notion of 'conjuncture' as related to the development of national political economies, see James H. Mittleman *Underdevelopment and the Transition to Socialism: Mozambique and Tanzania* (New York: Academic, 1981).
11. 'Declaration of the Conference of Foreign Minister of Non-Aligned Countries, New Delhi, February 1981: Economic Part', *Review of International Affairs* 32(741), 20 February 1981, 30. See also note 52 below.
12. Non-Aligned leaders are caught in a difficult dialectic: they are dependent upon external associates for support, capital, technology, markets, and imports yet they also require more of these goods than they

can ever hope to get. Hence the ambivalence generated by simultaneous conflict and co-operation as leaders at the periphery attempt to improve their position *vis-à-vis* those at the centre of the world system. Hence the gap between superstructural rhetoric and substructural reality with the former increasingly diverging from the latter.

13. On the adoption of such a rhetorical ploy by Third World leaders in their attempt to improve their position between external associates (who exploit as well as support) and internal demands, see Claude Ake *Revolutionary Pressures in Africa* (London: Zed, 1978) 92–4.
14. For an overview of these, see *World Bank World Development Report 1981* (New York: OUP, 1981) and *Financing Adjustment with Growth in Sub-Saharan Africa, 1986–90* (Washington, 1986).
15. On these two approaches, see Timothy M. Shaw 'The Non-Aligned Movement and the New International Economic Order' in Herb Addo (ed.) *Transforming the World Economy? Nine critical essays on the new international economic order* (London: Hodder & Stoughton, 1984 for UNU) 138–62.
16. A.W. Singham (ed.) 'Preface', of his collection on *The Non-Aligned Movement in World Politics* (Westport, Conn.: Lawrence Hill, 1977) iii.
17. A.W. Singham 'Conclusion' in *ibid*. 227. See also Dinesh Singh 'Non-Alignment and New International Economic Order', *Review of International Affairs* 32(755), 20 September 1981, 8–12, and Janez Stanovuik 'Non-Alignment and the New International Economic Order' *Review of International Affairs* 32(757), 20 October 1981,14–19.
18. H. Hveem and P. Willetts 'The Practice of Non-Alignment: On the Present and the Future of an International Movement' in Y.A. Tandon and D. Chandarana (eds) *Horizons of African Diplomacy* (Nairobi: EALB, 1974) 2.
19. Hveem and Willetts 'The Practice of Non-Alignment', 28.
20. Ibid., 21 and 22.
21. On this, see Timothy M. Shaw 'Dependence to (Inter)Dependence: Review of Debate on the (New) International Economic Order', *Alternatives* 4(4), March 1979, 557–78.
22. Singham 'Conclusion', 227. For more on the evolution of the Movement from political to economic preoccupations, see Miguel Angel de la Flor Valle, 'The Movement of Non-Alignment and the New International Order', *Review of International Affairs* 32(756), 5 October 1981, 15–18.
23. 'Final Document: Political Declaration 1986' para 21, 39.
24. See Craig Murphy, *The Emergence of the NIEO Ideology* (Boulder: Westview, 1984).
25. See Timothy M. Shaw 'Towards a political economy of the African crisis: diplomacy, debates and dialectics' in Michael H. Glantz (ed.) *Drought and Hunger in Africa: Denying Famine a Future* (Cambridge: Cambridge University Press, 1986) 127–47.
26. See Ankie M.M. Hoogvelt, *The Third World in Global Development* (London: Macmillan, 1982).
27. See Claude Ake 'NonAlignment in the Contemporary World: an

African perspective' *African Association of Political Science Newsletter* July-September 1986, 5–10 and L. Adele Jinadu and Ibbo Mandaza (eds) *African Perspectives on NonAlignment* (Harare: African Association of Political Science, 1986).

28. 'Political Declaration, 1976', para 167.
29. See Chidzero and Gauhar (eds) *Linking the South: the route to economic cooperation* especially ix–18 and 303–18.
30. See Hoogvelt, *The Third World in Global Development*, 73–102.
31. Ervin Laszlo, 'Introduction: the Objectives of the New International Economic Order in Historical and Global Perspective' in Ervin Laszlo *et al., The Objectives of the New International Economic Order* (New York: Pergamon for UNITAR, 1978) xviii.
32. 'Economic Declaration of the Fifth Summit Conference of the Non-Aligned Governments, Sri Lanka, August 1976' in Singham (ed.), *The Non-Aligned Movement in World Politics* (263–73) para 39.
33. 'Declaration of the Ministerial Conference, 1981: Economic Part', 31–2.
34. Laszlo, 'Introduction', xxi.
35. Cf. Timothy M. Shaw, 'Conclusion: African Development and the New International Division of Labour' in Adebayo Adedeji and Timothy M. Shaw (eds) *Economic Crisis in Africa* (Boulder: Westview and London: Frances Pinter, 1985) 267–83.
36. 'Economic Declaration, 1976', para 38.
37. Jack N. Barkenbus, 'Slowed Economic Growth and Third World Welfare' in Dennis Clark Pirages (ed.) *The Sustainable Society* (New York: Praeger, 1977) 317.
38. See Timothy M. Shaw, *Towards a Political Economy for Africa: the dialectics of dependence* (London: Macmillan, 1985).
39. On this range — from producer associations and nuclear energy to sports and women — see 'Review of Implementation of the Action Programme for Economic Cooperation', *Review of International Affairs* 32(641), 20 February 1981, 40–6.
40. See Mai Palmberg (ed.), *Problems of Socialist Orientation in Africa* (Stockholm: Almqvist & Wiksell and New York: Africana, 1978). For a rather partisan review of socialist-non-aligned relationships, see S.G. Sardesai, 'Achievements and Difficulties of Non-Alignment', *World Marxist Review*, 17 March 1974, 74–82.
41. 'Political Declaration, 1976', para 13.
42. 'Economic Declaration, 1976', para 19.
43. Ibid., paras 34 and 35.
44. Singham, 'Conclusion' 227–8. For further analysis of some of these contradictions, see Bojana Tadic, 'The Movement of the Non-Aligned and its Dilemmas Today', *Review of International Affairs* 32(756), 5 October 1981, 19–24.
45. Singham, 'Preface', x–xi.
46. See Wallerstein, *The Capitalist World-Economy*, 66–118 and Timothy M. Shaw, 'Kenya and South Africa: "Sub-Imperialist" States', *Orbis* 21(2), Summer 1977, 375–94, and 'International Stratification in Africa: Subimperialism in Eastern and Southern Africa, *Journal of South-*

ern African Affairs 2(2), April 1977, 145–64. See also Bahgat Korany 'Hierarchy within the South: in search of theory', *Third World Affairs 1986* (London: Third World Foundation, 1986), 85–100.

47. See Jerker Carlsson and Timothy M. Shaw (eds), *New-Industrialising Countries and the Political Economy of South-South Relations* (London: Macmillan, 1988.)
48. Ali A. Mazrui 'Technology, International Stratification and the Politics of Growth', *International Political Science Association*, Moscow, August 1979, 10-12. For more on inequality and interaction within the Third World, see his *The Barrel of the Gun and the Barrel of Oil in North-South Equation* (New York: World Order Models Project, 1978). Working Paper Number Five.
49. On this debate in the case of Nigeria in West Africa, see Timothy M. Shaw and Olajide Aluko (eds), *Nigerian Foreign Policy: Alternative Perceptions and Projections* (London: Macmillan, 1983). See also Timothy M. Shaw, 'Nigeria in the International System' in I. William Zartman (ed.), *The Political Economy of Nigeria* (New York: Praeger, 1983) 207–36.
50. 'Political Declaration, 1976', para 12.
51. Ibid., paras 32 and 33.
52. Fred Halliday, 'The maturing of the Non-Aligned: perspectives from New Delhi', *Third World Affairs 1985* (London: Third World Foundation, 1985) 52.
53. Ismail-Sabri Abdalla, 'Heterogeneity and Differentiation – the End for the Third World?, *Development Dialogue* 2, 1978, 11 and 10.
54. Ibid., 18.
55. 'Political Declaration, 1976', para 15.
56. Singham, 'Preface', xi.
57. Ibid. See also Singham & Hune, *Non-Alignment in an Age of Alignments*.
58. Wallerstein, *The Capitalist World-Economy*, 117–18.
59. 'Solemn Declaration to Mark the 25th Anniversary of the Non-Aligned Movement', *Review of International Affairs* 37(875), 20 September 1986, 27.
60. 'Economic Declaration, 1986', para 6, 66.

2 The Organisation of African Unity in World Politics

K. Mathews

> AFRICA is a paradox which illustrates and heightens neo-colonialism. Her earth is rich, yet the products that come from above and below her soil continue to enrich, not Africans predominantly, but groups and individuals who operate to Africa's impoverishment.[1]

> Africa is important to the United States for many reasons. Last year (1978) the United States exported $3.4 billion in goods annually and this total is expected to grow appreciably during the 1980s. Africa is also the source of many important raw materials, including 20% of imported oil and a majority of our diamonds, cobalt, platinum and other critical minerals. The 47 Sub-Saharan African countries play an important role in world diplomacy and international relations.[2]

> We African leaders must . . . realise that we cannot ask outside powers to leave us alone while, in most cases, it is our own actions which provide them with the excuse to interfere with our affairs.[3]

> As long as Africa cultivates its fields with a hoe of others, without being able to manufacture it, Africa is alienating itself. Africa will liberate itself and progress as long as it manufactures the hoe.[4]

INTRODUCTION

The present-day international system is characterised by varying degrees and types of interdependence, dependence and independence among the members of the system. It is said that not even the superpowers can act independently of each other; independence is a fantasy in a world in which all countries are interdependent. However, it is important to stress that within the international system some states are more independent than others. There is a qualitative difference between the independence of the superpowers and that of the poor Third World countries, including Africa.[5] Nevertheless, Africa is part of the international system and what happens in Africa affects the world and vice versa. Before the advent of colonialism in the 19th century Africa was a continent of autonomous regional empires and state systems. The colonial era was a period of great dependence on Europe. For obvious reasons neither the US nor the USSR had a particular interest in preserving European colonialism in Africa; it was only with the demise of European colonialism that they could begin to stake their own imperialist claims to the continent. Post-independence Africa is now characterised by varying degrees of dependence according to national ideology and resources and the issue area of interaction. However, Africa's contemporary membership in global organisations guarantees continued participation and visibility for it in the international system.[6]

At the time of the creation of the United Nations (UN) in 1945, Africa was represented by only four states: Egypt, Ethiopia, Liberia and South Africa. A decade later, the African presence in the UN had increased by only four. The independence of Ghana in March 1957 heralded a new era for Africa, however. By October 1960 25 African states were members of the UN, constituting 25 per cent of its total membership. By 1987 51 African states were members of the UN, signifying a growing importance of the 'African factor' in world politics.[7] Africa also accounts for over 50 per cent of the membership of the Non-Aligned Movement (NAM). However, the real significance of these figures is a matter of dispute.

We do not need to prove the obvious point about Africa's powerlessness to influence the international system. The ongoing crisis in the African economy, as highlighted in the May 1986 UN General Assembly Special Session on Africa, the continuing crisis in Southern Africa, among others, amply prove the point. It is an undeniable fact that political independence is a necessary, though far from sufficient, condition for autonomous participation of African states in world politics. And in the contemporary world, political independence and membership in the UN are virtually coterminous. The 1960s thus marked the formal emergence of African states as actors (or factors) in the international system. The Organization of African Unity (OAU), established in 1963, as the most important political organisation of all African states, has become an important instrument for the conduct of collective African diplomacy in the world context.

Although individual African states may be quite powerless in world politics, the collectivity of 51 members of the OAU has definitely more status and influence. The OAU provides numerous opportunities for multilateral interaction not only among African states themselves, but also facilitates Africa's collective interaction in the international system.[8] An attempt is made in this chapter to examine and analyse the role and impact of the OAU in the international system given the background of the place Africa occupies in the wider international political economy. I start with an examination of the nature and powers of the OAU itself.

THE OAU AND ITS POWERS

The OAU, which symbolises Africa, is both the largest and biggest regional organisation in world politics. It is pertinent to note that one of the main purposes of the OAU is specifically: 'to promote international cooperation, having due regard to the Charter of the United Nations and the Universal Declaration of Human Rights' [Article II(e)]. Likewise, one of the seven paramount principles of the OAU is the 'affirmation of a policy of non-alignment with regard to all blocs' [Article III(7)]. There are also other provisions of the OAU Charter which suggest an external policy role for the organisation. However, an analysis of the role of the OAU in the world context would depend on one's perception of the OAU itself. Many observers discuss the OAU's role in world affairs as if the organisation is an autonomous and independent body capable of making and exerting its own decisions. Others even perceive the organisation as a supranational body endowed with powers to influence and control decisions and actions of its member-states. Still others view the OAU as a body whose function should largely be integrative; that is, it should be concerned with promoting the harmonisation of external policies of its member-states. These various perceptions have obviously coloured the thinking and evaluation of observers regarding the role of the OAU in intra-African as well as extra-African politics.[9] A better understanding of the real nature and powers of the OAU, is, therefore, a precondition for evaluating its role in world politics.

A crucial characteristic of the OAU is the fact that it is essentially an organisation created by and for the African petty bourgeoisie. This fact is clearly observable in the Assembly of Heads of State and Government, the supreme organ of the OAU. Significantly, the opening words of the Charter are: 'WE THE HEADS OF AFRICAN STATES and Government . . . have agreed to this Charter.' According to the Charter the projected unity of Africa is to be forged and links established, not among African peoples, but 'between our

States' which means 'between our Governments' created by the African petty bourgeoisie. A study of the seven basic principles of the OAU contained in Article III of its Charter confirms this. Accordingly the Charter declares that member-states solemnly affirm and declare and resolve to respect the sovereign equality of all states, agree not to interfere in the internal affairs of other states, and honour each state's sovereignty and territorial integrity. Another principle denounces 'political assassination as well as subversive activities on the part of neighbouring states or any other state'.[10] Briefly, it would seem that the OAU was created to protect, almost exclusively, the interests of the African ruling class who constitute the Heads of State and Government rather than the peoples of Africa. This has made the OAU look like a sort of 'Trade Union of African Heads of State' far removed from and often working against the genuine interests of the African masses. This structural deformity is replicated in the Council of Ministers and Specialised Commissions.[11]

Historically, the OAU was created as a compromise between two groups, diametrically opposed in African politics, that emerged in the early 1960s, and which dominated the founding conference of the OAU at Addis Ababa in May 1963. They were represented by the 'conservative' Monrovia and the 'radical' Casablanca Groups. While the Casablanca Group viewed all African political integration as the only legitimate way of securing African independence and liberation, the Monrovia Group wanted only some sort of alliance and voluntary co-operation among the governing classes for the maintenance of the status quo. What the moderates wished to do under the umbrella of the OAU was to build on the common Africanness of the states in the region in order to promote co-operation and interdependence among them, to co-ordinate their policies and actions in certain areas and to reduce conflicts among them while maintaining their full independence and sovereign identities. In contrast, the radical group advocated essentially unity of the African peoples. The OAU was expected to be, if not a mass movement whose goal would be to transform Africa, at least a loose confederation of states aimed at bringing about a higher level of political integration among African states and, by implication, the dissolution of the territorial boundaries inherited from colonial powers.

The difference between the two opposing groups in African politics was not a mere disagreement over strategies for integration in Africa. It was a much more fundamental difference. It was a division between those who saw African underdevelopment as the product of imperialism and those who did not; between those who saw imperialism as simple colonialism and those who appreciated the more sinister implications and deeper roots of imperialism; between those who favoured the mobilisation of the African masses against imperialist domination of the continent and those who favoured collaboration with imperialism against both the progressive African leaders and their socialist allies; between those who favoured a progressive transformation of the continent through institutional integration and those who favoured gradual reform through inter-state collaboration. It is significant to stress that the struggle between the above two groups ended in favour of the conservative Monrovia bloc who constituted the vast majority at the founding conference of the OAU in Addis Ababa in May 1963. This dichotomous situation between groups of African states still prevails and considerably limits the role of the OAU in African and world affairs.

There are also other constraints on the role of the African sub-system. It is to be noted that the OAU is a corporate body which derives its power and authority from its members; that is, the extent to which it can act is limited by its member-states. It has no autonomy of its own, and cannot act independently. Its activities are derived largely from decisions and directives of the Assembly of Heads of State and Government and of the Council of Ministers. It is important to note that these organs of the OAU are composed of individual member-states acting collectively. In fact, the member-states have not found it easy to delegate their individual or collective powers to the body of their own creation. Briefly, it can be said that the extent to which the OAU can play a role in the international system, as in other areas, is limited in many ways.

SOME THEORETICAL CONSIDERATIONS

In simple terms an international system can be defined as the pattern of relations among actors in world politics.[12] A sub-system is, then, the pattern of relations among some but not all of the actors in world politics or the pattern of relations among all actors with respect to some but not all issue areas of world politics. The contemporary international system is characterised by both congruence and discontinuity, with similarities and dissimilarities between the global system and the regional sub-systems themselves.[13] A study of the interaction between the African sub-system and the international system will help systematic comparisons.

The most salient feature of the African sub-system is that it is penetrated. According to James Rosenau,

> A penetrated political system is one in which nonmembers of a national society participate directly and authoritatively, through actions taken jointly with the society's members, in either the allocation of its values or the mobilization of support on behalf of its goals.[14]

A penetrated sub-system would therefore be one in which external actors play a significant role in the processes within the system. Such a situation results from the low level of capabilities of the members of the sub-system *vis-à-vis* the external actors concerned, the dependence of the sub-system members on the external actors, and the importance of the sub-system to the external actors.

It is only too well known that the African sub-system is essentially composed of weak and underdeveloped states. In spite of Africa's possession of enormous natural and human resources, Africa is strikingly behind the rest of the Third World in development, with the largest concentration of the poorest countries of the world.[15] The populations of African countries are generally small and their economies underdeveloped (see Table 2.1).

In 1986, for example, only four out of the 53 African countries (Egypt, Ethiopia, Nigeria and South Africa) had populations of over 30 million; 26 had populations under 5 million (see Table 2.1); 12 had populations under 1 million.[16] In the same year only seven countries, including the oil producing countries, had a per capita GNP of US$ 1000 or above.[17] Although over 10 per cent of world's total population lives in Africa, its share of world industrial output is less than 1 per cent. In short, the economic and social position of most African countries is simply abysmal. It can be safely asserted that the poverty and weakness of African states is a negative factor in terms of power relationships with the external actors and is in part responsible for the penetration of the sub-system by the external powers.

A second factor that explains the penetration of a sub-system by external actors is the importance that the external actors attach to the sub-system. It may be noted that, with the exception of Ethiopia and Liberia, all African countries were formerly colonies of European powers. The result of this was that at the time of independence external actors had substantial economic interests in the African

TABLE 2.1 *Basic Data on African States, 1986*

State	*Area in Sq. km.*	*Population in millions 1986*	*GNP per capita 1986 US $*
1 Algeria	2 381 741	21.5	2 400
2 Angola	2 246 700	8.5	470
3 Benin	112 622	3.9	290
4 Botswana	582 000	1.0	900
5 Burkina Faso	274 200	6.6	180
6 Burundi	27 834	4.6	240
7 Cameroon	475 000	9.5	820
8 Cape Verde Republic	4 033	0.3	320
9 Central African Republic	622 984	2.5	280
10 Chad	1 284 000	4.9	80
11 Comoro Republic	2 171	0.4	340
12 Congo	342 000	1.7	1 220
13 Cote d'lvoire	322 463	9.4	710
14 Djibouti	22 000	0.4	480
15 Egypt	1 002 000	45.8	690
16 Equatorial Guinea	28 051	0.4	310
17 Ethiopia	1 221 900	43.3	120
18 Gabon	267 667	1.1	3 430
19 Gambia	11 295	0.6	290
20 Ghana	238 537	13.1	320
21 Guinea	245 957	5.9	300
22 Guinea-Bissau	36 125	0.9	190
23 Kenya	582 646	20.3	340
24 Lesotho	30 355	1.5	560
25 Liberia	111 369	2.2	480
26 Libya	1 759 540	3.6	8 460
27 Madagascar	587 041	9.7	310
28 Malawi	118 484	7.0	210
29 Mali	1 240 192	8.2	150
30 Mauritania	1 030 700	1.8	480
31 Mauritius	2 045	0.9	1 160
32 Morocco	446 550	21.4	760
33 Mozambique	801 590	13.6	270
34 Namibia	824 292	1.5	170
35 Niger	1 267 000	5.9	240
36 Nigeria	923 768	92.0	770
37 Rwanda	26 338	5.8	270
38 Sao Tome and Principe	964	0.09	340
39 Senegal	196 192	6.4	440
40 Seychelles	280	0.06	2 430
41 Sierra Leone	71 470	3.5	330
42 Somalia	637 657	4.5	250
43 South Africa	1 221 037	32.5	2 285

State	Area in Sq. km.	Population in millions 1986	GNP per capita 1986 US $
44 Sudan	2 505 813	21.0	400
45 Swaziland	17 363	0.6	870
46 Tanzania	945 087	21.7	240
47 Togo	56 000	2.8	280
48 Tunisia	163 610	6.9	1 290
49 Uganda	236 036	14.9	220
50 Western Sahara (SADR)	266 770	0.07	n.a.
51 Zaire	2 345 409	29.0	170
52 Zambia	752 614	6.4	580
53 Zimbabwe	390 580	8.3	740

SOURCE Based on participation at the Eighth Non-Aligned Summit, Harare, Zimbabwe, September 1986 (except for South Africa and Western Sahara). *Review of International Affairs* (Belgrade) vol. 37, no. 875, 20 September 1986.

states in the form of investments, access to raw materials especially minerals and extensive trade links. The desire of the former colonial powers to protect these interests coupled with efforts by other external actors (China, Cuba, Japan; the Soviet Union and the United States in recent years) to encroach on these interests made the African sub-system important to external actors.

The importance of the African sub-system derives also from geopolitical concerns. Strategically Africa is important because it borders on the Mediterranean, the Atlantic and the Indian Oceans, where the superpowers compete for dominance. Moreover, in the context of the East-West Cold War and the competition for influence and prestige between them, African states are important as potential allies as well as for their votes in the various international organisations and conferences.

In this context it is equally important to note that one of the cardinal features of the African sub-system is the entrenched dependence of its members on external powers. Although all the member states of the OAU are legally sovereign they lack actual power to act independently. All of them are economically and militarily dependent on states of Europe, America and the Soviet Union. African countries largely trade with Europe and America and receive financial and technical assistance from them. African states have very little (less than 3 per cent of the total) trade among themselves. African states, moreover, depend on the same external actors to train their soldiers, equip them and prepare them to ensure the defence and security of their territories.

In other words, in various ways African states are tied to the apron strings of the states of Europe and America. There is hardly any African state that can be said to enjoy a truly independent existence. As a result of this dependence, the decisions and actions of African states, concerning both domestic and external affairs, are determined and shaped by extra-African powers on which they depend for both survival and development. This condition of post-colonial Africa is the reality of neo-colonialism on the continent. Thus, in the mid-1960s, Nkrumah could argue that,

> The essence of neo-colonialism is that the state which is subject to it is, in theory independent and has all the outward trappings of international sovereignty. In reality its economic system and thus its political policy is directed from outside.[18]

Julius Nyerere, one of the foremost contemporary exponents of African thought on international affairs has noted:

> The reality of neo-colonialism quickly becomes obvious to a new African government which tries to act on economic matters in the interest of national development and for the betterment of its own masses. For, such a government immediately discovers that it inherited the power to make laws, to direct the civil service, to deal with foreign governments and so on, but it did not inherit effective power over economic developments in its own country. Indeed, it often discovers that there is no such thing as a national economy at all. Instead there exists in its land various economic activities which are owned by people outside its jurisdiction, which are directed at external needs, and which are run in the interests of external economic powers.[19]

As Greg Lanning and Marti Mueller point out:

> Foreign mining companies created Africa's dependent economic structure and incorporated the continent into the world economy. And today Africa's subordinate position in a world economy dominated by the advanced industrial nations is maintained by the giant international companies. The obstacles blocking the way are

too great, and the forces too powerful, for a poverty-stricken African state, however richly endowed with resources, to develop its potential as part of the world capitalist system.[20]

Briefly, as another analyst rightly argues,

Both the colonial and peripheral social formation can only be understood in terms of the more complex social formation to which they belong: the evolving world capitalist system. They are both an integral part of that system, by virtue of the fact that surplus was and is regularly and systematically transferred from them to the advanced part of the system. They differ, however, in that whereas surplus transfer from the colonial social formation was based, *in the last resort on the political domination* by one part of the system over the other, surplus transfer from the peripheral social formation to the centre of the world capitalist system is now essentially based on *economic constraints*, that is, on the peculiar relationships which economically bind both parts of the system to one another, and the peculiar type of class alignments and class contradictions which goes with that bond.[21]

In other words, neo-colonialism can be defined as 'the survival of the colonial system in spite of the formal recognition of political independence in emerging countries which become the victims of an indirect and subtle form of domination by political, economic, social, military, and technical means'.[22] The neo-colonial objective is accomplished through European colonialists relinquishing power to 'an (African) intermediary . . . the transmission belt between the nation and the capitalists . . . that puts on the mask of neo-colonialism'.[23] One of the main ploys of neo-colonialism is to make sure that the dominated countries do not have too much direct horizontal contacts among themselves, particularly not economic interaction or trade. Furthermore, contacts with the outside world must be vertical — towards the center — as established, in recent years, under the various Lomé Conventions (1975, 1980 and 1985) (see chapter 3).

Another vital area of Africa's current neo-colonial dependence on the West relates to the powerful role of the International Monetary Fund (IMF) and the World Bank — the foremost capitalist Western institutions — in African countries. Particularly in the 1980–85 period almost all countries of the continent have gone through the agonies of negotiating to borrow from the IMF.[24] Everywhere on the continent governments seem to be formulating their programmes in the image of the IMF, apparently indicating their greater acceptance of the IMF view of the world. More and more countries are beginning to accept that the IMF policies represent a reality with which a poor country has to live. This acceptance is clearly forced by circumstances, especially the absence of any easily accessible alternatives, since the adoption of the IMF programme (with its attendant conditions of all kinds of austerity measures: devaluation, retrenchment, wage freeze, higher prices, and so on) is now insisted on by the major donor countries as well as by the World Bank as a precondition for any assistance. It is commonly acknowledged that the IMF programmes are clearly directed at making the African countries perform better in their client relationship with the West.[25]

A more fundamental aspect of present-day neo-colonialism in Africa relates to the fast expansion of trans- or multinational corporations (MNCs) who control more than one-third of the GNP of the capitalist world and more than 50 per cent of its foreign trade besides four-fifths of the exchange of technological 'know-how'. In Africa, there has been a growing trend — even in the so-called socialist states like Angola and Mozambique — to lobby for MNC investment.[26]. In fact, one of the most disturbing aspects of recent African development has been the growing partnership between African governments and private or public financiers in the West. This race appears to bridge ideological differences. The cases of South Africa, Ivory Coast, Zaire, Nigeria, Kenya, and so on, are well-known.[27] Even Sékou Touré's socialist Guinea, after 25 years of close association with the Soviet bloc, has turned to Western companies to exploit Guinea's extensive resources of bauxite, iron ore and diamonds.[28] Countries like Nigeria and Angola in their craze for foreign earnings invited MNCs to expand the extractive sector, often with a single item export, fetching varying prices in the world market. This reduced whatever autonomy these countries had in the beginning to diversify their economics and trade linkages. Nigeria's oil has attracted partnership between the government and such giant oil companies as Shell-BP, Gulf, Mobil, Agip, Phillips and others.

One of the most critical outcomes of the ever-expanding role of MNCs in Africa (as elsewhere in the Third World) has been the accentuation of domestic and regional inequalities. The states which have mining or energy resources can attract foreign capital on a larger scale than those who do not have them. This aggravates uneven development between the two groups of states. As Timothy

Shaw and Malcolm Grieve have pointed out: 'Today African states with oil, uranium, phosphates and other minerals have enhanced economic prospects at least in the medium term'.[29] They also argue that 'states with large populations and initiatives and those most amenable to the interests of multinationals have come to dominate continental decision-making'. This trend towards inequality within and among African states, according to them, would give rise to 'sub-imperial states within the capitalist system, which though subordinates in world politics, may play regional hegemony. For, their ruling classes are able to perpetuate their internal power and international influence through association with one or more of the central actors of the multipolar international system'.[30] The combined impact of sub-imperialism, differential growth and alternative development strategies will together tend to revive ideological cleavages and conflicts on the continent, reminiscent of the pre-OAU Casablanca/Monrovia schisms. Tensions between the rich and the poor, between the 'moderates' and the 'radicals' in Africa will be exacerbated by regional conflicts supported by antagonistic external forces. I now look at the role of the OAU in this area.

OAU AND FOREIGN INTERVENTION IN AFRICAN CONFLICTS

Perhaps, nowhere is the imperialist and neo-colonialist domination of Africa and the OAU more clearly exposed than in the area of external intervention in intra-African conflicts (see chapters 7 and 8). For an understanding of the character and categories of intra-African conflicts and their relationship to external intervention and the role of the OAU it is necessary to appreciate the character of international conflicts generally. Intra-African conflicts manifest themselves in different forms — in 'hot' wars (that is, armed conflicts) or in 'cold' wars (namely, ideological struggles or contests). A more detailed categorisation of intra-African conflicts may be obtained by looking at the different sources of conflict in contemporary Africa.[31] In the early years of African independence the main source of intra-African conflicts lay in the struggle for territories and disagreement over boundaries.[32] Examples of such early conflicts include among others: Algeria versus Morocco; Somalia versus Ethiopia and Kenya; Nigeria versus Cameroon; and Morocco versus Mauritania.[33] The Somalian-Ethiopian conflict, for example, has its roots, in the first place, in colonialism and the armed aspect of it involved the intervention by the two superpowers and their African, Arab and Latin American allies.[34]

Many inter-state conflicts in Africa often result from the overflow and consequences of internal conflicts. It is also becoming increasingly clear that such conflicts themselves do not always or necessarily originate, in internal sources. Moreover, intra-state conflicts in Africa are, in the main, the consequence rather than the cause of external intervention and once in progress attract further such intervention.

There are several ways in which, and several reasons why, external actors create dissention, rebellion and conflict in African states. Firstly, for example, foreign powers often intervene against emerging radical regimes in Africa regarded as a threat to the *status quo* in the region or sub-region. Such intervention takes several forms: sponsored *coups d'état*; creation of and/or support for opposition groups; economic sanctions and 'press war' designed to undermine the legitimacy of the regime; the isolated or combined use of neighbouring states, mercenaries, and direct military intervention to destabilise the regime. Patrice Lumumba's government in Congo (Zaire) was one of the earliest victims of such attempts. Other examples include: Nkrumah of Ghana (1966); Obote of Uganda (1971); Sékou Touré of Guinea (1970); Mathieu Kerekou of Benin (1977); Albert René of Seychelles (1981); and Muammar Gaddafi of Libya (1986).

Secondly, an extra-African power could also set out to depose a pliant regime and replace it with another if it has already served its purpose, has outlived its usefulness and now constitutes an embarrassment to the external power. Often such a change is effected in order to prevent a total breakdown of law and order in the state. Examples of this category in recent years include those of: Ngarta Tombalbaye of Chad (1974); Jean-Bedel Bokassa of Central African Republic (1979); and Jafar-El Nimeiry of Sudan (1985). Also intra-state conflict could result if the pro-imperialist regime is surrounded by anti-imperialist states. They could take sides with the factions within the pro-imperialist state and complicate the problem of external intervention. Alternatively, the anti-imperialist regime could see the continuance in power of the pliant, pro-imperialist regime as a danger to its own security. In either case, the result is usually conflict.

Besides, the action of an extra-African power to buttress a neocolonialist regime generates intra-African conflict in another way. Usually, a regime which relies primarily on external powers for its continued stay in office is inherently a source of both internal and external conflicts. Such a regime finds it unnecessary to build up internal/domestic popular support. Relying on external powers for survival, neo-colonialist regimes provoke internal hostility which ultimately leads to their removal. This in turn further exacerbates domestic tension, attracting greater external intervention. The cycle of the relationship between external intervention and intra-African conflicts become complete.[35] Examples include the conflicts in South Africa and Namibia and those surrounding the states of Sudan and Chad.

The question of intra-African conflicts is related to the African struggle against neo-colonial domination and exploitation of the continent. The achievement of political independence has indeed been a major step forward. Obviously, with the political withdrawal of colonial powers from Africa and the installation of 'independent' African governments, even inter-imperialist conflicts can only be waged through and against these governments. Thus, what may appear at first sight to be a purely 'territorial' dispute between African states (for instance, Western Sahara) may only be a continuing struggle of the people against imperialism, which is now in its neo-colonial phase. What may appear to be a case of subversion (for example, the Shaba crisis of 1977–78) may again be a continuation of the old story in a new form.

In order to assess the response of the OAU towards foreign intervention in intra-African conflicts, it is necessary to study each situation individually, which is beyond the scope of this chapter. At a general level one may make two observations, however. The first is that external intervention, as indicated earlier on, takes many overt and covert forms. The deployment of Moroccan troops to quell the Shaba rebellion is clearly a covert proxy intervention by Western imperialism; that is to say, the use of the troops of one African state in another African state, just as in an earlier decade the United States used Thai and Filipino troops to fight its battles in another Asian country — Vietnam. The installation of a new government in the Comoro Republic by 'Colonel Denard' and his band of mercenaries is another case of covert intervention by French imperialism. The South African mercenary attempt to overthrow the socialist government of President Albert René in Seychelles in 1981 falls into the same category. On the other side, the use of Cuban troops to quash the democratic aspirations of the oppressed nationalities in Ethiopia and Eritrea, though this one has a revolutionary veneer to it, is no less a case of intervention by the Soviet Union in the struggles of the peoples of Africa. Even the Nigerian civil war (1967–70), which at first sight appeared to be an ethnic war, was a war in which the superpowers fought through proxies to protect or advance their own interests.[36]

The second observation relates to the role of the OAU in alerting its members about these overt and covert forms of foreign interventions that either initiate or compound intra-African contradictions. The usual reaction among the OAU members is to see the mote in the other's eyes, while not seeing it in their own. Thus Angola could accuse Zaire of the presence of French troops in its territory, and be accused in turn of depending on Cuban troops. In fact, the economic and military stakes in Africa are too high to allow the foreign powers to quit the continent. Hence we are likely to witness an intensification of superpower confrontations on the continent which would variously appear as a 'border problem', or a problem of 'subversion' or an 'ethnic' war. This is the greatest danger that lurks in Africa. At the moment, the OAU can only reflect the weakness and contradictions of its general membership.

In recent years, particularly since its 15th summit in Khartoum in July 1978, the OAU has been trying seriously to grapple with the problem of foreign intervention in Africa.[37] As Colin Legum has pointed out, three distinctly different attitudes have emerged over the question of foreign intervention and its role in African politics. One minority attitude, representing perhaps eight OAU members,[38] strongly endorsed the role of the Soviet bloc and Cuba in all the current conflicts on the continent. A second minority attitude, representing about a dozen OAU members,[39] condemned all forms of Soviet/Cuban intervention and favoured greater Western involvement instead. But a third attitude, representing the majority of the OAU members, remained true to the principles of non-alignment; yet they qualified their opposition by endorsing foreign intervention in particular situations. The former Tanzanian President, Julius Nyerere, reflected this position when he stated:

> We regret, even while we recognise its occasional necessity, that an African government should ask for military assistance from a non-African country when it is faced with an external threat to its national sovereignty. We know that a response to such a request by any of the big Powers is determined by what that big Power sees as its own interest. We have been forced to recognise that most of the

> countries acknowledged as world Powers do not find it beneath their dignity to exacerbate existing and genuine African problems and conflicts when they believe they can benefit by doing so. We . . . believe that African countries, separately and through the OAU, need to guard against such actions. But we need to guard Africa against Africa being used by any other nation or group of nations. The danger to Africa does not come just from nations in the Eastern bloc. The West still considers Africa to be within its sphere of influence, and acts accordingly. Current developments show that the greater immediate danger to Africa's freedom comes from nations in that Western bloc. We reject the right of Western European countries to dominate Africa, just as much as we would reject attempts by Eastern bloc countries to dominate Africa.[40]

Nigeria's former President, General Olusegun Obasanjo's strictures about the share of responsibility Africans must themselves shoulder for inviting foreign intervention (see opening quotation) were strongly reinforced by Guinea's President Sékou Touré in his address to the Khartoum summit: 'We Africans are more responsible for our misfortunes than imperialism'.[41] A totally different view was expressed by Senegal's former President, Leopold Senghor when he stated:

> The West is illogical. If it wants us to defend ourselves against the forces of external aggression, against the forces of international communism, it must give us the means to do so. Otherwise, it can sit back and watch Africa fall to international communism. The West doesn't want that to happen, but also it doesn't want to spend money to aid us. What we are experiencing at present is the first phase of World War III — and the East has the edge on us because it has definite objectives and is prepared to commit very efficient, modern and expensive means towards attaining them.[42]

Obviously, Senghor was not speaking for himself alone.

Briefly, as recent developments (for instance, ever-escalating foreign intervention in Southern Africa, Chad, the Horn of Africa and the overt American military attack on Libya in April 1986) indicate, foreign intervention in Africa is endemic and seems likely to grow rather than diminish in the near future. All major foreign powers and a number of minor ones (including Arab states, Israel, Cuba and so on) are actively involved in African conflicts. Their intervention is made possible mainly because of the policies pursued by African leaders.

With regard to the responses of the OAU to foreign intervention in African conflicts it must be stressed that they merely reflect the attitude of African leaders and remain a poor testimony of that organisation's ability either to aid the victims of external intervention or to stamp out such instances. It is well known that the OAU has been quite ineffective in the conflicts in Southern Africa, in the Horn of Africa, in Chad, in Western Sahara and elsewhere.[43] These and other conflicts are all symptoms of a deep-seated malaise; namely, the vulnerability of the continent to imperialist machinations and the utter impotence of the OAU in maintaining peace and security in Africa. Unlike other regional organisations (for example, the Arab League and the OAS) the OAU Charter contains no provision for collective security in Africa in the sense that member states are legally obliged to come to the assistance of other members in the event of aggression. An African High Command, though advocated by Nkrumah and others, was never created.[44] There is also no standing peace-keeping force under the command of the OAU and the fiasco of the one attempted by the OAU in Chad in 1981 is well known.[45] The Chadian and other experiences of the OAU are a sad commentary on the lack of readiness on the part of the OAU and serve as a good reminder to all African states of the urgent need to reform and restructure the organisation's machinery.

As indicated earlier, even the verbal pronouncements of African leaders on external intervention quite often contradict each other. Similar contradictions can be discerned in the OAU's pronounced policy on non-alignment.

THE OAU AND AFRICAN NON-ALIGNMENT

If one carefully examines the general characteristics of non-alignment in world politics as understood by its proponents, one also sees it as an active policy designed to exploit the Cold War for those who accept the East-West divide as the basis of their foreign policy. According to the proponents of non-alignment, its benefits range over a wide area. It has been justified: (1) as a means of ensuring freedom and independence; (2) for keeping small powers out of larger conflicts of no concern to them; (3) as a means of avoiding alliances which make local problems more difficult to solve; (4) as a

TABLE 2.2 *Africa in the Non-Aligned Conferences*

Year	*Conference*	*Total Participants*	*African States*	*Percentage African*
1955	Bandung Conference	24	6	25%
1961	Belgrade Summit	25	11	44%
1964	Cairo Summit	47	28	59.6%
1970	Lusaka Summit	53	33	62%
1973	Algiers Summit	75	41	54.7%
1976	Colombo Summit	86	47	55.8%
1979	Havana Summit	95	51	53.5%
1983	New Delhi Summit	100	51	51%
1986	Harare Summit	101	51	50%

SOURCE Various records of the Non-Aligned Conferences.

means of preventing the diversion of scarce resources to military obligations; and (5) as a means of obtaining aid from both sides. It was no wonder that African countries saw non-alignment as a logical ideology capable of guiding the continent in world politics in an endeavour to secure a favourable atmosphere for the realisation of their national aspirations.

At the first summit conference of the non-aligned countries in Belgrade in 1961, Africa, though not as yet a numerical majority (see Table 2.2), made a forceful entry into the movement. All African countries had by then declared non-alignment as the basis of their individual foreign policies, though direction and degree of commitment varied from state to state. Thus, the 1963 Addis Ababa summit, which founded the OAU, had no difficulty in including as one of its basic principles 'an affirmation of a policy of non-alignment with regard to all blocs'. Discussing the role of the OAU in non-alignment, Diallo Telli, its first Secretary-General stated at the second summit of the non-aligned countries in Cairo in October 1964:

> Non-alignment has been written into the OAU Charter as a positive principle to guide the external policy of African governments. Thus a concept that could have been at best elaborated into a policy is elevated to the level of a principle. The significance of this can hardly be over emphasised. It was born out of a deep conviction that if Africa is to contribute to the maintenance of peace it can do so only by effectively insulating itself from the cold war. There is also a sincere belief that the essentials of the cold war have nothing to do with present problems.[46]

As indicated in Table 2.2 African participation in the various non-aligned summits was consistently impressive as all the newly independent African countries were admitted to the movement. A glance at the documents and resolutions of these conferences would show that African problems, particularly the question of Southern Africa, Chad, Western Sahara and the deepening economic crisis on the continent, received particular attention. These conferences — particularly the sixth summit in Havana (Cuba) in September 1979 — were also indicative of the basically anti-imperialist character of the NAM.[47] They called for total decolonisation of Africa and sternly opposed the destabilising and divisive tactics of imperialism. It may be said that the four (out of eight) non-aligned summit conferences held in Africa (that is, Cairo 1964, Lusaka 1970, Algiers 1973 and Harare 1986) were collective high-water marks indicating the concern this movement has shown towards the problems and predicaments of Africa. In a sense, by sheer weight of numbers, African states have made the NAM more representative and broad-based than what it had been in the early 1960s.

However, (as noted elsewhere in this book), Africa's adherence to and the OAU's advocacy of the policy of non-alignment is fraught with contradictions. The flexible attitude of African countries encouraged them to pursue divergent goals in their foreign relations. Some African states professed non-alignment even as they became closely integrated with the defence arrangements of external powers. This is particularly so in the case of most francophone states which have retained French military bases in their territories in order to secure larger economic benefits from France. Some even pleaded for active French intervention to defend and preserve their own national integrity. Some African states offered military facilities to the superpowers. Thus, Angola and post-revolutionary Ethiopia turned to the Soviet Union and accepted a large number of Cuban troops to defend and guard their territorial integrity against foreign invaders. This caused the neighbouring states to turn to American and Western sources for countervailing military assistance. The United States obtained naval facilities from Somalia and Kenya before offering them large amounts of economic and military assistance. The cases of Egypt, Morocco, Liberia, Zaire, and others are well-known. Many of these countries could be, strictly speaking, disqualified from membership in NAM. It is rightly said that, in the process of increasing its own ranks, the movement has maximised membership at the expense of homogeneity.[48]

Moreover, at the economic level, Africa's integration into the world capitalist system and increasing dependence on external powers, as shown earlier, continues to be crucial. Despite the OAU's Lagos Plan of Action and the call for collective self-reliance, few African countries have shown the capacity to move out of their dependency on the major Western economies. Africa's association with the European Economic Community (EEC) under the Lomé Conventions shows that for trade and economic co-operation African countries have turned increasingly to the very same quarters which they have otherwise condemned as neo-colonial. Moreover, African states have continued borrowing from Western sources at an alarming rate — resulting in an external debt of about $200 billion by 1987. In short, most African countries are tied to the apron-strings of the Western powers. Many African governments, in fact, have decided to compromise on much of their non-aligned stance for the sake of economic advantage.

In brief, it may be said that non-alignment reflects a clear understanding of the realities and contradictions in the contemporary international system. It is primarily an attempt by weaker nations to combine their strength to develop a critical counterforce to promote their common interests in the face of opposition by the powerful nations. The weak nations cannot do much about the critical aspects of their weakness without combining their strength. This is particularly true of Africa which is decidedly the weakest and most marginalised region in the international system. Among the major problems and weaknesses which Africa hopes to overcome with the help of non-alignment are those associated with her colonial past and neo-colonial present which shape and reshape Africa's socio-economic conditions. Africa has to fight the colonialism and imperialism of both apartheid South Africa and its Western allies. One major attraction of NAM for Africa is the possibility of strengthening the anti-colonial struggle through the solidarity of other Third World countries such as India and Cuba.

Another equally compelling attraction of non-alignment for Africa is that it offers some potential for the redress of economic imbalances and inequities in the present world economic order. In this regard Africa's interest in non-alignment is more in tune with the major thrust of the movement in recent years. Nothing has shaped the solidarity and the profile of the contemporary NAM as much as the economic question. The doctrine of non-alignment has itself undergone critical changes in recent years. While the emphasis in earlier days was on military disengagement, non-alignment, since the early 1970s, has become predominantly a doctrine of economic liberation. The role of the NAM in the Third World struggle for the establishment of a New International Economic Order (NIEO) in recent years illustrates this point. I now turn to a consideration of the OAU's role in the quest for a NIEO.

THE OAU, AFRICA AND A NEW INTERNATIONAL ECONOMIC ORDER

As noted earlier, no other region of the world establishes so sharply and so starkly the need for a New International Economic Order (NIEO) as does the continent of Africa. It is, therefore, to be expected that the continent with the most to lose by the continuation of the existing economic order would be the most vigorous in working towards a new one. It is no wonder then, that Africa and the OAU have shown keen interest in and have been at the centre of the Third World struggle for a NIEO over the past decade. It should be noted that the question of African economic development was a serious concern of the early Pan-African movement. A major objective enshrined in the OAU Charter placed a duty on the members 'to achieve a better life for the peoples of Africa' (Art. II(b)). Moreover, a Special Resolution adopted at the founding OAU summit in Addis Ababa in May 1963 on Problems of African Economic Co-operation and Development made far-reaching recommendations on various aspects of the problem, including the establishment of a common external tariff, restructuring of international trade, establishment of a Pan-African monetary system, and harmonisation of national development plans. In 1963 the majority of the African leaders also believed that African unity could be realised only through economic co-operation.

Unlike in the 1960s when the OAU was primarily preoccupied with political problems, in the 1970s and 1980s, the OAU, in conjunction with the ECA, has made some efforts to deal with the grave social and economic problems of Africa.[49] Significantly, the OAU's 10th anniversary summit in Addis Ababa in 1973 adopted the 'African Declaration on Co-operation, Development and Economic Independence'. It put forward, among other things, Africa's demand for the establishment of a NIEO which was later taken up at the fourth summit of the non-aligned countries in Algiers in September 1973, where the OAU members commanded a majority. Thus, it was as a result of the demands of the OAU, later endorsed by the NAM, that the UN General Assembly met in the Sixth Special Session (the first of its kind on economic issues) in April-May 1974 and adopted the well-known 'Declaration' and 'Programme of Action' on the establishment of a NIEO.[50] In December 1974 the General Assembly also adopted the 'Charter of Economic Rights and Duties of States'.[51] In 1975, at the Seventh Special Session of the General Assembly, another resolution was adopted on 'Development and International Economic Co-operation'.[52] The above four resolutions formed the basis of the Third World demand for the establishment of a NIEO as a means of bringing about more radical changes for the development of the African and Third World countries.

However, it is to be pointed out that the OAU's role with regard to a NIEO has largely remained marginal. Nevertheless, the OAU Council of Ministers did pass a resolution on the NIEO which was adopted by the 12th OAU Summit in Kampala, Uganda in July 1975.[53] This noted significantly that 'the responsibility for their [African] development rests on the African countries themselves'.

Most of the OAU resolutions on economic relations, among other things, have called for the strengthening of solidarity within the Group of 77 and the reform of the machinery of UNCTAD in order to reflect the aspirations of the expanded world community. For understandable reasons, OAU members have not been happy with the outcome of the various UNCTAD Conferences,[54] mainly because of the rigid attitude and lack of realistic understanding on the part of the developed countries who are resistant to the necessary changes being demanded by the developing countries. As the OAU Council of Ministers has noted, it appeared that the governments of developed countries wanted to replace the multinational framework of negotiation, the pooling of ideas and endeavours to combat injustices, with a preponderance of bilateral relations with developing countries, such as the world still condemns in the existing system of international trade and aid development. It was as if a preference had been abruptly shown for altruistic aid bound up solely with the overriding needs and political interests of the developed countries.[55]

The devastating effects of the oil crisis and the rapid deterioration of African economies in the mid-1970s forced African countries and the OAU to pay continued attention to the continent's economic and social problems, as symbolised in the OAU's 'Kinshasa Declaration' of December 1976, which made far-reaching recommendations including the creation of an African Economic Community (AEC). In 1979 the OAU and the ECA jointly organised a colloquium in

Monrovia (Liberia) on the 'Future Development Prospects of Africa by the year 2000'. Some of the major conclusions of this symposium formed the basic text of the now well known book, *What Kind of Africa by the Year 2000?*[56]

The most significant OAU initiative in the economic field, however, was the adoption in 1980 of the *Lagos Plan of Action* (*LPA*) which set out comprehensively the actions which African countries should take at the national, sub-regional and regional levels in order to achieve economic integration by the year 2000. It was envisaged and hoped that the various measures recommended therein when (and if!) successfully executed would lead to the creation of an African Economic Community (AEC) by the end of the century.[57] In a separate Resolution on the Participation of Africa in International Negotiations, the African Heads of State deplored the lack of political will and the negative attitude of industrialised countries in international negotiations relating to the restructuring of the world economy for the establishment of a NIEO. The resolution also appealed to the OAU member-states to participate fully and actively in the international economic negotiations especially at the 11th Special Session of the UN General Assembly (the third on economic issues) in September 1980. It is noteworthy that this Special Session was held only a few months after the OAU's Lagos economic summit. By appending the LPA to the basic UN Document (A/S–11/14), the African Group succeeded in letting the world know of what Africa planned to do for itself and what the world community could contribute towards African programmes.

In 1981 the World Bank published a key report entitled *Accelerated Development in Sub-Saharan Africa: An Agenda for Action*. It was said that the study was commissioned at the request of the African Governors of the Bank. It focused on how 'growth' could be 'accelerated' and how the resources to achieve the long-term objectives set out by African governments could be generated with the support of the international community. Briefly, the World Bank's attempt was to find short-term solutions to the urgent economic problems of Africa which it felt should follow the development strategy dictated by market forces. The Report also stressed the comparative advantages which Sub-Saharan African economies could derive by specialising in the production of primary commodities.

The OAU's reaction to the World Bank Report was quick and unequivocal.[58] In a resolution passed by the OAU Council of Ministers in February 1982, it expressed serious concern:

> [T]he strategy to development and economic growth recommended in the World Bank Report is *inconsistent* with the basic objectives, guidelines, and targets of the Lagos Plan of Action and would in fact perpetuate the present structure of African economies and make them more dependent on agricultural exports and on external markets.[59]

The OAU resolution also deplored the attempt by the World Bank to divide Africa by confining its Report to Sub-Saharan Africa which is inconsistent with the overall objectives and orientation of the *LPA*.

Between 1983 and 1986 Sub-Saharan Africa faced what was perhaps the worst famine and drought in modern history. It paralysed production and created a grave food crisis in many African countries. The OAU in collaboration with the ECA and other UN agencies has taken a number of initiatives to deal with the problem, including seeking the support of the UN Secretary-General on this matter. The Secretary-General in 1984 established an 'African Economic Crisis Office' in Nairobi and appointed Dr Adebayo Adedeji, Executive Secretary of the ECA, as his personal representative to head it. An important 'Declaration on the Critical Economic Situation in Africa' made by the 20th Summit of the OAU in 1984 stated among other things, that at the international level the main effort should concentrate on alleviating externally-induced constraints which would increase African countries' capability to mobilise more resources for relief and emergency needs of the stricken populations. The OAU Declaration also welcomed the proposal contained in the subsequent 1984 World Bank Report on Africa[60] calling for additional bilateral and multilateral disbursements of about $2 billion annually for Sub-Saharan Africa.

The 21st OAU Summit held in Addis Ababa in July 1985 was basically devoted to discussion of Africa's economic crisis. It significantly adopted a document called *Africa's Priority Programme for Economic Recovery 1986–1990* (APPER), aimed at advancing the provisions of the LPA for self-sustaining growth. The OAU Summit also called for the convening of a Special UN General Assembly Session on Africa's critical economic situation in 1986.

The most outstanding success of OAU diplomacy on the economic front at the international level was the holding of the first-ever Special Session of the UN General Assembly exclusively devoted to Africa in May 1986. Although Africa's economic plight is a matter with which the international community has been conversant for some time, it was the drought-induced emergency situation of 1983–86 that forced it upon the centre stage of global events. The then Chairman of the OAU (1985–86), President Aboudu Diouf of Senegal, in his opening address in New York spoke of Africa's new resolve to do right by itself economically if only the developed world would show faith in Africa and its destiny in the spirit of international solidarity.[61]

African states had hoped that their commitment to Western-inspired economic reforms embodied in their paper (APPER), which formed the basis of discussions at the Special Session, would impress the Western nations sufficiently for them to announce a commitment to meet the African request for additional resources in aid and debt relief. But the final document, 'United Nations Programme of Action for African Economic Recovery and Development 1986–1990' merely stated that the international community 'commits itself to making every effort to provide sufficient resources to support and supplement the African development effort'. The UN document was based primarily on Africa's APPER prepared by the OAU and ECA. The African commitment embodied in APPER is to mobilise Africa's internal resources and take all necessary actions to reorder their priorities (with emphasis on agriculture and food production) in order to establish more dynamic self-reliant and self-sustained economies. The Programme is estimated to cost $128 billion, of which African countries expect to contribute $82.5 billion or 65 per cent. The international community was called upon to commit itself to provide the balance of $45.6 billion over five years; an average of $9.1 billion per year.

The crucial question, however, is whether the OAU's LPA or its APPER or the UN Programme or any other programme can really: (1) stop the ever-widening gap between the poor African countries and the rich Western countries; (2) solve the problem of ineffectiveness of measures adopted in the past quarter of a century of independence to combat under-development; and (3) mobilise the continent's vast resources to lead to a rapid transformation of African economies. It may be pointed out that the UN's 1984 programme for Africa has highlighted the imperative need for African countries to struggle for a new domestic economic order rather than to pursue the so-called NIEO, which has proved to be a mirage. Africa's problems would not be solved by the mere acceptance of the IMF view of the world. The widespread and blind acceptance in Africa of the IMF philosophy could be dangerous if it killed-off the old dream of a strong, united, self-reliant Africa that is not just an appendage of the industrialised world.

CONCLUSIONS

It is the main contention of this chapter that the broad parameters of African political economy, including the OAU, are defined and determined primarily by the international system. Given Africa's place at the periphery of the global system, it is obvious that it is unable to influence the international system in any meaningful way. The relative powerlessness of Africa to influence the economy and polity of the region is clear from the nature and extent of neo-colonial domination and control of the continent. With the increasing intervention of the superpowers in Africa, especially in more recent years, the options open to the OAU and independent African states to influence the international system have become even more circumscribed than before. Independence merely created an illusion of power rather than its reality. African states and the OAU can join the international chorus of moral exhortations for a NIEO, for disarmament and protection of human rights, and for the granting of the right to self-determination in Afghanistan, Kampuchea or Grenada, but they can do very little to alter the actual global balance of power. The limits to moral pressures are apparent when superpower interests are at stake. The situation in Southern Africa is a clear indicator of this.

The reality of neo-colonialism in post-independence Africa is too serious to be wished away. Indeed, the tragedy of Africa and the OAU, which can only reflect African realities, today lies in the triumph of neo-colonialism and the defeat of Pan-Africanism. The birth of the OAU in 1963 marked a historic turning point at which the African nationalist petty bourgeoisie renounced genuine African unity, a unity that would correspond to the real interests and aspirations of the people of Africa.[62]

The present organisation of Africa into 50-odd small and mainly unviable states provides a most suitable climate for neo-colonialism. It is well-known that 'divide-and-rule' as a policy towards Africa has served world imperialism well. It was used to plunder and colonise Africa, it worked in delaying the decolonisation process, and since 1963 it has been used to prevent unity among independent states. The struggle against neo-colonialism in Africa is likely to be much more disruptive of African unity than the struggle against colonialism and racialism. The present neo-colonial phase of African struggle against the continued domination and exploitation of the continent by imperialism is fraught with greater dangers. Much of this struggle may take the form of intra- and inter-African disputes, though lurking behind these are likely to be one or the other superpower. Unless the masses of Africa become politically conscious of the lurking dangers and demand that their leaders preserve the independence and integrity of the African continent as a whole, we shall witness not only the inevitable polarisation of African states as between the superpowers but also the final and inevitable collapse of the OAU.

Indeed, the main reason for the continued success of neo-colonialism in Africa can be traced to the very nature of the regimes in Africa which are benefitting from such a relationship. Whatever the factors behind Africa's continued underdevelopment, what strikes one most is the persistent refusal of Africa's ruling classes to overcome their dependency complex. Most governments are trying to achieve instant development by turning to external sources of assistance, by accepting IMF conditions and solutions to the problems, by seeking special relationships with the international community such as the Lomé Conventions (1975, 1980 and 1985) (see Chapter 3), Afro-Arab Co-operation or Euro-Arab-African co-operation ('triangularism').[63] However, experience has proven that such strategies only help consolidation of a political, military and bureaucratic élite which is far removed from the masses of the people. And these African élites from sheer pride and self-interest prefer to be unequal partners in economic and political arrangements with Europe and America rather than developing Pan-African economic and political organisations.

The role of this neo-colonial bourgeoisie, who identify most with their counterparts in the West, is that of a transmission line between the nation and international capitalism, assuming the role of managers of Western enterprise. As Frantz Fanon said, this national fraction will in practice set up the country as a brothel for Europe and America.[64] Not surprisingly, African élites have found it advantageous to their own political power equation to compromise with exploitation and accept easy short-term solutions to complex economic problems. And most African regimes who have become involved in neo-colonial relationships find that continuing them poses less immediate danger to the regime than changing them. For many others, the vicious circle of poverty and underdevelopment which led them to accept a neo-colonial relationship in the first instance, has not proved amenable to solution. Moreover, the legacy of European colonialism has left Africa's new nations singularly ill-equipped to break out of the clutches of neo-colonialism.

From the foregoing, it is clear that Africa faces a troublesome future. The configuration of internal and international forces does not augur well for Africa. The present weakness of the African leadership, arising partly from its class character but mainly out of the circumstances in which it finds itself, combined with the ideological power vacuum created by the ending of formal colonialism, has created the ideal setting for superpower intervention into conflict situations in Africa. The economic and military stakes in Africa are too high to allow the superpowers to quit the continent. Hence, we are likely to witness the intensification of superpower confrontation on the continent in the coming years with disastrous consequences for the OAU and a greater occurrence of foreign intervention in African affairs.

The OAU's continental system can work well only if it persuades outside powers to keep out of Africa's affairs. But when member states themselves (see Obasanjo's opening quotation) invite foreign powers to send arms or troops to back up their rival claims, the system will collapse. A Swahili proverb says that 'When two elephants fight, it is the grass that suffers'. Africa's frustration can best be summarised with a quotation from Leo Tolstoy:

> I sit on a man's back chocking him, and making him carry me and yet assure myself and others that I am very sorry for him and wish to lighten his load by every means possible except by getting off his back.

Africa would do well to heed the advice of one of the fathers of Pan-Africanism, W.E.B. Dubois, who wrote: 'You [Africa] are not helpless. . . . You can wait. You can starve a while longer rather than sell your heritage for a mess of Western capitalist pottage'.[65]

NOTES

1. Kwame Nkrumah, *Neo-Colonialism: the last stage of imperialism*, (London, 1968) 1, quoted in Timothy M. Shaw, 'Beyond Neo-Colonialism: varieties of corporatism in Africa', *Journal of Modern African Studies*, 20:2 (1982) 239.

2. Stephen B. Cohen, United States Department of State, Bureau of Public Affairs, *Current Policy*, 119 (January 1980) 3.
3. General Olusegun Obasanjo, Speech at the 15th Summit of the OAU in Khartoum, Sudan, July 1978, quoted in Colin Legum, 'Foreign Intervention in Africa', *Yearbook of World Affairs*, 35 (London; Stevens, 1981) 23.
4. Edem Kodjo (former OAU Secretary-General), Speech at the OAU Special Economic Summit, Lagos, Nigeria, 28–29 April 1980.
5. See Yashpal Tandon, 'Africa Within the Context of Global Superpower Struggle', in E. Hanson (ed.) *Africa: Perspectives on Peace and Development* (London: United Nations University/Zed Books, 1987) 34–51.
6. Timothy M. Shaw, 'Actors in African International Politics', in Timothy M. Shaw and Kenneth A. Heard (eds) *The Politics of Africa: dependence and development* (New York: Africana, 1979) 358, 361.
7. See Timothy M. Shaw and 'Sola Ojo (eds) *Africa and the International Political System* (Washington: University Press of America, 1982), especially 2–9, 104–38.
8. See R.A. Akindele, 'Reflections on the Preoccupation and Conduct of African Diplomacy', *Journal of Modern African Studies*, 14:4 (1976) 556–76.
9. See A. Sesay, O. Ojo and O. Fasehun, *The OAU After Twenty Years* (Boulder: Westview, 1986).
10. See K. Mathews, 'The Organisation of African Unity', in D. Mazzeo (ed.), *African Regional Organisations* (Cambridge: Cambridge University Press, 1984) 49–85.
11. See Chimelu Chime, *Integration and Politics Among African States* (Uppsala: The Scandinavian Institute of African Studies, 1977), especially 200–11.
12. Stanley Hoffman, *The State of War* (New York: Praeger, 1965) 90.
13. I. William Zartman, 'Africa as a Subordinate State System in International Relations', *International Organisation*, 21:3 (Summer 1967) 545–64.
14. James Rosenau, *The Scientific Study of Foreign Policy* (New York: Free Press, 1971) 127–8.
15. According to UNCTAD reports, 21 of the 30 poorest countries of the world are in Africa.
16. They are: Botswana, Cape Verde Republic, Comoro Republic, Djibouti, Equatorial Guinea, Gambia, Guinea-Bissau, Mauritius, Sao Tome and Principe, Sahrawi Arab Democratic Republic (SADR), Seychelles and Swaziland.
17. They are: Algeria, Gabon, Libya, Mauritius, Seychelles, South Africa and Tunisia.
18. Nkrumah, *Neo-Colonialism*, ix.
19. Julius K. Nyerere, 'The Process of Liberation', Address to the Convocation of Ibadan University (Nigeria), 17 November 1976. For the full text of this address, see K. Mathews and S.S. Mushi (eds), *Foreign Policy of Tanzania 1961–1981: a reader* (Dar es Salaam: Tanzania Publishing House, 1982) 246–53.

20. Greg Lanning, with Marti Mueller, *Africa Undermined: mining companies and the underdevelopment of Africa* (Harmondsworth: Pelican, 1979) 495.
21. See Fawsy Mansour, 'Some Notes on Social Stratification and Social Change in Africa: Some Theoretical Considerations', *Africa Development*, 3:3 (July-September, 1978) 6.
22. Definition given by the All African Peoples' Conference, Cairo, March 1961.
23. See Frantz Fanon, *The Wretched of the Earth* (New York: Random House, 1963) 152.
24. See *West Africa*, 10 March 1986, 511.
25. See Cheryl Payer, *The World Bank: a critical analysis* (New York: Monthly Review, 1982); and Tony Killick (ed.) *The Quest for Economic Stabilisation: The IMF and the Third World* (New York: St. Martin's, 1984).
26. See Carl G. Widstrand (ed.), *Multinational Firms in Africa*, (Uppsala: SIAS, 1975).
27. For a list of the top 400 MNCs operating in Africa, see *South* (London, March 1987) 65–80.
28. For details see, *Africa Research Bulletin*, 15 October - 14 November 1978, 4883–4.
29. See Timothy M. Shaw and Malcolm J. Grieve, 'The Political Economy of Resources; Africa's future in the global environment', *Journal of Modern African Studies*, 16:1 (1978) 1–32.
30. Ibid, 12.
31. For a list of conflicts in Africa and the role of the OAU, see Amadu Sesay, 'The OAU and Continental Order', in Shaw and Ojo (eds), *Africa and the International Political System*, 178–97.
32. See H.A. Asobie, 'Peace in Africa, Inter-African Conflicts and External Intervention', mimeo, Department of Political Science, University of Nigeria, Nsukka, October 1986.
33. See Saadia Touval, *The Boundary Politics of Independent Africa* (Cambridge, Mass: Harvard University Press, 1972).
34. See Bereket H. Sellassie, 'The American Dilemma on the Horn', in Gerald Bender, *et al.* (eds), *African Crisis Areas and U.S. Foreign Policy* (Berkeley: University of California Press, 1985) 163–77.
35. For details see, Asobie, 'Peace in Africa', 8–9.
36. See Colin Legum, 'International Involvement in Nigeria 1966–1970', in Yash Tandon and D. Chandarana (eds), *Horizons of African Diplomacy*, (Nairobi: East African Literature Bureau, 1974) 45–85.
37. For details see, Zdenek Cervenka and Colin Legum, 'The OAU's Year in Africa', *Africa Contemporary Record, XI, 1978–79* (London: Rex Collings, 1979).
38. OAU members which fall into this category are: Angola, Benin, Cape Verde, Congo Peoples' Republic, Ethiopia, Guinea-Bissau, Mozambique, Sao Tome and Principe. See Legum, 'Foreign Intervention in Africa'.
39. The leading members of this group are: Cote d'Ivoire, Egypt, Liberia, Morocco, Senegal, Somalia, Sudan, Togo, Tunisia and Zaire.

40. Julius Nyerere, Statement in Dar es Salaam, 8 June 1978, quoted in Legum, 'Foreign Intervention in Africa', 78–9.
41. Ibid, 79.
42. Ibid.
43. See Robert O. Matthews, 'Domestic and interstate conflict in Africa', *International Journal*, 25:3 (Summer 1970) 459–85; and David B. Myers, 'Intraregional conflict management by the OAU', *International Organisation*, 28:3 (Summer 1974) 345–73.
44. See T.A. Imobhighe, 'An African High Command: the search for a feasible strategy of continental defence', *African Affairs*, 79:315, (April 1980) 241–54.
45. See C.N.O. Agbakoba, 'The OAU Forces in Chad', *Nigerian Journal of International Affairs*, 8:2 (1982) 31–56.
46. Diallo Telli, 'The Organisation of African Unity in Historical Perspective', *African Forum*, 1:2 (1965) 46.
47. For details of the Sixth Non-Aligned Summit in Havana, Cuba, see *Review of International Affairs*, (Belgrade) 300:707 (Special Issue) 20 September 1979.
48. See H. Hveem and Peter Willetts, 'The Practice of Non-Alignment: on the present and future of an international movement', in Tandon and Chandarana (eds), *Horizons of African Diplomacy*, 28.
49. See Zdenek Cervenka, *The Unfinished Quest for Unity: Africa and the OAU* (London: Friedmann, 1977), chapter 10.
50. See UN General Assembly Resolutions 3201 (S-6) and 3206 (S-6), 1 May 1974, on the 'Declaration and Programme of Action on the Establishment of a New International Economic Order'.
51. See UNGA Resolution 3281 (S-6), 12 December 1974.
52. See UNGA Resolution 3362 (S-7), 16 December 1975.
53. CM/Res. 437 (XXV), July 1975.
54. The following seven UNCTAD Conferences have so far been held: (1) Geneva, 1964; (2) New Delhi,1968; (3) Santiago, 1972; (4) Nairobi, 1976; (5) Manila, 1979; (6) Belgrade, 1983; and (7) Geneva, 1987.
55. CM/ST. 7 (XIX), June 1972.
56. OAU, *What Kind of Africa by the Year 2000?* (Geneva: Institute of Labour Studies, 1979).
57. OAU, *Lagos Plan of Action for the Economic Development of Africa* (Geneva: Institute of Labour Studies, 1981).
58. See 'Accelerated Development in Sub-Saharan Africa: an assessment by the OAU, ECA, and ADB Secretariats', in *Africa Development*, (Dakar), 7:3 (1982), 112–13; see also CM/1177 (XXXVIII), February 1982.
59. CM/Res. 921 (XXXVIII), February 1982.
60. World Bank, *Towards Sustained Development of Sub-Saharan Africa: a joint programme of action* (Washington, D.C., 1984).
61. See *West Africa*, 9 June 1986, 1199.
62. See K. Mathews, 'The OAU and the Problem of African Unity', *Africa Quarterly*, 23:1–2 (1986) 1–27.
63. See Thandika Mkandawire, 'The New International Economic Order,

Basic Needs, Strategies and the Future of Africa', *Africa Development*, 5:3 (1980) 85–6.
64. See Fanon, *The Wretched of the Earth*, 122.
65. See W.E.B. Dubois, *The World and Africa* (New York: International Publishers, 1965) 308.

3 Beyond Lomé III: Prospects for Symmetrical EurAfrican Relations

Ralph I. Onwuka

The African states constitute more than four-fifths of the total members of the African, Caribbean and Pacific (ACP) Group associated with the European Economic Community (EEC), and dominate, in a more significant manner, in the subculture of the ACP class classified as 'least developed'. Specifically, only 13 African member-states, namely, Angola, Cameroon, Congo, Equatorial Guinea, Gabon, Ghana, Ivory Coast, Kenya, Liberia, Nigeria, Senegal, Zaire and Zimbabwe, fall outside the periphery of the 'least developed and landlocked' class within the ACP. This is because these 13 African states are either endowed with huge reserves of petroleum (Nigeria, Gabon and Cameroon), possess other valuable export products (Angola, Cameroon, Equatorial Guinea, Liberia, Ghana and Zimbabwe) and/or operate relatively diversified and stable economies (Ivory Coast, Kenya, Nigeria and Senegal). The other least developed and landlocked ACP countries are basically 'fictitious states' who exist in the 'minimal sense'[1] because they are maximally and helplessly insulated from the world market forces or/and because of the prevailing reckless personal rule of the leadership in these countries. Because of their deplorable, though varying, poverty levels, the Lomé Conventions accorded these states 'special treatment', thereby recognising the need for them to catch up with their more privileged counterparts.

These classifications notwithstanding, all the 66 ACP states belong to the deprived group of the world economy. They are undeveloped and are significant members of the agitating club of the Group of 77, demanding in a consistent, though sometimes unorganised manner the restructuring of the prevailing international economic order in such a way that international finance, technology and trade facilities would be made readily accessible to them. The ACP states in conjunction with other members of the Non-Aligned Movement (see chapter 1) play a role, sometimes more symbolic than significant, in lessening East-West tensions and world conflicts in general, in and outside the United Nations. Most of these conflicts are rooted in the management of world resources, and in the attempt by the developing countries to reduce the level of their dependence on the developed industrial countries.

The African states have not succeeded in any consistent way in freeing themselves from the clutches of economic dependence still similar to that which operated earlier under British, French, Portuguese and Spanish colonialisms. The Lomé Convention emerged as a broad-based European attempt to restructure EurAfrican economic relations founded primarily on unequal exchange. This attempt has not changed the pattern of relationships between the partners fostered by the Yaounde Conventions which preceded Lomé.

The dependence structures of the Yaounde Conventions I and II, well-articulated elsewhere,[2] were clearly evidenced in the magnitude of the Associated African and Malagasy States'(AASM) reliance on France. The three Lomé Conventions have not seriously deviated from the dependence patterns of the Yaounde accords. The purpose of this chapter is to demonstrate that the Lomé Conventions, though remarkable in introducing novel trade relations between the parties, have nevertheless consolidated the dependence of the ACP countries on the 12 member countries of the European Economic Community (EEC). Thus the optimistic hope for an interdependent relationship between the two groups emerging from the Agreements was dashed when the Lomé I, II and III Conventions, expected to initiate dynamic features that would inject a more symmetrical relationship between the two parties, fell far short of doing this.

What the Conventions have done, in fact, has been to institutionalise a gradual incorporation of the economies of the ACP countries into the advanced European economic system. As the AASM economic system was functionally incomplete and structurally dependent on France under the Yaounde Agreements so are the ACP states on the 12 under the Lomé Conventions, particularly on such issues as trade, technical co-operation and transfer of resources. Lomé II and III are particularly disappointing because they barely offer cosmetic and non-economic changes to the previous treaty, thus consolidating the *status quo* of the established dependent relationship. In order to analyse the neo-dependence attributes of the 1980 and 1984 treaties it is necessary to diagnose the 1975 Convention with a view to identifying its areas of innovation and structures of dependence.

LOMÉ CONVENTION: FEATURES OF INNOVATION AND DEPENDENCE

The first Lomé Convention has been described by optimists as 'a pioneering model of co-operation between equal partners' or simply as 'an exemplary type of co-operation'.[3] Certainly the Convention was both 'exemplary' and 'pioneering' in that it constituted the largest trading bloc between a group of developing countries and a set of industrialised countries in Europe in the post-colonial era. The membership of the ACP group has been ever-increasing: from 46 in 1975 to 60 in 1980, and 66 in 1984 with the accession of Mozambique. For the first time, a successor to the Yaounde Convention was not restricted to the former colonies of the Community member states. Thus such countries as Ethiopia, and Liberia, which had no formal colonial links with Europe were incorporated into the ACP group.[4] With this new group, which included associable members of the Commonwealth, the scope of EEC development policy was extended beyond the AASM states so that the new Commonwealth members came to be treated equally to the former colonies of France.

There is an interesting parallel between the situation which resulted in the French government persisting on the inclusion of Part IV of the Treaty of Rome as a condition for it being a party to the Agreement, and that in which the British government insisted, under Protocol 22 of the Accession Treaty of 1972,[5] on enlarging the associables to include most Commonwealth states. Both France and Britain were keenly interested in retaining 'post-colonial economic relations'[6] within the framework of the EEC. Some non-French speaking states, particularly Nigeria,[7] expected that the spread of membership of the ACP group beyond the AASM would signal the beginning of a new economic relationship that would consequently end France's exploitative and superordinate relationship with its former colonies. Yet the liberalisation of the associable group has perhaps loosened but not removed the dependent relationship between the former AASM states and France but certainly the EEC-ACP relationship has created a new system of unequal exchange structured to serve Europe rather than Africa.

The trade dependence matrix of the Yaounde Conventions was replaced in the Lomé Conventions with provisions on non-reciprocity which allowed free entry of ACP exports, including some of the EEC's Common Agricultural Policy (CAP) products into the Community market. No measures were demanded of the ACP countries to dismantle their tariffs and/or quotas with respect to imports from the Community. In addition, the ACP members were allowed to give preferential treatment to other developing countries at terms of higher benefits than those extended to the Community.[8] In precise terms, Lomé I allowed all industrial and 96 per cent of all agricultural ACP exports into the Community without either quantitative restrictions or duty. Lomé I was remarkable in allowing trade concessions in keeping with UNCTAD demands in various meetings. Such concessions, though inadequate, were helpful in lowering the prevailing high level of asymmetry between the two contracting parties.

A crucial innovative scheme under Lomé which has recognised the prevailing asymmetry in trade performance is that for the Stabilisation of Exports (Stabex). This is a compensatory finance scheme for certain exports of the ACP countries to the Community. The scheme applied where a country's export earnings from the selected 34 products during the year preceding the year of application represented at least 7.5 per cent of its total earnings from merchandise exports; for sisal, however, the percentage was 5 per cent. For the least developed, landlocked or island ACP states the percentage was 2.5 per cent. The difference between the reference level and actual earnings constituted the basis of the transfer of the compensatory finance from the Community to the concerned ACP states.

The Stabex scheme was, no doubt, pivotal to the positive reception of the Convention by the ACP group. The scheme recognises, as the late Raul Prebisch advocated, that the poor performance of the developing countries in world trade directly reflects on their balance of payments position and indeed on their development performance. Stabex was thus welcomed as it involved a large number of products crucial to most participating African states. Under Lomé I the Stabex scheme covered 19 products, of which iron ore was the only non-agricultural product. Funds available under the scheme amounted to 380 million European Units of Account (EUA).

Under the scheme West Africa alone received transfers for losses in export earnings from groundnuts, cocoa, coffee, palm nuts and oil, wood, raw hides and skins, bananas and iron ore. Payments made to the West African beneficiaries, the exporters of the above-named products, constituted 65 per cent of the released fund under Stabex I. And of the eight main recipients of the Stabex funds, six were francophone states — Senegal, Mauritania, Niger, Benin, Ivory Coast and Gabon.[9] Although this scheme has the merit of being excluded from the financial resources tied to EEC-approved projects 'drawn up or programmed in consultation with ACP government'[10] its method of disbursement remained clumsy, arbitrary and mostly along colonial lines.

The 1975 Treaty also provided for industrial co-operation, and towards that end the Community was to assist the ACP states in such areas as transfer of technological resources, education and promotion of small- and medium-scale industrial firms. A Committee on Industrial Co-operation established for this purpose was supervised by another committee composed of ambassadors. The Centre for Industrial Development (CID) based in Brussels is the co-ordinating point for Community actions towards the acceleration of the industrialisation process in ACP countries. Also, various forms of financial transfers similar to those under the Yaounde Convention were made available from the Fourth European Development Fund and the European Development Bank. For example, part of the sum of 150 million EUA set aside as exception aid had been utilised by most least-developed and landlocked countries. In 1978 alone, seven West African states affected by the Sahel drought benefited from this exceptional aid programme.[11] As Figure 3.1 shows this dispensation continued in both Lomé II and III. Under more desperate circumstances such aid is often supplemented with Stabex funds and by emergency food aid financed by the Community budget.

Equally significant was the fact that the Lomé Conventions recognised and positively supported economic integration efforts within the ACP group. The Economic Comunity of West African States (ECOWAS) has received constant logistic and moral assistance and the possibility of significant technical and financial aid. For example, the EEC in co-operation with the ECOWAS Secretariat, held a workshop in 1978 to look into the possibility of setting up new industries in the West African sub-region.[12] And 10 per cent of the Community's regional aid programme was earmarked for regional co-operation projects.[13] It was from such funds that projects were promoted within the *Organisation pour la mise en valeur du fleuve Sénégal* (OMVS).

It is noteworthy that the total individual aid from the governments of the Community is higher than that from the collective Community aid programme to the ACP countries. The European powers would be more readily prepared to make aid available where and when the demands of geopolitical and strategic considerations are satisfied. The fact that individual members of the Community prefer to channel more of their aid to ACP countries separately denotes the

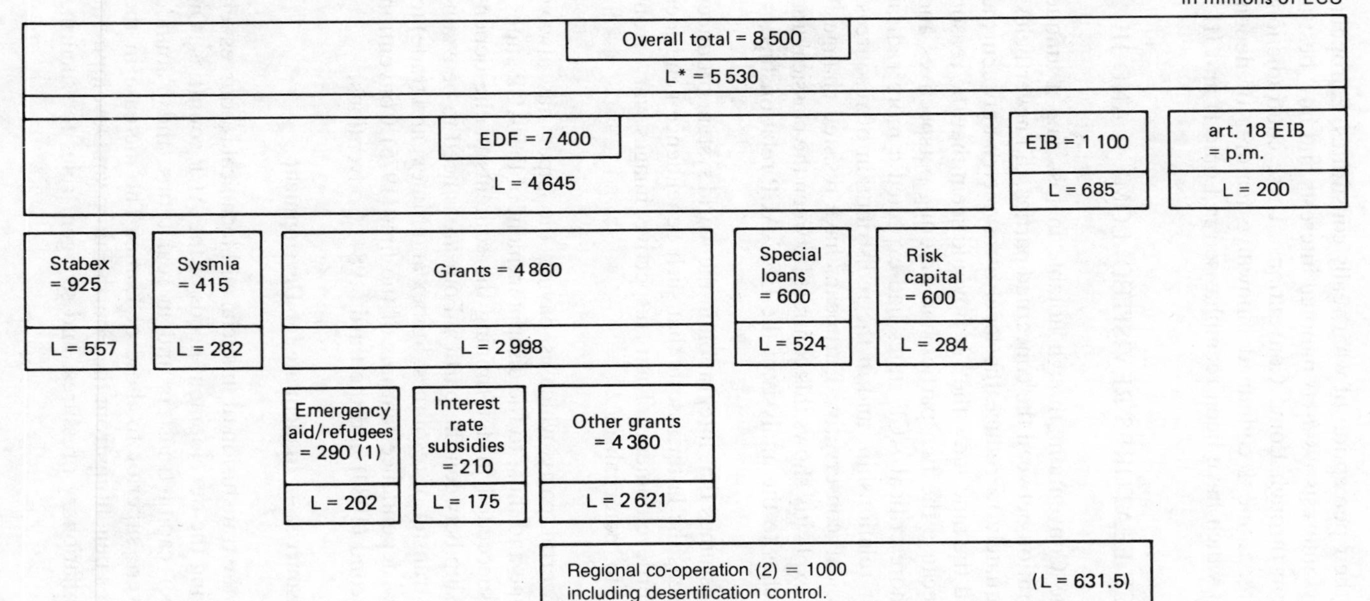

FIGURE 3.1 *Breakdown of resources under Lomé III Convention (1985–90)*
SOURCE *The Courier*, No. 89 January-February 1985, 24.

proclivities in their perception of what really constitutes 'European' or 'Community' interests *vis-à-vis* national interests and how best to perpetuate them through Lomé Conventions. These contradictions notwithstanding, Lomé I contained innovative features of dependence, most of which have been reemphasised in Lomé II and III.

DEPENDENCE FEATURES REVISITED: LOMÉ II AND III

The first Lomé Convention, though notable in fostering a unique type of co-operation between the concerned parties, did nevertheless not serve adequately to reduce the level of asymetry between the ACP states and the nine, now the 12. It would seem that the reason for this was because the two parties had differing perspectives and images. The more critical ACP states had expected a more radical change in their relationship, and in the redistribution of resources, while the 'classical' conservative Europeans have resisted change.[14] Timothy Shaw explicitly shows this contrast between the classical and critical approaches to the analysis of the EEC-ACP relationship:

> The former assumes that integration in the world system produces growth whereas the latter asserts that such dependence generates further underdevelopment. Their respective images vary from 'partnership' to 'paternalism'.[15]

The more powerful party which is paying the piper has always dictated the tune and thus, to the disappointment of the ACP states, the EEC has succeeded in determining the contents of the dependence relationship between the parties. Four areas need to be examined critically (transfer of resources, Stabex and Minex, and trade) to see clearly how dependence features of the first (1975) Convention recur in the second (1980) and the third (1984) Conventions.

Transfer of Resources — Inadequate for Development

Under Lomé I the transfusion of financial and technical resources fell short of satisfying the development needs of the ACP countries. On the basis of per capita transfers and in real terms, the Yaounde Conventions were superior to those of Lomé. The increase in the number of states benefiting from the Fourth European Development Fund, world inflationary pressures, and stringent rules for securing the transfers were some of the important set-backs to a liberally-constituted and democratically-committed Fund. As against 18 AASM countries under Yaounde, the associates under Lomé I numbered 46 in 1975, and under Lomé II in 1980 the total had risen to 60, with Zimbabwe joining the group of ACP countries benefiting from the Fifth Development Fund. By 1984 the number was 66.

The renegotiation of Lomé I proved to be intractable and prolonged on the issue of total EEC aid to ACP states because the ACP group felt dissatisfied with the programme under the previous treaty. Under Lomé II, the ACP countries lamented that the financial assistance was inadequate and asserted their belief that what was decided upon should be regarded as the minimum. Even after grudgingly accepting the total aid package under the new treaty, the ACP in a unilateral declaration (and there were four of such annexes) made the following reservation to the Convention:

> While the ACP states have, in a spirit of co-operation accepted for the purposes of this Convention, the total amount of assistance of 5607 million EUA, the ACP states wish to record that in their opinion this amount is neither adequate nor fully reflects the understanding reached on the volume of financial assistance between the Co-Presidents of the Council of Ministers in the course of the negotiations in June 1979.[16]

Other than the inadequacy of the available funds, the modality for committing the aid distressed the ACP states. The method of disbursing the aid under the Lomé Conventions is similar to that under the Yaounde Accord. The ACP states participated in framing the objectives and priorities of the intending programmes, but were carefully excluded from the EDF Committee responsible for taking crucial final decisions on the financing of projects. The net result of the Community having an exclusive right in the decision-making progress of the EDF Committee was that not all the available funds were committed. Because of the rigorous conditions and bureaucratic processes involved, there existed a gap between funds available and those committed. For example, at the end of Lomé I only 66 per cent of the available funds were charged to commitments, and of the financial resources (300m EUA) available for regional aid, only 65 per cent (195m EUA) was committed.[17]

Because of administrative problems in and the unilateral methods of disbursing the fund, the ACP states persistently sought 'real and effective participation' in the joint management of the EDF. This request was not conceded to them in Lomé II. Had they succeeded, the Convention would have shed one of its strategic mechanisms for sustaining a dependence relationship. Control over the disbursement of financial resources is control over the development capabilities of the ACP states. Herein lies a central feature of the dependence tendencies of the Lomé Conventions. The reason for depriving the weaker partner of facilities for self-reliant development is to make sure that the stronger partner continues to determine the nature and content of their relationship and, subsequently, mode of production. It is, in fact, arguable that it is in the interest of the stronger partner to maintain the prevailing economic asymmetry and not establish an interdependent relationship between them and the ACP countries. This is because one of the Community's strategies in the Accord has been to supply less than adequate financial resources for ACP development.

Financial pledges under Lomé I were, for example, inferior to those under Lomé II and III. Under Lomé II the sum of 5227 million EUA was granted as against 3466 million EUA in Lomé I. Also the total financial resources for transfers to ACP countries has increased by 51 per cent, while the fifth EDF has increased over the Fourth EDF by 48 per cent. These seemingly large increases have, however, been critically analysed from three angles:

(1) from a change based on 1975 constant prices;
(2) from a change based on a real annual basis; and
(3) from a change based on a real annual per capita basis.

Using 40 per cent annual inflation based on the index of OECD export unit values over the period 1975–9, the percentage of Lomé II over Lomé I as reflected in (2) is far less than that in (1). The situation is further depressed to negative values in (3) when the fact is considered that Lomé I had a four-year life span while Lomé II has a five-year life period. If the resources are further adjusted to reflect change in ACP population the transfers to the ACP countries will be seen to be even less generous in (3) than in either (1) or (2).

It has been coherently argued by the Overseas Development Institute, that because the population of the ACP countries was 270 million in 1975 and rose to 305 million, in 1979, even at an annual population growth rate of 2.5 per cent the EEC's pledges required a compensatory growth of 13 per cent to maintain the ACP's former per capita aid. The Institute concludes convincingly that,

> the EEC's aid pledge in Lomé II is worth 16 per cent less than that of Lomé I in real terms, and the ACP, far from achieving an increase in their per capita aid allocation have negotiated a real per capita decrease of 25 per cent.[18]

Thus, in terms of the real value of the financial transfers from the Community to the ACP countries, Lomé II contains more neo-dependence structures than Lomé I. Lomé III has re-emphasised the profiles of the preceeding Lomé Conventions. I. William Zartman has confirmed this observation with reference to the financial transfers under Lomé III, where he maintains that 'because of the increase both in member countries and in their population the real annual per capita value of the aid has gradually dropped slightly'.[19] He quickly added that the ECU 8.5 billion of Lomé III is almost equal to the combined values of the European Development Funds (FED) of previous Lomé (I and II) Conventions and this represents a sizeable increment of Official Development Assistance (ODA). But in spite of these assertions, much of the financial aid to ACP states usually finds its way back to the European donors' economies, as Zartman has testified:

> As church-goers know, more baskets generally mean more offerings. Furthermore, the FED reinforces a privileged relationship that the Convention countries already hold in the European bilateral ODA distributions, so that the FED is not a substitute for others aid. That much of the FED money returns to the donors' economies through contracts and purchases is more a feature of ODA in general and indeed more broadly of developed-underdeveloped relations than of Lomé arrangements.[20]

Other than the fact that much of the FED money finds its way to Europe, the financial mismanagement of EEC development projects in the Third World further reduces the utility of the financial transfers to ACP countries.[21] The EEC's Court of Auditors, the financial watchdog of the body, has confirmed this in its findings based on evaluation of 63 EEC-financed projects in Ghana, Guinea, Cape Verde, Madagascar, Mauritius, Kenya, and Somalia.

Three major failings were identified by the Court. The first is related to the EEC's faulty identification of Third World priorities. Second, in many instances, the officials in Brussels neglected to take into consideration 'the precarious situation of many national budgets and the chronic lack of foreign exchange'[22] as in the cases of Kenya, Guinea and Somalia. And third, the Court discovered that there was a serious problem of lack of complementarity between EEC projects and national development efforts as demonstrated in the livestock project in Mauritius, Madagascar's coconut production, and the soguiplast factory in Guinea. In each case little attempt was made to relate production relations to production and market forces. The result was the production of tons of goods which were virtually beyond the purchasing power of the population. The neo-dependence profile of the Lomé Conventions is equally notable in the aim and spirit of both the Stabex and Minex schemes.

Neo-Dependence Structures of Stabex and Minex (Sysmin) Insurance Schemes

The Stabex scheme under Lomé I was, as acknowledged earlier, very innovative. But despite the remarkable features of the scheme, it has inadequately satisfied the conditions for establishing a balanced relationship between the parties. The ACP countries because of this, during negotiations for Lomé II, had sought to enlarge the product coverage of the scheme in such a way that all their exports would be covered under it. They also sought significant reforms that included the indexation of transfers in order to reduce the effect of inflation on their export earnings, and the abolition of all repayment obligations usually attached to the scheme. If these reforms had been granted, the ACP countries would have secured more favourable financial resources from trade, and thus greater possibilities for accelerated development.

The modifications granted by the EEC embodied in Lomé II were concentrated in six areas. First, the available Stabex fund was increased from 381 million EUA to 550 million EUA. However, this increase suffered from a similar deficiency in the EDF in general; namely, the monetary increase in real terms was eroded by world inflation and increases in the populations of participating ACP states. Second, there was an addition of ten products including rubber, pepper, cashew nuts, shrimps and prawns to bring to 44 the number of products covered by the scheme. Yet this enlargement of product coverage still fell short of the demand by the ACP countries. Third, iron-ore (the only mineral in Lomé I) continued under the scheme until 1984 when it was transferred to the mineral exporting scheme

(Minex). Fourth, a separate facility for minerals was to be organised along similar lines to Stabex. Fifth, the 'dependence' and 'trigger thresholds' were liberated in such a way that the relevant qualifying rates were reduced from 7.5 per cent to 6.5 per cent, and from 2.5 per cent to 2 per cent for the 44 least-developed, landlocked and island countries. Finally, instead of totally abolishing repayment obligations, modifications were made such that for richer ACP countries not qualifying for grant transfers repayments were spread over seven years with two years of grace. These modifications brought added pressures to bear on the Stabex fund and, with the battle for its indexation to the purchasing power of exports lost, this fund is bound to decrease in both money and real terms.

Claude Cheysson, the EEC Development Commissioner, in 1975 called the Stabex arrangement an insurance scheme, a safety net, so that if drought or other natural calamity hits a country and export earnings fall then compensation is available. This is equally true of the Minex scheme with regards to transnational corporations operating in ACP areas. Lomé III, for example, gives its reason for providing for the special financing facility for mining products as:

> To re-establish the viability of the mining sector or remedy the harmful effects on their development of serious temporary unforeseeable disruptions affecting those mining sectors and beyond the control of the ACP states concerned.[23]

It is obvious from the implications of Article 276 that the objective of the parties to the Convention was primarily to safeguard against risks the interests of international corporations operating in mining sectors. Such provision encourages MNCs from EEC countries to invest their capital and technology in the mining of manganese, copper, cobalt, bauxite, tin, iron ore, aluminium and phosphates in ACP states. In this way, these strategic minerals are securely guaranteed for European industries.

The provisions for a special facility for mineral exports was a new feature of Lomé II launched with the sum of 282 million EUA increasing to 415 million EUA in Lomé III. The 'dependence threshold' of the Minex scheme is higher than that of Stabex in that the mineral concerned must account for 15 per cent of exports (or 10 per cent for the least developed, landlocked and island countries). The 'trigger' threshold is placed at a 10 per cent drop in either production or export earnings as in Stabex. Table 3.1 shows the

TABLE 3.1 *Term's of the ECC's Minex Scheme*

Producer Country	*Dependence Threshold Average 1972/76*	*ECC share of Exports Average*
Copper		
Zambia	91%	60%
Zaire	55%	91%
Papua New Guinea	51.7%	40%
Phosphates		
Togo	59%	92%
Senegal	17.6%	54%
Bauxite		
Guinea	90%	34% (bauxite 76)
Alumina		
Jamaica	67%	19% (alumina 76)
Suriname	70%	29% (alumina 76)
Guyana	40%	29% (alumina 76)
Manganese		
Gabon	15%	32% (1976)
Iron Ore		
Liberia	69%	74%
Mauritania	71%	75%
Tin		
Rwanda	13%	75%

SOURCE Peter Afolabi, *The New ACP-EEC Convention*, NIIA Lecture Series No 37, 35.

minerals covered by the Minex scheme and the major countries where these are exploited. In its purpose and implication, the Lomé II and III Minex scheme had a close semblance to the ill-fated International Resource Bank (IRB) suggested by Henry Kissinger at UNCTAD IV in Nairobi. As the mining areas in the ACP group are mainly on the African continent (Liberia, Guinea, Gabon, Mauritania, Togo, Senegal, Zaire and Zambia), an area of imminent or latent instability, the scheme acts as a ready and easy source of financial resources to cushion the losses of the operating corporations, occasioned by unforseeable circumstances. Thus by implication, the Minex scheme, like the IRB, to a large extent serves the interests of the European-based transnational corporations operating in the ACP countries in general and in Africa in particular. To this extent the scheme is a neo-dependence arm of the Community. Lomé III has gone further in its protection of the interests of transnational corporations through the inclusion of a special chapter designed to encourage European investors in Africa. This is seen to consolidate further the neo-colonial profiles of the previous Conventions.

UNEQUAL EXCHANGE OF RAW MATERIALS FOR MANUFACTURED GOODS

The trade provisions of the successive Lomé Conventions have not favoured a balanced trade relationship between the parties in that the ACP countries had, under all three treaties, consistent balance of trade deficits. The Lomé II and III Conventions were designed to maintain a metropolitan-periphery relationship similar to that of Lomé I. The trade package under Lomé II gave free access of 99.5 per cent of the current ACP exports, of which 75 per cent are not only raw materials but would otherwise have entered duty free under the most-favoured nation treatment. Additional concessions made to the ACP under the Lomé II were inadequate although tomatoes, carrots, onions and asparagus were for the first time liberalised. No concessions were secured for rice, nor for most of the 60 products for which the ACP demanded free access. Generally the new concessions were made on products falling under the EEC's Common Agricultural Policy (CAP), which represented only 9 per cent of ACP trade with the Community.

Writing of the practical results which the first Lomé Convention offered for the succeeding Conventions, Katharina Focke, in a report presented to the 1980 meeting of the ACP-EEC Consultative Assembly, regretted that the free access to the Community for ACP products had been 'more spectacular than effective'.[24] According to her report, the implementation of the trade provisions of the 1975 Treaty had been disappointing because the few trade surpluses achieved by the ACP group were a function of changes in prices rather than of volume of trade — an indication that the trade-promotion measures embedded in the Convention were ineffective. This situation seems to have been modified in theory in Lomé II where trade co-operation covered not just EEC and non-EEC (including ACP) markets but also national and regional (including ECOWAS) trade.

Other than ineffective trade promotion measures limiting the access of the ACP products to the EEC, it has also been the undisguised policy of the Community to discourage manufacturing in ACP countries where such industrialisation would place similar industries in Europe in a poor competitive position. For example, the 12 are opposed to any expansion in textile manufacturing in ACP countries that would further depress the fortunes of Europe's textile industries. While European textile industries are fast declining those of the Third World countries have been expanding at an unprecedented rate, almost 30 times, due mainly to cheap labour. According to *The Economist* in 1984, 'while the number of cotton spindles in the nine EEC member countries declined from 30m to 16 between 1960 and 1976, Asian capacity increased 50 per cent. In weaving of fabrics, European countries suffered capacity drops of 40–68 per cent, while capacity increased in Asia by 54 per cent, in Africa by 152 per cent, in Taiwan by 125 per cent and in Thailand by nearly 100 percent'.[25]

As a result of the decline in textile industries in most of the EEC, its textiles lagged behind others in manufacturing and investment throughout the 1970s — by 40 per cent in Britain, 27 per cent in France, and 63 per cent in Belgium. Only in Germany were new investments made, despite the closing of about 46 per cent of textile capacity. The EEC countries have therefore subscribed to protectionist measures either through the North-South trade regulation system, as seen under the multi-fibre arrangement (MFA) within the GATT orbit, or through voluntary export restraint agreements, quota and administrative constraints under EEC-ACP co-operation. For similar reasons, the EEC has persuaded the Ivory Coast to abandon its sugar processing facilities already under construction. Thus the Lomé Convention is an instrument for discouraging industrialisation and consequently encouraging continued ACP dependence on the EEC's manufactured goods.

The rules of origin governing ACP goods are added facilities designed not only to weaken the participation of ACP countries but also to exclude Japanese and North American manufactured goods from the EEC-ACP market. For example, the condition that a 'minimum amount of manufacturing should occur in ACP countries' excludes non-EEC input in the manufacture of goods likely to seek access to the Community market.

If one takes a second look at the countries within the ACP trading most with the EEC, one witnesses the domination of the former members of the AASM states under the Yaounde Accord. In 1977, for example, the countries with the highest concentration of imports from the Community were the francophone states of Cameroon, Gabon, Ivory Coast, Madagascar, Mali and Mauritania; an indication that despite the liberalisation of the membership of the EEC associates, the pattern of trade is still along Yaounde lines. In this way, the three Lomé Conventions have reinforced more than ever before the dependence of the francophone states on France in particular and on the EEC in general.

The trade package of Lomé II included neo-dependence facilities in three main areas. First, the Convention encouraged the exportation of raw materials to the Community in exchange for the industrial goods of the then nine European countries of the EEC. Second, the Convention did not allow entry of all the goods — raw materials, manufactured and semi-manufactured — from the ACP countries to the Community. Rather, the flow of goods from ACP to EEC was and is restricted by rigorous rules of origin, quota systems and voluntary export agreements. These restraints on ACP exports inhibited rapid industrialisation in these developing states in spite of the provisions on industrial co-operation.

And third, through the technical co-operation programme of the Convention, firms from the nine member-states of the Community had individual but unequal stakes in the ACP countries. Between 1976 and 1978 French firms won the highest number of contracts, while Germans and Italians followed in that order. Countries like Denmark and Ireland, with no colonial experience, won the least number of contracts under the Fourth Development Fund. Like those under the larger framework of UNCTAD, arguments posited by the parties on the transfer of technology are usually politicised. There is normally a conflict of interest between the technology bearer, its host partner, and the state. Community firms are reluctant to participate fully in the industrialisation of the ACP countries without guarantees.

This impression was conveyed by the Commission of the Community during the negotiations for Lomé II, when the Commission recommended to the Council two possible guarantees aimed at preserving the interests of European companies in Third World countries. The first involved negotiating agreements between the Community and individual developing countries or groups of developing countries in order to settle the 'norms of good conduct' on such issues as stability of 'investment conditions' and 'non-discriminatory treatment of investment'. The second involved 'specific-project agreements linked to Community guarantees in terms of financial protection against non-commercial risks'. These were partially taken care of by Lomé III. It would seem that the Minex scheme is designed to meet many of the guarantees sought by the Commission for the Community firms operating in the mining area of the ACP countries.

HUMAN DIMENSIONS OF LOMÉ III

One can readily acknowledge that Lomé III has introduced a human face to the EEC-ACP relationship by stressing the need for food aid and self-sufficiency, and by generally advocating adherence to human rights without excluding apartheid. In a way more than ever before, the sovereignty of man is fully acknowledged in 'what has essentially been a commercial and economic relationship'.[26] This is obvious in the EEC-ACP joint declaration where the contracting parties reaffirmed 'their obligation and their commitments under international law to fight for the elimination of all forms of discrimination based on ethnic, group origin, race nationality, colour, sex, language, religion or any other situation'.[27] The two sides also proclaimed their determination 'to work effectively for the eradication of apartheid which constitutes a violation of human rights and an affront to human dignity'. This seems to be the first time that the apartheid system of South Africa has been unequivocally condemned by the European grand patrons of the racist system in a collective manner. Though the individual policies of the EEC countries towards South Africa have always depended on their respective interpretation of national interest, collectively the mood of international politics, as influenced by East-West relations, has resulted in a more positive stance against apartheid.

Much more positive, though, with its underlying implications, is the provision for fighting rapid desertification, famine and drought in Africa. To emergency aid and refugees the sum of 290 million EUA was allocated in answer to the continental situation which worsened during the 14 months of negotiations for Lomé III up to the time of the Convention's signing in 1984 and thereafter.

The attention of the UN has been drawn to the critical situation, as indicated by the Special General Assembly on the African crisis in mid-1986, while European Non-Governmental Organisations (NGOs) in collaboration with the EEC in 1986 adopted in Brussels *The Natali Plan*[28] intended to take collective action against famine and drought in Africa. This plan directed its attention towards securing medical assistance, food aid and, most importantly, agricultural rehabilitation in Africa in both short- and long-term strategies. This EEC-NGO effort has led to the financing of the agricultural rehabilitation of the eight African states hardest hit by famine (Angola, Chad, Ethiopia, Mali, Mauritania, Mozambique, Nigeria and Sudan). The 12 also agreed to the ACP's 'demand for access to surplus farm products in the EEC. And the Convention provides for the possibility of specific agreements on food supplies to requesting ACP states'.[29] Food aid alone represents about a third of the Community's total co-operation budget.

The major criticism of the EEC's food aid programmes is the same as towards virtually all food aid strategies; namely, that it leads to food-dependency as it discourages self-help and reliance on traditional food. Thus it can be logically argued that although Lomé III represents a continuation of Lomé II, in a few respects, particularly in its human dimensions, it constitutes a departure from it, too.

OTHER SETBACKS TO A BALANCED RELATIONSHIP

There are issues not broadly discussed in the earlier sections which directly or indirectly have contributed, or are bound to contribute in the future, to the ACP-EEC relationship not 'inching towards inter-dependence'[30] but rather towards a relationship which reinforces the dominance of the more prosperous partners over the weaker.

One of these additional issues is the bureaucratic and institutional instruments for carrying out the provisions of the Lomé Conventions — the joint ACP-EEC consultative institutions, the Council of Ministers, Committee of Ambassadors, Consultative Assembly and the Committtee for Industrial Development. Of these four, the last organ is the only executive institution which is run jointly by the two parties. Other than the need to democratise the range of decision-making processes on crucial development issues, there is over-bureaucratisation of the decision-making process which sometimes breeds distrust and suspicion between the parties. It was mainly because of these reason that there was an unfulfilled gap between funds available and those committed under the Fourth Development Fund. It could also be argued that it was because of the bureaucratic style of the Community that the crucial Centre for Industrial Development — set up to serve 'as a liaison between ACP projects and European capital and technology' — was only established in 1979 and never operationalised any single scheme throughout the first Convention. Institutional factors aided in wrecking the grand designs of the industrial co-operation sector of the general agreement which did not genuinely focus on the industrial and technological needs of the ACP countries.

Because of the nature, content and modality of implementing the

Conventions, the development of the ACP states has been deprived of an objective and integrated appraisal. Although the Conventions have no doubt taken due consideration of the least developed countries, landlocked, and island states within the ACP group, the provisions for accelerated growth of these nine deprived states have been inadequate and piecemeal.

At best the EEC has committed itself to the 'dependent development' of the ACP states. This is a state of development where only low degrees of industrialisation and accumulation of capital are allowed. It was hoped that through 'export-oriented growth' and 'consolidation of internal markets'[31] the ACP would be developed under the directives of the EEC countries. Such, according to Peter Evans, is 'dependent development'; that is 'dependence' combined with 'development'.[32] E. Antola's criticism of the Lomé Conventions rests on their neo-colonial profiles — 'subordinate capitalist development' based on the intervention and calculations of international private capital aimed at the consolidation of the international division of labour.[33]

The results of the first two Lomé Conventions have clearly shown, particularly in the areas of trade and the transfer of technical and financial resources, that a dependent relationship (without development) prevails, and is bound to continue under the provisions of the succeeding conventions. Evidence has shown that Lomé III refines Lomé II but in many respects does not depart from it. Thus, as long as the European attitude remains in outline 'imprecise and unprovable in thier material particulars'[34] the dependence parameters of the Lomé Conventions will continue to be accompanied by at best stagnation.

Another crucial but not direct fact that has contributed to a dependent (without development) relationship is the recent enlargement of the EEC. When Greece, Portugal and Spain joined the Community the chances were that these less developed members would place more pressures on the available aid to the Associates. It was suggested that the southern enlargement of the Community would necessitate a massive aid programme for these new members, similar to the Marshall Plan of the late 1940s.[35] It was also possible that the Community would have to redefine its interests and make adjusted provisions with reference to its Common Agricultural Policy. If the interests of the ACP states become conflictual and competitive with those of the new southern countries of Europe, there is no gainsaying the fact that the EEC will first protect and promote these vital 'European interests'. This would leave the ACP countries in a worse position in their desperate plight to procure financial and technological assistance from the Community towards their development efforts.

CONCLUSIONS

The ACP countries, particularly the African component of the group, are in a frenzied rush to develop their economies which stagnated because of the savagery of colonialism, ignorance and economic deprivation. The initial Lomé Convention was acclaimed as 'innovative' and 'pioneering' because it was perceived, during its negotiation, as a means to solve the economic development problems of the ACP states. The Convention introduced 'model' trade co-operation arrangements along the lines demanded by UNCTAD. The Stabex scheme was central to the uniqueness of the first treaty. Equally commendable, though not executed satisfactorily, were provisions for the transfusion of diverse financial and technical resources from the rich EEC countries to the ailing economies of the ACP countries.

But by the end of its first term of life the Convention clearly proved itself in demonstrating that its unique features were indeed structures for maintaining the dependence of the weaker signatories. The annual growth in ACP's exports to the EEC was erratic and unimpressive. The EEC continued to maintain a dominant share of the ACP countries' markets, a colonial pattern of trade similar to that under the Yaounde Accord which persists still under Lomé III. France still retains a dominant share of the market of the francophone members of the ACP group and, by the same token, these French-speaking associates are the main Stabex recipients from the Fourth Development Fund. Asymmetrical features are also traceable in the disbursement of the financial resources under the European Development Fund.

In the intricate EEC-ACP decision-making system, the ACP states are refused full consultation before committing funds for projects, while the conditions for granting some aid are time-consuming and generally dissuasive. The 'policy dialogues' introduced under Lomé III are admittedly a further method of EEC-ACP co-operation by which in-depth dialogue and agreement on ACP states' sector policies and programmes would become a prerequisite for Community financial assistance in the particular sector. The net result remains, however, that all the funds promised were not always committed, a situation that gave the ACP countries great cause for concern but bothered the EEC countries less. In the end, the ACP countries' development requirements were largely unattended to.

Thus Lomé I reinforced conditions of dependence (without development); and such conditions were revamped in Lomé II and III in most sectors. First, the funds made available under the Fifth European Development Fund were in real terms inferior to those under the Fourth EDF as the Sixth is most probably to the Fifth; that is, in making provision for inflationary pressures and the exponential nature of population growth among ACP members. Second, EEC members have refused to allow for equal participation, despite repeated appeals from and agitations by the ACP group, either in the disbursement and management of the European Development Fund or in the formulation of policies on related key issues. Third, the Minex scheme, though a new facility, has neo-dependence implications. The scheme will protect European-based transnational corporations in mining operations, in particular in Africa, an area of imminent and latent political instability from unforeseeable heavy investment and non-commercial risks. Fourth, neither Lomé II nor III removed the anomaly contained in Lomé I, namely, the subtle discouragement of industrialisation in ACP areas. The 12 under the new Convention continued to discourage the manufacture of goods, particularly textiles, in the ACP states, by not allowing such products access to the Community market, and/or encouraging voluntary export restraint on the part of the exporting developing countries concerned. Finally, and fifth, issues such as the over-bureaucratisation of decision-making and the enlargement of the EEC to 12 members have placed added pressures on the EEC-ACP relationship which may further thwart the development capability of the ACP countries. Prospects for symmetrical EurAfrica relations remain therefore dim despite all the rhetoric to the contrary.

NOTES

1. Richard Sandbrook, *The Politics of African Economic Stagnation* (Cambridge: Cambridge University Press, 1986) 35.
2. See, for example, Ralph I. Onwuka, 'The Lomé Convention: a machinery for economic dependence or interdependence', *Quarterly Journal of Administration*, Ife, (April 1979); Nicholas Hutton, 'Afri-

ca's Changing Relationship with the EEC', *The World Today*, (October 1974) 426–35; Eric Djamson, *The Dynamics of Euro-African Cooperation* (The Hague: Martinus Nijhoff, 1976); Douglas Evans, *The Politics of Trade: the evolution of the superbloc* (London: Macmillan, 1974); Peter Tulloch, *The Politics of Preferences* (London: Croom Helm/ODI, 1975); E. Olu Sanu, *The Lomé Convention and the New International Economic Order*, Lecture Series No. 18 (Lagos, Nigeria: NIIA); Christopher Stevens (ed.) *EEC and the Third World: A Survey, 4 Renegotiating Lomé* (New York: Holmes and Meier, 1984); and Robert Boardman, Timothy M. Shaw and Panayotis Soldatos (eds), *Europe, Africa, and Lomé III* (Lanham: University Press of America, 1985).

3. 'Lomé II', *Overseas Development Institute Briefing Paper*, No. 1, London (February 1980).
4. Onwuka, 'The Lomé Convention', 282.
5. E. Rhein, 'The Lomé Agreement: political and juridical aspects of the Community's policies towards less developed countries', *Common Market Law Review*, 12 (August 1975) 390.
6. See James Mayall, 'The Implications for Africa of the Enlarged European Economic Community', in Timothy M. Shaw and Kenneth A. Heard (eds) *The Politics of Africa: dependence and development*, (London: Longman and Dalhousie University Press, 1979) 295–7.
7. W. Briggs, 'Negotiations Between the Enlarged European Economic Community', *Journal of International Affairs* (July 1975) 12–32.
8. See arguments on this issue presented in Isabill V. Gruhn, 'The Lomé Convention: inching towards interdependence,' *International Organisation*, 30:2 (Spring 1976) 241–62.
9. *ODI Briefing Paper*, No. 1, Table 5.
10. See Article 92(3) of Lomé Convention II.
11. *West Africa*, 3177 (5 June 1978) 1083.
12. *Telex-Africa* (Brussels), 118 (27 February 1979) 6.
13. Ibid., 110 (31 October 1978) 8.
14. See Timothy M. Shaw's alternative modes of analysis for EEC-ACP relations and results in 'EEC-ACP Interactions and Images as Redefinitions of Eur-Africa: exemplary, exclusive, and/or exploitative', *Journal of Common Market Studies*, 18:2 (December 1979) 139.
15. Ibid.
16. John Ravenhill, 'From Lomé I to Lomé II: Plus ça change', quoted in Colin Legum (ed.) *Africa Contemporary Record, Volume 12, 1979–80* (New York: Africana, 1980) A87-A97.
17. *ODI Briefing Paper*, No. 1.
18. Ibid.
19. I. William Zartman, 'Lomé III: relic of the 1970s or model for the 1990s?', paper presented at the Symposium on European Community Development Policy: the Strategies for Africa, College of Europe-Bruges, July 1985.
20. Ibid.
21. *West Africa*, 3622 (9 February 1987) 276.
22. Ibid.

23. Article 176 of the Lomé III Convention.
24. *West Africa*, 3513 (17 December 1984) 2602.
25. *New Nigerian*, (Kaduna), 4607 (23 December 1980) 5.
26. *West Africa*, 3513 (17 December 1984) 2602.
27. Ibid.
28. *The Courier ACP-EEC* (Brussels) 98 (July-August 1986) 14–15.
29. *West Africa*, 3511 (3 December 1984) 2443.
30. Gruhn, 'The Lomé Convention', 241–62.
31. Peter Evans, *Dependent Development: the alliance of multinational, state, and local capital in Brazil* (Princeton: Princeton University Press, 1979) 327–33.
32. Ibid., 33.
33. Peter Afolabi, *The New ACP-EEC Convention*, Lecture Series No. 32 (Lagos: NIIA, 1981) 50–7.
34. Djamson, *The Dynamics of Euro-African Cooperation*, 247.
35. See, for example, Christian Deubner, 'The Southern Enlargement of the European Community', *Journal of Common Market Studies*, 18:3 (March 1980) 238.

4 CMEA-African Economic Relations[1]

Ralph I. Onwuka

Africans, particularly their business élites and political leaders, relate more to the Western centres of the United States of America and the EEC countries than to socialist Russia and its major partners in the Council for Mutual Economic Assistance (CMEA).[2] The two opposing ideologies — Western imperialism and Eastern Marxism-Leninism — should share responsibility for the low level of co-operation, particularly in economic and trade areas, between African states and CMEA countries.

Western imperialism through colonialism, neo-colonialism and capitalism, has in various ways affected the cultural, psychological and economic stability of the African continent. Through colonialism and, after independence, neo-colonialism the Western powers secured Africa, perhaps permanently, as an industrial and trading sphere. Thus their monopolisation of the means of production and consumption in Africa has become the veritable outcome of Western capitalism.[3] In spite of the antagonism and contradictions inherent in capitalism most African leaders prefer to adopt only Western economic theories as development strategies. With their high economic and cultural dependence on the West, little attempt is made in Africa to extend in an appreciable measure meaningful economic relations with the CMEA countries.

Marxism-Leninism, the common idiology of CMEA, aims principally at 'building socialism and communism and combating in fighting for peace, democracy and social progress'.[4] However, the CMEA, set up in 1949 for the development and expansion of socialist and communist construction, has not relentlessly fought for its ideals. And thus its effort to combat Western imperialism has not yielded satisfactory results in Africa. Mainly because of this, the continuing Westernisation process of many African states has not met with difficulty. The effort of the Eastern ideologies has yielded little dividend in Africa not only because their strategies have lacked sufficient aggressive content and sophisticated diplomatic drive, but also because the CMEA states have failed in some sectors — for example, in trade relations — to adapt Marxist-Leninist ideology to prevailing African conditions. As a result of this Marxist failure in interpreting and implementing African (development) intentions, the war against the predominant influence of the West in Africa has been lost by the CMEA partners.

The deepening structural adjustments within Africa, and between that continent and the Western and Eastern worlds, have in most parts multiplied the distortions and contradictions. Western capital as an agent of development has not freely and always embraced the development objectives of Africa without enslaving preconditions. The Marxist hope for the elimination of exploitation and oppression is still alive in Africa where the objectives remain most attractive in view of the prevailing limitations of material development and racial freedom in the continent.[5]

The objective of this chapter is to examine CMEA-African economic relations in three areas — political (particularly at UNCTAD), trade, and industrial co-operation. The intention is to identify the pattern of relations and establish in the process the problems and prospects for a mutually advantageous relationship.

POLITICAL RELATIONS: AREAS OF SUCCESSFUL CO-OPERATION

If one singled out the activities of CMEA partners at the United Nations (UN), particularly at UNCTAD, and Soviet military assistance to independence fighters it would be easy to maintain that CMEA-African relations are excellent. Many African countries have in various circumstances received Soviet military aid in the form of advisers and equipment. Between 1970 and 1975, a period of political challenges to African lenders' legitimacy, the Soviet Union gave military assistance not only to Angola, Mozambique and Nigeria that had survival problems but also to Somalia, Uganda, Guinea, Mali, Egypt, Libya, and Algeria suffering economic difficulties. The highest concentration of Soviet aid went to Egypt and Libya, while Soviet advisers were sent to Somalia, Algeria and Libya in large numbers. Where the Soviets are not engaged directly, Czechoslovakia was used to supply arms and instructors. The most successful military efforts of the Soviets and some of its allies were

> in their opposition to the intervention by imperialism and racists in the internal affairs of African peoples . . . and in dealing with the

problem of eliminating the vestiges of racism and colonialism and opposing neo-colonialism.[6]

In Angola and Mozambique massive Soviet military aid influenced the eventual attainment of political independence, while in Nigeria fragile unity was acquired through Soviet military aid. It can be safely argued that the period 1970–75 represents a high watermark in Soviet military assistance to Africa. This is more so with Angola, Congo and Nigeria. In Angola the Soviet offensive was mainly carried out through the military intervention of Cuban proxies. Christopher Stevens put this highpoint in definitive terms:

> Whether Angola is a landmark in the sense of a turning point in Afro-Soviet relations is not yet clear, but what is clear is that it is a landmark in the sense of a conspicuous beacon against which to take one's bearings. The present stark crisis provides an opportunity to assess the maturation of Soviet-African links during the 15 years from the Congo to Angola.[7]

With the Nigerian government relinquishing its peacetime pro-Western stand, the Soviets confidently seized the opportunity to forge a mutually beneficial Soviet-Nigerian relationship:

> The Soviets welcomed this change for the simple reason that it offered them the opportunity of securing influence — political, economic and diplomatic — in a country they had long coveted. They made various attempts to consolidate their presence in Nigeria. Apart from the anxiety to open consulates in all the States, they were reported to have adopted a tough line on becoming the sole supplier of arms in quantities that would ensure a quick victory.[8]

It is estimated that the procurement of arms through direct purchase by African states increased tenfold between 1972 and 1982 (amounting to $40 billion). Moreover, a few African states, notably Ethiopia and Libya, concluded treaties of mutual security with the Soviet Union.

Other CMEA-African co-operation issues that have political implications are the idea of 'proclaiming the African continent a nuclear free zone and the Mediterranean and the Indian Ocean peace zones and the prohibition of the use of force in outer space'.[9] There is also visible success in political co-operation between the two groups on the issue of self-determination at the United Nations.

The formation of UNCTAD represented a high watermark in CMEA-African political co-operation. The formation of UNCTAD would have been virtually impossible at the time without collaboration between the CMEA, under Soviet leadership, and the Group of 77 countries. With the demise of the International Trade Organisation (ITO) proposal initiated by the USSR, UNCTAD was conceived by its promoters as a preferred alternative to GATT, advocated by the US. R. M. Cutler has rightly asserted in a diagnosis on this issue that one of the main goals of ITO would have been

> to increase the legitimacy of the Soviet state in the system of international trade and in the legal regime governing that system.[10]

Thus, by implication, ITO would have significantly improved CMEA-African trade. The Soviet's reasons for initiating the establishment of ITO and later supporting the formation of UNCTAD were basically founded on its desire to promote East bloc trade with the Less Developed Countries (LDCs), which included the African states. For example, the USSR, Czechoslovakia, Hungary, and Poland had under the framework of UNCTAD intended to import more primary goods from the LDCs. It was the final support of the Soviets as partners in the LDCs' resolution 'that foresaw the establishment of the UNCTAD institutions suggested by Raul Prebisch'.[11] But once UNCTAD was formed, the CMEA countries — the Group B states — consciously and jealously guarded their collective interests, sometimes against African interests. So in spite of the ideals of the promotion of world trade that remained the *raison d'être* for the institutionalisation of UNCTAD, CMEA-African Trade has remained at a low ebb.

TRADE RELATIONS — LOW AND UNINSPIRING

It is necessary to remember that the major exports of the 50 odd states of Africa are agricultural products, a few minerals, and oil. Such exports include crude coffee, cocoa, groundnuts, soya beans, cotton and hides and skins. And more than three-quarters of African states depend largely on the agricultural industry for the financing of their imports. On the other hand, metal commodities, for example, copper, iron ore, phosphates and so on, monopolise the export industries in few countries. Nigeria, Libya, Algeria, Angola, Cameroon and Gabon are the major oil-exporting countries in Africa, and of these, Libya is the only capital-surplus country in the continent.[12] Studies conducted by Reinhard Muckhoff have shown that such consumer commodities as sugar, vegetable oils, coffee and tea constituted in 1970–75 the largest imports from African states. Sugar alone absorbed more than 50 per cent of the total import value of the 18 imported commodities studied.[13]

CMEA states are not, by any means, major trading partners of the African states. The Nigerian case is typical. Nigerian-CMEA non-oil trade promotion between Nigeria on the one side and Hungary, the USSR, Yugoslavia, Czechoslovakia, Poland, and the other socialist economies on the other confirms this. The Central Bank of Nigeria Annual Report of 1981, for example, reveals depressingly low trade relations between Nigeria and its CMEA partners. Nigeria's exports to the USSR were mainly cocoa, beans, coffee and other primary goods, while the Soviet Union exported to Nigeria such manufactured goods as cement, machines, electrical equipment, medicines, sugar and some other wares.[14] Generally the volume of trade between Nigeria and Western Europe is over 30 times larger than CMEA-Nigerian trade, manifesting the presence in Nigeria, as in most African states, of the more efficient and familiar Western superstructure of trade promotion.

The successful imperialist drive in Africa can be seen in the light of Western arm-twisting negotiating prowess and search for liberal concessions and cheap raw materials in return for Western manufactured goods. Nevertheless, the socialist countries' trade with the developing world is improving, though very slowly. Between 1960 and 1979 it grew from 1700 million Roubles to 19 400 Roubles. The socialist states of Africa, Asia and Latin America, according to this record, account for about 20 per cent of their total volume of trade with these three continents.[15] In Africa, for example, Angola, Ethiopia and Mozambique, compared with other states of comparable size, have reasonable trade dealings with the CMEA states. This is because these states operate socialist political structures.

Many factors contribute to the token and uninspiring trade relations between the two groups under discussion. The conduct of foreign trade of the CMEA group is based primarily on bilateralism. But recently bilateralism has been increasingly supplemented by such multilateral arrangements as 'tripartite co-operation, co-operation in Third World countries and co-operation arrangements linking individual countries with the CMEA member countries'.[16] Equally recent is the extension of co-operation arrangements to more than ten years. Multilateralism is, nevertheless, hampered by the poor and rigid transferability of the Soviet rouble, the international currency of the socialist countries. CMEA-African trade relations in no way parallel multilateral EEC-ACP relations. The socialists have denounced the Lomé relationship as exploitative of the African economy through the monopolisation of crucial exports of the African, Caribbean and Pacific countries. But nothing prevents the CMEA from institutionalising similar CMEA-African relations, or a CMEA-ECOWAS[17] accord, under a mutually beneficial framework. Here lies the weakness of the *modus operandi* of the socialist regional institutions — the Council Session, the Executive Committee, the Standing Commissions and the Secretariat. They are afflicted by an innate desire to promote intra-CMEA 'economic relations and co-operation in individual sectors of the economies of the member country'[18] under the leadership of the Soviet Union.

The Eastern mode of conducting foreign trade is in effect restrictive. But under bilateralism long-term trade agreements among themselves and between individual CMEA states and third parties, the CMEA states claim, are much more binding and respected. Thus under UNCTAD negotiations the bilateral regime of trade is preferred by the CMEA states. They would individually 'prefer barter arrangements in commodity trade with the LDCs,[19] even for long-term agreements.

Barter arrangements are central to the trade system of bilateralism. There seems to be a link between investment and trade in the conduct of bilateralism. In the late 1970s the Soviet Union's single largest investment was in Morocco's Meskala phosphate mine, which had reserves of between 8000 million and 10 000 million tonnes. This direct capital investment in Morocco was paid for with Moroccan phosphate rocks, triple-super-phosphate and phosphoric acid exported to the Soviet Union. These exports were bartered for Soviet capital investment in Morocco as in many other CMEA investments in Africa. In the case of the Soviet Union and Morocco, when the investment was paid-off, phosphates continued to be exchanged for Soviet crude oil.[20] The price of phosphates and derivatives were to be renegotiated after 30 years. The Soviets also imported about a third of the total of Moroccan citrus production as a way of balancing trade between the two countries.[21] There are also trade by barter relations between Ghana and Bulgaria where, in an agreement reached in 1983, Ghana was to supply Bulgaria with $5million of products while

Bulgaria in return would export $8million worth of goods to Ghana. The trade deficit of $3million was given to Ghana as a commodity credit repayable over a three-years period.[22]

Similar to the Ghana-Bulgaria agreement is the Tanzanian-East German trade arrangement where, in exchange for about 10 000 East German bicycles, Tanzania is sending cotton, tea, and tobacco to Berlin. Sometimes the CMEA countries finance the purchase of their goods by the African states. Romania in 1979, for example, granted Guinea $80million credit for the delivery by Romania of machinery and tools needed for a joint industrial venture between the two countries.[23] Hungary on its own allowed Kenyan businessmen a credit loan of Shs 65million to boost trade between the two countries.[24] Similar trade arrangements have existed between East Germany and Cameroon,[25] East Germany and Egypt,[26] and Czechoslovakia and Ethiopia.

The system of bilateral trade as a mechanism for operating both internal and international trade is adopted by the CMEA states as a way of facing up to the dilemma of currency and commodity inconvertibility. This has sometimes upset African traders, and sometimes it reduces the volume of trade to the amount that the weaker of the two partners can sell to the stronger. According to Holzman, when such imbalances do occur arrangements are made for the deficit country to pay in convertible currency.[27] When the LDCs are in trade surpluses with the CMEA states the problem of 'commodity inconvertibility' may emerge. This might force the LDCs concerned to purchase unrequired goods from the CMEA states. This may be to the disadvantage of the particular African countries involved.

Other than the above constraints, because African commodities are mainly agricultural with unpredictably long periods of gestation and high vulnerability to weather conditions, it is difficult to determine the supply line of the market. This leaves the Africans with little room for manoeuvrability, particularly under bilateralism. For example, under Nigerian-Soviet trade relations, Nigeria is in a deficit balance of trade because it has insufficient non-oil products to sell to the Soviet Union, which itself is a producer of oil.

Finally, because the African leaders relate more with the Western market they are more used to Western pricing and exchange regimes. To Africans, the CMEA pricing and exchange rates are arbitrary and irrational and sometimes seem to bear no relationship to the values of currencies in the international market.

INDUSTRIAL RELATIONS — MUTUALLY BENEFICIAL

Like trade, industrial relations between CMEA countries and African states are bilaterally implemented sometimes on credit-financed barter or even on an outright cash basis, possibly dollar. The major consideration for the numerous mutually beneficial industrial agreements of co-operation and friendship signed in the continent is the desire to acquire socialist technology for African industrialisation. But the general argument against CMEA technology is the fact that CMEA states are themselves as eager to develop as are the Africans and in terms of development

> Only the triangle encompassing Western Czechoslovakia and Southern Poland (Bohemia-Silesia) could be described as a significant area of industrial development.[28]

No doubt CMEA states have placed high priority on industrialisation through socialist integration and through international links and co-operation. Thus, despite the much politised issue of codes of conduct for the transfer of technology, the conditionality for the technology transfer from the socialist to African states stems principally from the mutuality of interest in bilateral intergovernmental business agreements.

The socialist-African business connection can be grouped into (1) those relations that aim at promoting trade; (2) joint ventures; and (3) other general business agreements that encompass (1) and (2).

Trade promoting business relations can be seen in the light of socialist capital investment in the mining sector of the African economy with a view to generating export goods destined for the investing CMEA state. The Soviet Union has numerous such industrial investments in Congo (mining), Uganda (cotton), Algeria (iron and steel) and Morocco (phosphates). Czechoslovakia and East Germany have similar bilateral business agreements with Ethiopia intended to promote agricultural exports needed in the signatory socialist states. Thus, like the Western-based multinational corporations, (MNCs) the primary motive in CMEA business ventures in Africa is self-serving, especially when such an industrial set-up is designed to fuel the barter relationship or supply raw materials for home industries.

There are, nevertheless, some joint ventures between the CMEA states and the African countries. Joint ventures are necessary in most cases, where national (African) laws have stipulated compulsory indigenous participation in certain businesses or, as in all cases, where the local technological resources are too lean and inferior to be absorbed into the project. Under this class of business relations are, for example, the Soviet-Madagascan mining project; the Libyan-Italian-Bulgarian refinery project; the Czechoslovakian-Nigerian leaf spring factory in Bauchi; the Soviet-Libyan nuclear station; the Romanian-Guinean joint industrial venture; the East-German-Egyptian power station; the Soviet-Nigerian iron and steel works, and the various joint projects between Nigeria and Poland. The points of conflicts in such joint business enterprises are usually the mode of financing and operationalisation and the nature of priorities placed on such ventures. Disagreements have led to breakdowns and renegotiations on the conditions for joint participation, particularly those between Nigeria and the Soviet Union, and between Nigeria and Poland. In addition sometimes political consideration may be conclusive in determining the viability of business relations, like the ideological controversy that led to the expulsion of the Soviet technical experts from Somalia in late 1970s. In such a situation, the return of Western experts is easily guaranteed by the US or the EEC countries.

Lastly, there are many other business accords between the CMEA and African states that fill the technical and capital needs of the host countries. The fishing agreements between the Soviet Union and Angola or those between the former and Morocco are good examples. Here Soviet fishing techniques were imported into Angola and Morocco, perhaps at the expense of the local fishing entrepreneurs.

Other agreements are for capital finance projects (for instance, direct loans). The socialist nations have given credits to and rescheduled or even cancelled debts of the African states. Such concessions are usually given in the appropriate political environment. It was easy for Yugoslavia to cancel the ($7million debt owed it by Guinea in 1979, but in early 1983 when Guinea was disengaging from the East and consequently made advances to the West such a liberal act of kindness from the East would have been difficult. The USSR has given all sorts of loans to Ethiopia, a passionate socialist African state, while it had good reason to reschedule its loan with Guinea-Bissau in 1978. Between 1979 and 1983 the Soviet Union alone had 70 per cent of total CMEA investment projects in Africa. And 51 per cent of these projects were in such socialist countries as Algeria, Angola, Congo-Brazzaville, Ethiopia, Libya, Madagascar, and Mozambique.[29] This constitutes in essence an attempt by the Soviets to reinforce economic and social changes in these basically centrally-planned African states against contrary Western, especially IBRD, pressures. The Soviet Union dominates its CMEA partners in terms of capital involvement in Africa. By 1979 the USSR had economic and technical agreements with 30 African countries and had 380 projects in operation with more than half completed.[30] By 1982 the number of projects had increased to 500 in 35 African countries.[31] Important Soviet investments are in metallurgical, hydrochloric, nuclear and bauxite ventures. Other CMEA countries, such as Bulgaria, East Germany, Czechoslovakia and Poland trail behind the USSR in investment distribution and concentration in Africa.

CONCLUSION

CMEA-African relations are still at a primitive stage with great room for development. Africa is bedevilled by problems of underdevelopment in independent countries and the war against racism in other areas. Ideology becomes useful in the African context if it promotes the process of economic development and liberation. Western imperialism has had both negative and positive impacts on this process. Yet the CMEA states have not fully exploited their natural advantages over the Western powers in Africa. The socialist countries never colonised Africa but their strict adherence to the Marxist-Leninist ideology in their relations with African states has led to the prevailing low level of trade relations, and, except for the special case of the Soviet Union, to inadequate involvement in advancing the industrialisation of Africa. The continent may be marginal in the world economy but it remains more central in the Western capitalist system than in the Eastern non-capitalist one.

NOTES

1. This chapter originally appeared in *Co-Existence: a Review of East-West and Development Issues* published by the Department of Politics at the University of Glasgow.
2. The original member states of CMEA were Bulgaria, Czechoslovakia, Hungary, Poland, Romania and the Soviet Union. Albania joined in February 1949, and East Germany in September 1950. China (1956), North Korea (1957), North Vietnam (1958) and Mongolia (1958) have since been admitted. China has not made use of its observer status

since the end of 1961 because of its dispute with the USSR. See M.A.G. Van Meerheaghe, *International Economic Institutions* (London: Longman, 1974) 217.
3. R. I. Onwuka, 'Western Imperialism and Africa's International Trade', *Renaissance Universal Journal* (Burlington, Ontario) vol. 3 (1982) nos. 2–3, 53–7.
4. K.I. Mikulsky (ed.), *CMEA-International Significance of Socialist Integration* (Moscow: Progress Publishers 1982) 16.
5. André Gunder Frank, 'Real Marxism is Marxist Realism' *Viertel Jahres Berichte* (Bonn), No. 93, September 1983, 219.
6. V. Morozov, 'The Struggle for Peace and Soviet-African Relations', a paper presented at the International Conference on *OAU/ECA Lagos Plan of Action and the Future of Africa*, Department of International Relations, University of Ife, March 1984.
7. C. Stevens, 'The Soviet Union and Angola' *African Affairs* (London), vol. 75 (April 1976) no. 299, 137.
8. Oye Ogunbadejo, 'Nigeria and the Great Powers: The Impact of the Civil War on Nigeria Foreign Relations', *African Affairs*, vol 75 (January 1976) no. 298, 24.
9. Morozov, 'The Struggle for Peace'.
10. Robert M. Cutler, 'East-South Relations at UNCTAD', *International Organization* (Massachusetts), vol. 37 (Winter 1983) no. 1, 124.
11. Ibid.
12. R. I. Onwuka, 'The African Resource-Exporting States: An Examination of the Frustration of the Periphery of the World Periphery', Proceedings of the 10th International Conference on the Unity of Sciences, November 1981, Seoul, 156.
13. R.O.F. Muckhoff, *Africa: World Trade Significance of Commodities*, Forchungsinstitut det Fredrick-Ebert-Stiftung (Bonn) No. 67, 1978.
14. A. Laurincukas, 'Nigeria: Achievements and Problems', *International Affairs* (Moscow) 11 November 1983, 140.
15. Mikulsky (ed.), *CMEA*, 327.
16. M. S. Davydov 'The Socialist Countries of Europe' in A. B. Akinyemi (ed.), *Economic Co-operation Between Nigeria and Eastern Europe* (Lagos; NIIA, 1986) 8.
17. The Economic Community of West African States (ECOWAS) comprises the 16 West African States of Nigeria, Ghana, Benin, Togo, Ivory Coast, Senegal, Niger, Guinea, Guinea-Bissau, Sierra Leone, Mali, Mauritania, Upper Volta, Gambia, Cape Verde and Liberia.
18. Article 8(1) of the Treaty of CMEA.
19. F. D. Holzman, *International Trade Under Communism: Politics and Economics* (London: Macmillan, 1976) 24.
20. *Africa Research Bulletin* (Exeter) 15 January-14 February, 1978.
21. Ibid.
22. Ibid., 15 February - 14 March 1983, 6787.
23. Ibid., 15 July - 14 August 1979, 5220.
24. Ibid., 15 November - 14 December 1983, 7098.
25. Ibid., 15 February - 14 March 1979, 5428.
26. Ibid., 15 December 1980 - 14 January 1981, 5524.

27. Holzman, *International Trade Under Communism*
28. A. I. Macbean and P. N. Snowden, *International Institutions in Trade and Finance* (London: Allen & Unwin, 1981) 195.
29. Eugene Zaleski, 'Socialist Multinational in Developing Countries' in Geoffrey Hamilton (ed.), *Red Multinationals or Red Herrings*? (London: Frances Printer, 1986) 173–4.
30. *Africa Research Bulletin*, 15 July - 14 August 1978, 4800.
31. Morozov, '*The Struggle for Peace*'.

5 The Revival of Regionalism: Cure for Crisis or Prescription for Conflict?[1]

Timothy M. Shaw

> Regional cooperation is not new in Africa. In fact the myriad regional and sub-regional organisations testify to the intensive efforts made to harness regional cooperation to the task of African development . . . Yet, as elsewhere, the results have not been impresssive. While this record has caused disenchantment among integration theorists, [my] thesis. . . . is that for Africa the realities still point to the imperative of regional cooperation.[2]

> There is no doubt that in spite of all the difficulties and all the constraints, there has been some remarkable progress in laying the foundation for meaningful economic cooperation in Africa. Although there has been no breakthrough yet, there is cause for hope, if not for optimism . . .
> The balkanisation of Africa is one of the major constraints to the economic transformation of the continent . . . it is imperative that African countries should strengthen their solidarity in all fields and stress the factors that unite rather than those that divide them.[3]

The continuing continental crisis, of underdevelopment rather than drought, highlights the distance between rhetoric and reality in African regionalism. It also draws attention to the distinction between 'old' and 'new' regionalisms, that is, between formal and comprehensive declarations on the one hand and informal and specific arrangements on the other. If the crisis led to re-evaluations of development direction — the *Lagos Plan of Action* (LPA) and self-reliance[4] — it also generated reconsiderations of regionalist doctrine — from free trade areas and common services to sectoral and infrastructural agreements. In short, the future of Africa's development policies in general and regional proposals in particular has led over the last difficult decade to a redefinition of both, in which national and collective self-reliance are taken to be the criterion of development. Regionalism remains an imperative but it has been largely restated to fit current needs, experiences and contexts. As Sam Asante laments:

> By 1980 — when the LPA was adopted — almost all the economic cooperation schemes optimistically launched in the 1960s — the halcyon years of African integration — had become largely moribund.[5]

INTRODUCTION

Since the turn of the decade there has been a marked conjuncture in continental affairs: the post-Bretton Woods and post-oil shocks economic (dis)order finally caught up with Africa. The Sahel famine was merely symptomatic of a larger failure, not of rain but of development. Fortuitously, a few more enlightened African leaders had anticipated such a collapse by gathering in 1979 in Monrovia, where they designed a collective strategy subsequently embodied in the LPA. The pair of continental economic summits — in 1981 in Lagos and 1986 in Addis Ababa — mark a turning point in African affairs: from a preoccupation with short-term, political rhetoric towards longer-term economic reform. The LPA and Addis Ababa Declaration, prepared for the Special UN General Assembly of mid-1986, signify a cluster of forces and factors:

(1) Africa's reluctant recognition that contemporary rates of development were either unsatisfactory or negative;
(2) a belated appreciation that global recovery would not necessarily help Africa and that many external agencies had only a temporary interest in continental development;
(3) recognition that international recommendations were not always appropriate, so Africa had to design its own strategy;
(4) agreement that continental balkanisation had to be overcome to provide the basis for sustained recovery;
(5) insistence that indigenous interests, exchange and policies

should be primary so that both South-South and South-North negotiations could proceed from a position of cohesion rather than division; and

(6) consensus that Africa needs self-confidence as well as self-reliance and self-sustainment to advance towards redevelopment, redirection and a continental country by the end of the century.[6]

The failure of national economies, regional integration, South-South relations and South-North redistribution combined with inflation, recession (often with regression), desertification, regional conflicts and debt reschedulings[7] meant that Africa had to re-evaluate its development directions rapidly and critically. With the encouragement of the UN Economic Commission for Africa (ECA) this process has resulted in a new framework for regional endeavours if not yet unequivocal regional benefits. According to the major *animateur*, Adebayo Adedeji, the LPA and related declarations and documents made collective co-operation and self-reliance an all-pervasive issue with the ultimate goal of an African Economic Community by the year 2000, approached in a series of stages:

> Thus, it calls, during the 1980s, for the strengthening of existing regional economic communities and for establishing new ones so as to cover the continent as a whole; for the strengthening of sectoral integration at the continental level; and for promoting coordination and harmonization among existing and future economic groupings. And during the decade of the 1990s, it calls for sectoral integration.[8]

Adedeji proceeded to identify a trio of novel regional groupings as indicative of such stages of integration, pointing to the Economic Communities for West and for Central African States (ECOWAS and ECCAS) and to the ECA-sponsored Preferential Trade Area (PTA) (for Eastern and Southern Africa) rather than the Front Line States (FLS)-supported Southern African Development Coordination Conference (SADCC):

> Excessive openness and external dependence of African economies are inimical to the achievement not only of national but also

of collective self-reliance so that progressive inter-African economic penetration is a *sine qua non* for the achievement of national and collective self-reliance.

There is no doubt that the developments of the past few years have heralded the emergence of a sound foundation for achieving this objective. ECOWAS, PTA and ECCAS constitute the main instrumentalities for achieving this goal. Among them these three institutions cover the entire area of sub-Saharan Africa. Therefore, we need urgently to put them into the position of helping direct African economic policy.[9]

But these institutional developments take place in a continent chracterised not only by cyclical droughts but also by exponential declines and inequalities and in a world system preoccupied by a new international division of labour rather than a new international economic order. In short, the national, continental and global galaxies of forces are hardly in a propitious orbit.[10]

To advance development, let alone co-operation, substantial changes need to take place in the character of production, relations and institutions within and between African political economies. And such changes are a function of history as well as of ideology and diplomacy. Together these determine whether the continent can advance from old to new forms of regionalism, from extroversion to self-reliance, and from orthodox to radical analysis and *praxis*.[11]

However, Africa is not only the largest regional sub-system in terms of territorial size and number of states[12]; it is also the least industrialised and the one characterised by the most inequality. Its colonial inheritance — 'dualistic' economies, authoritarian regimes and high levels of ethnic and racial consciousness — is not an advantageous one and if current projections materialise with regard to both its continued inability to meet Basic Human Needs (BHN) and the incidence and impact of growing inequalities, its future prospects are rather gloomy.[13] Nevertheless, despite its unfortunate inheritance and mixed performance, Africa has emerged as an important actor in the contemporary arena of world politics.

Ambiguities and contradictions in the past and present characterise the political economy of Africa; in addition it is a Southern continent in a global system still dominated essentially by the interests and actions of the North. The discontinuities and dilemmas of 'economic' dependence and 'political' interdependence are revealed most poignantly in the very tenuous and vulnerable form of 'independence' presently achieved by African countries. The uneven rates and results of development — with their interrelated political, economic, social and strategic components — have served to exacerbate inequalities and tensions both within and between the states of Africa as well as between continental and global actors.[14]

The position and prospects of Africa in an unequal world order pose problems for both analysis and action, perception and prediction. This chapter is concerned, therefore, not only with the comparative study of two African regions, but also with alternative approaches to analysis as well as alternative development strategies. In particular, it will consider and contrast both the more 'orthodox' and 'radical' modes of analysis and modes of production, taking into account the interrelationship between theory and policy. The paradoxes and dilemmas of Africa's role in the world system are relevant to the comparative analysis of regionalism, to comparative explanations of integration and to comparative policy choices. They also inform contrasts between ECOWAS and SADCC as case studies.

ALTERNATIVE MODES OF ANALYSIS AND ADVOCACY

The revival of ideology in Africa is one aspect of a broader trend towards divergent political economies caused by the highly uneven impact of incorporation into the world system. The myth of equality dies hard amongst scholars as well as statesmen, and the emergence of a few leading powers on the continent is forcing a reassessment in both perception and policy. Nevertheless, the orthodox school sticks doggedly to the assumption that the continental system consists of essentially equal and similar actors, while the radical approach attempts to relate novel concepts — such as that of 'sub-imperialism'[15] — to changes in Africa's position in the world order. Both modes of analysis retain their currency in a global system characterised by a return to *realpolitik* and power politics. Nevertheless, I. William Zartman continues to assert that it is simply not possible to understand the relations of the continental system through a study of the few states which, through a combination of such elements of national strength as location, area, population, GNP and foreign policy interest, might be counted as the powerful of the continent.[16]

Nonetheless, the orthodox approach has moved some way towards recognition of the growing inequalities on the continent, conceiving of them, however, as changeable and unstable phenomena rather than as reflections of a gradual evolution in Africa's substructure. Instead of treating Africa's new group of 'middle powers' as indicative of changes in the international division of labour, Zartman views them merely as centres of momentary conflicts and coalitions. According to him, the three major features of the leading African states are:

> temporary initiatives on the regional level, delicate positions of predominance within a subregion, and limited arrays of resources available as a power base even for the strongest . . . in short, African states have little with which to threaten and little to share, and they are not in a position to win or enforce long-term commitments. At best, they can command temporary advantages, since most African states' resources are meagre.[17]

By contrast, the radical mode sees regional powers as being less transitional, not restricted to strategic issues alone and more structurally defined. From this viewpoint the emergence of sub-imperialism on the continent is related to the evolving international division of labour in which some limited forms of industrialism can take place — albeit under the auspices of the multinational corporation, in the 'semi-periphery'.[18] As production is restructured within corporations and centre states so certain countries may advance from the periphery into the semi-periphery; but technological, financial and administrative controls are largely retained in the centre.

Internationalisation of production does not mean internationalisation of control. Rather, the centre is able to secure favourable terms and attitudes by offering some limited degree of semi-industrialisation to co-operative regimes or countries with particularly valuable natural or organisational resources. According to Immanuel Wallerstein's world system framework, a few African states, either by invitation or by accident, will come to enjoy upward mobility in the international hierarchy, while the majority will continue to stagnate and remain underdeveloped in the periphery.[19] The possibility or prospect of advancing into the semi-periphery serves to reinforce confidence in orthodox development theory as well as to encourage quiescence in established spheres of influence. In turn, a few semi-industrial states dominate their own regions of the continent, partially on behalf of centre interests.

In the mid-term future, semi-industrialism in the semi-periphery may reinforce confidence in orthodox development strategies and in the continent's ability to maintain order. However, in the longer term, as Steven Langdon and Lynn Mytelka suggest, the sub-imperial 'solution' may generate its own contradictions and demise because of its association with the established capitalist international division of labour:

> Export manufacturing in Africa, then, will undoubtedly increase — as the signs of change in such countries as the Ivory Coast, Senegal, Ghana and Kenya suggest. But this manufacturing is likely to be largely under the direction of foreign enterprises and integrated into the structure of internationalized production. In consequence, the linkage, employment, and income effects of such manufacturing will be fairly limited within Africa — and probably will be enjoyed mainly by those local elites who will extend their import substitution symbiosis to the export sector. Significant restructuring of African economies, with wide dynamic advantages for African majorities, cannot be expected to emerge from this export-manufacturing growth.[20]

The emergence of inequalities and regional powers on the continent may, paradoxically, serve to increase the level of interaction in Africa, at least in the short run and amongst the group of emergent middle powers. To date, the proportion of intra- versus extra-continental exchange has been very limited, because of Africa's dependent status within the world system. Economic interaction and military relations have been concentrated at the subregional level, increasingly under the dominance of a few regional centres and cities — such as Abidjan, Cairo, Dakar, Harare, Lagos and Nairobi — that serve as intermediaries between metropolises and peripheries.

Interdependences based on integration in Africa remain largely an aspiration rather than a reality. Despite declarations and diplomacy, integration as measured in terms of economic, communications and social transactions remains at a stubbornly low level. The orthodox view of this situation is that integration takes time and that, given Africa's colonial inheritance, its post-independence performance is quite promising. By contrast, the radical perspective sees extra-continental economic dependence as an essential characteristic of the capitalist world system; it does not expect high levels of continental integration while Africa remains incorporated within global networks. These divergent perspectives have informed alternative current policies, as indicated below.

So, whereas the orthodox approach sees no necessary incompatibility between global, continental and regional integration, the radical school considers continental and regional self-reliance to be incompatible with global and transnational integration. Regional exchange has a rather mixed record, with inter-African trade other than 'informal' exchange rising more slowly than extra-African trade; that is, inter-African exchange continues to fall as a percentage of total African trade. Moreover, most of this official trade is either transit of non-African goods to landlocked states, or the export of manufactures by multinational branches located in regional centres such as Abidjan, Harare, Lagos and Nairobi.

Inter-African trade is unlikely to increase much other than through smuggling and the black market until the continent escapes from its colonial heritage of North-South links and produces goods with markets on the continent as well as outside. A regional industrialisation policy is necessary to maximise compatibility and exchange; yet this cannot be designed or realised until decisions made by foreign countries and corporations are transcended.[21] This, in turn, requires a degree of autonomy that can only be achieved through collective action. Hence, the vicious circle of exogenous rather than endogenous growth, of a highly open rather than relatively closed continental system. The elusiveness of inter-African exchange is reflected in the underdeveloped state of the continental infrastructure. Communications by land, sea, air and telex are improving but still by no means balance extra-African connections.

POLITICAL ECONOMY AND FOREIGN POLICY

The established African response to colonialism and underdevelopment has been advocacy of nationalism at the state level, Pan-Africanism at the continental level and non-alignment at the Third World level; all these reactions call for a redistribution of authority and resources without involving a real transformation in Africa's world position. These three clusters of values have constituted the core of Africa's collective foreign policy and have led to current demands for a NIEO.[22] However, with the emergence of inequalities on the continent and the reappearance of ideological cleavages, common international positions have tended to fragment. The espousal of 'alternative' development strategies, such as the 'non-capitalist path' and various forms of socialism, inspired by Marxist-

Leninist rather than traditional thought, have undermined the continent's ideological consensus and have led to a variety of foreign policy orientations and emphases at least until the recent period of widespread structural adjustments.[23]

The orthodox approach, recognising Africa's common heritage and transition, still emphasises commonalities in the continent's foreign policies; the radical approach, reflecting changes in the political economy of parts of the continent, accepts and examines contradictions in the foreign relations of participating state and non-state institutions. The orthodox perspective, based on certain sociological, cultural and psychological affinities conceives of Africa's foreign policy as being singular and consensual. It appreciates the imperative of unity if Africa's voice is to be heard. Under the impact of various associations, however, it has begun to accept that there may be different foreign policy emphases or nuances, particularly based on membership in, say, the Commonwealth, *la francophonie*, the Arab League or Islamic states:

> The recognition of overlapping systems in interpreting foreign policy alternatives and possibilities for states with dual membership is both a more helpful and more realistic way of looking at foreign policies than is the attempt to force such states exclusively into one area or the other.[24]

While African states may belong to a variety of international institutions, their foreign policy choices may be quite limited, particularly by their selection of a development strategy. The comparative study of foreign policy in Africa remains rather embryonic although a few frameworks for analysis now exist.[25] One major factor in foreign policy-making is, of course, choice of development strategy which, given Africa's dependence and openness, means essentially how to respond to external pressures and opportunities. Donald Rothchild and Robert Curry have proposed a trilateral typology of such responses that may also serve as a framework for comparative foreign policy analysis. They identify three policy options — accommodation, reorganisation and transformation (revolution?)[26] — which span the spectrum from acquiescence to resistance, respectively. But, in agreement with the general tenor of the orthodox school, they treat these as mere policy responses rather than as political strategies that reflect underlying structural contradictions.

By contrast, the radical perspective concentrates on development alternatives rather than on foreign policy, and attempts to relate these to modes of production and incorporation rather than to international associations and ideologies. More radical African scholars such as Micah Tsomondo and Teti Kofi argue in this genre that Pan-Africanism is representative of 'bourgeois' interests and needs to be transcended both in analysis and practice by a more 'scientific' variety of socialism. Moreover, they see the adoption of socialism at the continental level as a prerequisite for effective unity based on an appreciation of class politics and the adoption of a continental industrial strategy. In other words, they conceive of socialism as a response to fragmentation and functionalism on the one hand, and to dependence and underdevelopment on the other.[27]

The orthodox approach, however, still sees Pan-Africanism as a reaction to colonialism and does not go much beyond the re-Africanisation of the continent as an objective. It still has faith in orthodox theories of convergence and 'trickle-down' development, and extroverted strategies of growth. By contrast, the radical approach has largely abandoned the assumptions and remedies of the orthodox perspective in favour of an approach that is more introverted and self-reliant, based on an appreciation of the international division of labour as it affects Africa.[28]

OLD AND NEW REGIONALISMS

The orthodox approach has analysed attempts at regional integration in Africa as part of a diplomatic strategy to improve the balance of forces between the continent and the rest of the global system. This approach conceives of regionalism, not as a development strategy or an attempt to restructure the international division of labour, so much as a diplomatic tactic designed to enhance Africa's visibility and autonomy — a collective form of decolonisation. Its focus has been on regional constitutions and institutions — the form rather than the relationship — and on mediation and liberation rather than structural transformation. From this perspective, the process is as important as, if not more than, the results. And although one motive of the Pan-African movement has been to reduce balkanisation and to transcend nationalism, in fact the record of the OAU to date has served to reinforce fragmentation and to reify the state:

> From the start the existence of the OAU has been far more important to African statesmen and policiticians than any func-

> tional role it may perform in promoting economic cooperation or even the alignment of foreign policies . . . By merely being there, the OAU does indeed perform one vital role in African diplomacy — it bestows legitimacy on its members and on the movements and causes which they choose to recognise . . . It has always been the OAU's main task to set the seal of legitimacy on both the distribution of power within African states and on those liberation movements, mainly in Southern Africa, which were contesting power with colonial or minority regimes.[29]

By contrast to the orthodox school's focus on diplomacy and legitimacy, the radical approach considers the developmental and economic impact of nationalism. And whereas the orthodox school tends to produce relatively positive evaluations, the radical approach leads to essentially negative conclusions. The OAU network may have served to stabilise the continental system in terms of decolonisation, mediation and consultation, but the ECA and its 'subregional' associates have not yet begun to escape from a position of economic dependence on the world system.

The OAU displayed a remarkable resilience over its first 20 years in its ability to weather the storms of 'dialogue' and '*détente*' with South Africa, of conflict in Shaba, Sudan, Chad and Sahara, and of OPEC and Afro-Arab divisions.[30] But these rather ephemeral, 'diplomatic crises' are seen by the radical school as merely reflections of fundamental contradictions that the OAU-ECA system has yet seriously to confront. Despite a growing range of proposals and scenarios, regional interactions did not lead to significant advances at least until the 1980s, and then because of destabilisation and desertification in South and West, respectively.

The radical school suggests that the reason for this condition is the continued integration of Africa into the world system.[31] Whereas at the level of diplomacy and ideology the OAU can score pyrrhic victories, at the level of productive accumulation and the continental political economy it cannot, with profound implications for both metropolitan and African élite interests. Given the close transnational links between the new élite and foreign countries, corporations and classes, such a prospect is likely to continue, unless and until global and national conditions change. In an attempt to make Africa's powerlessness and assertiveness compatible with each other, Zartman has recognised the discontinuity between continental dependence and demand while ignoring the structural contradictions that generated such ambiguity:

> In a world where Africa does not have the power to protect itself and promote its own goals, it proposes a new system of international relations that emphasises its rights and deemphasises the classical means to attain them. The inherent contradiction, sharpened by the fact that the faster developing states in Africa do in fact seek to increase their power and use it in classical ways, is typical of an idealistic view of international relations.[32]

If the orthodox approach, with its emphasis on the new diplomacy, is 'idealistic' in tone then the radical perspective, with its emphasis on the old dependence, is 'realistic' in orientation. This analytic and existential dichotomy is reflected in patterns of contemporary regional co-operation and conflict — that is, ECOWAS versus SADCC — which are themselves but aspects of contemporary contradictions within and around the continent. These extend to continued advocacy of extra-continental regionalism — EurAfrica — as well as intra-continental, despite repeated nationalist critiques of dominance and dependence.

REVISIONISM, REGIONALISM AND THE CONTINENTAL CRISIS

Contemporary contradictions between regionalisms within and around Africa take place in a world system characterised then by recession, inflation and transition. The demise of the post-war Bretton Woods order of relative expansion and diffusion has resulted in a more anarchic, unyielding world of general contraction and highly uneven patterns of growth and decline; from the resilience of South Korea and Singapore to the stagnation of Senegal and Zambia, and the decay of Ghana and Tanzania, that is, the new division between Newly Industrialising Countries (NICs)[33] and Least Developed Countries (LLDCs), between 'Third' and 'Fourth' Worlds.

The last decade, then, has seen a relatively or aspiring homogeneous continent become considerably more heterogeneous, with myriad implications for cohesion and regionalism. It has also witnessed a growing tension between the political and the economic, as well as an emerging set of contradictory responses symbolised by the OAU's *Lagos Plan of Action*, on the one hand, and the World Bank's *Agenda for Action* on the other (see previous chapters).[34] If the latter advocates extroverted growth, compatible with EurAfricanism, then the former advances African self-reliance, compatible with continental regionalism.

In short, the present conjuncture of global and continental crises has stimulated a variety of responses at the levels of politics and economics on the one hand and of EurAfrican and continental regionalisms on the other. Given the new diversity of political economies on the continent, these alternatives, and not necessarily compatible policies and preferences, are advocated by different states, classes and fractions. The myth of Pan-Africanism is thus under attack from both extra- and intra-African forces of either disinterest, division or dominance.

Regionalism a hundred years after the Berlin Conference is a controversial ideology and policy because of a multiplicity of interpretations, interests and implications. Its tendency to manipulation and ambiguity is a reflection of the range of contradictions generated by the current crisis and the intensity of competition for scarce resources in a period of no or negative growth. Regionalism becomes more problematic and antagonistic as growth is elusive and projections are unpromising. Hence the willingness of diverse interests to define it in different ways to maximise their prospects of (renewed) growth, if not development.

Thus, regionalism has had a rather checkered history in Africa; yet, despite many cautionary tales, optimism still abounds over the latest efforts at regionalism in the continent. In many ways a 'second-generation' institution, ECOWAS is, despite the subsequent appearance of SADCC, both bigger and more ambitious than most previous experiments in either Africa or elsewhere. Nevertheless, its prospects remain problematic, and its aspirations remain ambiguous. Its tenuous situation and support lead to a set of questions about its future that are posed in the concluding section, although the turbulent future of Southern Africa — the conjuncture of racism and repression, destabilisation and disengagement — may yet spill over to affect ECOWAS.

If regionalism was difficult in previous decades, it is likely to be even more so in the 1990s because of interrelated changes in the global and continental divisions of labour and economic priorities. Until the mid-1970s international growth was sufficiently large for the marginal redistribution of surplus and opportunity from the centre to the periphery to be neither impossible nor controversial. However, in the less benign and more calculating world of the 1980s — a world of recession and inflation still trying to live with fluctuating exchange and interest rates and with unstable higher prices for energy — Third World regional development at the expense of metropolitan growth is most unlikely. International economics are once again zero- rather than mixed-sum; the environment for regionalism is no longer tolerant, let alone supportive. If ECOWAS fails, the causes may well be extra- rather than intra-African: and, if it succeeds, the benefits may well flow outside rather than inside the region. Yet, despite the problems of regionalism in Africa over the last 20 years, many of which arose in less difficult times than today, West African leaders retain the faith that ECOWAS will be the exception. Given the lack of visible, viable options, such faith may spring from the lack of any alternative; that is, regionalism and self-reliance by default.

The rest of this chapter attempts to explain and evaluate the elusiveness of regionalism in Africa by contrast to the seeming resilience of EurAfricanism, by situating it in the context of the changing global political economy. The prospects for unity and development on the continent in the 1980s and 1990s are profoundly affected by pressures on the international division of labour elsewhere. Likewise, any projections for regionalism in Africa in general and West Africa in particular cannot exclude world trends and forecasts: the ambiguity of dominance, especially of EurAfrica (see chapter 3).[35]

International capitalism has evolved considerably in the two decades that Africa has been formally independent. This evolution — from liberalism to protectionism, from American hegemony to 'trilateralism', and from growth to recession — has important implications for the African continent. If most African states failed to grow before the mid-1970s, their prospects have since deteriorated. And any improvement that has occurred — before but especially after the mid-1970s — has been unevenly generated and distributed, both between and within countries. Growing inequalities in Africa have important implications for unity as well as for development.[36]

AFRICAN DEVELOPMENT IN THE 1980S: DEPENDENT OR SELF-RELIANT?

African unity is increasingly tenuous, because African states have increasingly divergent positions within the world system; a divergence which Lomé Conventions do not transcend and may even exacerbate (see chapter 3). The majority of primary commodity producers have suffered declining terms of trade as the prices of manufactures and petroleum have increased; over the last decade the LLDCs have hardly grown at all, with several enduring negative growth rates in the second half of the 1970s. By contrast, the would-be NICs grew at an almost exponential rate, at least until the bursting of the oil bubble in the early 1980s. Africa is, therefore, an increasingly unequal continent in which growth, industrialisation and optimism are concentrated in a few aspiring NICs, while the majority of countries and peoples suffer minimal growth, continued marginalisation and a bleak outlook. In these circumstances, development strategies diverge, as do growth rates, despite collective economic policies in the OAU, Lomé and Group of 77 arrangements.

In general the LLDCs have looked inwards, while the NICs looked outwards; poorer African states advocate self-reliance, while the richer favour further incorporation. These 'back-to-back' developmental orientations have important implications for regional as well as continental co-operation. TheLLDCs tend to favour collective as well as national self-reliance, but the prospects for autonomy through regionalism are reduced when the 'core' of each potential region is more extroverted in policy and in practice: African and EurAfrican regionalisms become contradictory at such junctures. The periphery cannot effectively turn regional institutions towards disengagement when the semi-periphery seeks to play an intermediary role, involving continued association with metropolitan countries and corporations. In other words, regional integration in Africa is now jeopardised because regional leaders are either disinterested or diverted: successive Lomé arrangements provide alternative avenues for pressure and position.

The logic of the semi-periphery has negative implications for successful integration within the periphery except as an extension of ubiquitous EurAfrican connections. Regional powers grow not only because of their relatively large extractive, manufacturing or service sectors but also because they have come to dominate regional relations, diplomatic and strategic as well as economic. In an era of relative superpower withdrawal, they have had their intermediary role recognised and expanded. So they play effectively the role of regional leader — catalyst and core — but their connections with metropolitan countries and corporations make them linkages in the centre-periphery chain. In other words, their interest in regionalism as the semi-periphery — dominance and growth — may be quite different from that of the periphery — development and self-reliance.

The conception of regionalisms within Africa and EurAfrica are quite distinctive and may be dialectical.

This also means that the semi-periphery has an orientation quite different from that of the other major continental organisation — the ECA. Yet, in an era when the Pan-African *political* consensus within the OAU has become elusive — see disputes over Angola, Chad, Sahara, Shaba, Somalia and so on — the apparent Pan-African *economic* consensus within the ECA has become broader and more solid. Given projections of increased inequalities, dependence and underdevelopment, the ECA has called for a collective response outside of the EEC-ACP nexus to head-off an unpromising future.[37] In other words, at a time when the definition and implementation of (political) non-alignment and Pan-Africanism have become diluted advocacy of (economic) self-reliance has become relatively commonplace.

The ECA, in suggesting designs for national and collective self-reliance, is taking the part of the majority of peripheral, Fourth World states rather than advancing the interests of the minority in the semi-periphery (see chapter 2). Instead of being permissive about Africa's inheritance of integration within the world system, especially within EurAfrica, the ECA has called for a reconsideration of unequal exchange, a re-evaluation of international economic relations:

> Their significance lies in the role they play in facilitating or inhibiting (a) the establishment of self-reliance, i.e. the substitution of domestic for foreign factor imports, and (b) the promotion of self-sustainment, i.e. the substitution of internally generated forces determining the speed and direction of economic growth . . .[38]

AFRICAN REGIONALISM IN THE 1980S: FROM EURAFRICA TO PAN-AFRICA? FROM ECOWAS TO SADCC?

The site of the first economic summit — Lagos — is also the headquarters of the latest attempt at comprehensive regional integration — ECOWAS; it was also the centre of ACP strategy in the negotiations for Lomé I. Despite the problems of effective collective self-reliance at the regional level in Africa since independence, optimism persists that this largest-ever grouping can succeed[39] and so become one of the foundations for the proposed continental common market.

This scenario of regionalism paving the way for continentalism serves to resolve the historic debates over the primacy of regionalism or continentalism, functionalism or federalism that have bedeviled previous attempts at development through integration. Yet contradictions remain within Pan-African integration despite increasing disinterest in Europe and growing diversity in Africa.

Paradoxically, ECOWAS was being discussed and designed at the same time as on the other coast the East African Community (EAC) was in a state of disorder and decay. Some ECOWAS institutions were structured with the failure of EAC in mind, but there are limits to which West African political economies can be pushed to avoid a similar tragedy on the west coast. The interests of dominant regional forces — those of indigenous and international capitalisms and of the semi-periphery — cannot be easily disregarded unless regionalism is defined in more radical terms than collective self-reliance. But, given the central role of elements within incumbent ruling classes[40] in espousing regionalist causes, any such redefinition in practice is quite unlikely, unless national and global pressures combine to change the position of such fractions. In short, unless more regimes go beyond the constraints of state capitalism and state socialism towards more genuine forms of socialism, regionalism may still serve established national and transnational class interests rather than advancing the BHN of the poor countries and communities. Despite frequent claims to the contrary, the continuing popularity of Pan-African regionalism may lie in its compatibility with dominant interests. And it is these very interests which are still attracted to EurAfrica, too, recognising that some fractions are more Pan-African and others more EurAfrican in orientation.

Thus, John Renninger is sceptical about the formulation and implementation of the ECOWAS treaty.[41] He concludes that it is unlikely to overcome either dependence or underdevelopment because of diverse economic and political interests within the region clustered around the competing EurAfrican nexus: transnational class linkages and uneven development work against a more fundamental definition or interpretation of regional integration. 'Thus, although ECOWAS can undoubtedly contribute to the achievement of collective self-reliance in West African sub-regions, it will not, by itself, lead to collective self-reliance.'[42] More basic issues of political economy would have to be addressed for such regional plans to be designed and effected. But the post-colonial ruling class has little interest in going beyond reform towards a more radical definition of regionalism, especially the ruling classes within regional centres like the Ivory Coast, Nigeria and Senegal with their EurAfrican connections.

ECOWAS is then essentially an orthodox common market with some developmental content (cf. chapter 6). Its structural intent is quite limited: it seeks free trade in goods and peoples rather than the creation of a more self-reliant regional political economy, the rhetoric of collective self-reliance notwithstanding. Although the diversity of interests and resources — and learning from the demise of EAC — was reflected in the creation of a Fund for Co-operation, Compensation and Development, this Fund is not central to ECOWAS's structure or success. Moreover, its novel 'collective defence' potential, reflective as it is of the centrality of 'security' issues as a prerequisite for sustained regional integration is thereby an adjunct to its central purpose rather than integral to its design; it may also raise questions about the compatibility of ECOWAS with the OAU, given the latter's off-on interest in an African High Command (see chapter 7). However, the basic issue confronting regionalism in Africa is not compatibility with either the EEC or the OAU, although these remain important issues; rather, it is compatibility with established political economies and ruling classes. And, when these are oriented towards extra-continental integration, intra-continental connections remain undeveloped and unimportant.

In a critical vein, James Sackey from a comparative Caribbean perspective has raised some of these major concerns about regionalism: their external support and their regional consequences. On extra-African advocates, he laments that 'the role of class interest and the transnational domination through peripheral organisations, such as the local merchants, in shaping the ultimate destiny of ECOWAS appears not to be recognised by authors in the area'.[43] And on regional class solidarity — as expressed in plans for regional collective security — he warns that regionalism may constrain experimentation in political economy:

> The presence of class interest and political opportunism in the formation of ECOWAS would, as in the case of CARICOM, mean the endorsement of a developmental ideology which favour (sic) capitalism as the only solution to the poverty of the region. This, in turn, would create a favorable atmosphere for the development and consolidation of the class interests of the rapidly rising national bourgeoisies and petty bourgeoisies within the region.[44]

With remarkable foresight — he wrote before the Rawlings and Doe coups and before the anti-Pereira *putsch* in Guinea-Bissau and the abortive uprising in Gambia — Sackey warned progressive forces in West Africa about collective conservatism rather than collective self-reliance:

> This might take several forms, such as military coup in Guinea or support for further state capitalist development in Guinea-Bissau. The ultimate of these developments is the entrenchment of an authoritarian central state, at the service of capitalism.[45]

In which case, regionalism would not only fail to advance either development or disengagement, it would also serve to limit the range of choice of African states: regional political order may be achieved at the cost of regional powers — to maïntain regional stability. The felt need for this 'interventive' role may grow, as semi-periphery and periphery diverge in the future. Moreover, protectionist pressures in the world system may make development ever more elusive, generating more contradictions and antagonisms.

In short, the prospects for regionalism advancing either development or self-reliance in Africa would appear to be less promising for the next 15-year period than in the previous 25 years. Neo-mercantilism in the north may reinforce the regional dominance of the semi-periphery and serve to marginalise the periphery further. In which case Pan-African regionalism may seek to contain increased contradictions rather than advance self-reliance. Yet, even the maintenance of the *status quo* is problematic, given divisive external pressures, especially those within the EurAfrican regionalist nexus. In sum, for different fractions, different forms of regionalism may come to represent control and connections rather than autonomy and development.

The stand-off between the EEC-supported SADCC and the ECA-supported PTA illustrates these differences.[46] SADCC as an instrumental development of the FLS — from rather exclusive diplomatic to a more inclusive economic grouping — is concerned about two forms of dependence: first, on South Africa, and second, on the industrialised states. It is a reaction to the achievements of and constraints on African liberation given the intransigence and interference of the white regime: authoritarianism at home and destabilisation in the region. Despite SADCC's assistance from the EEC and other Western states and its primary goal of transcending South

Africa's dominance through infrastructural projects — it is also determined to increase its collective self-reliance in relation to the advanced capitalist states.[47] By contrast, the PTA as a broader and more orthodox free trade allocation has proposed distinctive rules of origin for intra-African trade. As in the short-lived Andean Pact, local products require local control of companies.[48]

By comparison, ECOWAS lacks the focus on the indigenous capitalism of PTA and on the development projects of SADCC, in part because it lacks the immediate threat, economic and strategic, posed to the region by South Africa. Moreover, somewhat akin to Zimbabwe's role in SADCC and those of Zimbabwe and Kenya in PTA, in ECOWAS the sub-imperial powers are internal — Cote d'Ivoire, Nigeria and Senegal — as South Africa will be after apartheid. But in emphasising the structural bases of regionalism — infrastructure and ownership, respectively — SADCC and PTA go beyond orthodox formulations. To this extent they are suggestive of the degree to which liberation rather than nationalist struggles in the region has made a difference to policies on development and integration. ECOWAS may be in danger of merely rationalising the periphery on behalf of extra-African capital. Both SADCC and PTA in different ways repesent a challenge to South African and Western capitalisms and so constitute a redefinition of African regionalism reflective of innovative responses (1) to world crises and conditions, and (2) to revisionist analyses and insights.

THE FUTURE OF UNITY AND DEVELOPMENT IN AFRICA: BEYOND EURAFRICA

Given (1) changes in the global and regional political economies and (2) ambiguities in the design and direction of regionalisms in Africa, predictive scenarios are rather problematic. However, the distinction in the literature between orthodox and radical investigations and prescriptions can be extended into the mid-term future. This at least provides a framework for evaluating the prospects for and progress of ECOWAS. Nevertheless, such a task remains hazardous, as unforeseen eventualities can arise (for example, dramatic increases in the prices of energy or money) and social relations are not readily predictable (for instance, the expansion, contraction and reaction of the indigenous proletariats and bourgeoisies). Quite clearly, however, linkages amongst the centre, semi-periphery and periphery are not static, while the impact of regionalist schemes on them is likely to be rather marginal. Nevertheless, the outcome of the dialectic between semi-periphery and periphery is of considerable importance to the definition and orientation of regional communities like ECOWAS.

At least five central questions can be raised about the intention and direction of regional integration in Africa before the year 2000, the answers to which will depend on whether a more orthodox or a more radical mode of analysis is applied. In turn, any projections will be informed by the different positions and perceptions of these divergent approaches. All need to be situated in the context of prevailing and pervasive security and economic structures.

First, who are the major advocates of regionalism? They may be located outside the region (for example, multinational corporations and international organisations versus national bourgeois fractions or the labour aristocracy within the proletariat). Which of these social formations is dominant in designing and establishing regional institutions will be reflected in regional priorities and processes. In general, the more national the bourgeois forces and the more proletarian the advocates, the greater the prospects for African self-reliance, even if not necessarily for socialism. Conversely, the more comprador the bourgeois fraction and 'aristocratic' the labour, the greater the prospects for EurAfrican connections.

Second, and related to the first point, does regionalism seek to reform or refine the international division of labour? If on the one hand its concern is with increased self-reliance rather than with increased trade, it would seek to reform or transform the regional and global divisions of labour away from the 'peripheral capitalism' of extraction and towards a greater degree of industrialisation. If, on the other hand, its concern is with increased exchange, as in EurAfrica, it will attempt to refine but not reform its position: producing more and selling higher, but not altering its place in the global hierarchy. Clearly some regionalists (inside and outside Southern and West Africa) would prefer reform — Pan-African regionalism — while others would support just a refinement in the region's place in the international division of labour — EurAfrican regionalism.

Third, depending on which transnational coalition of regionalists prevails and the degree of reform thereby advanced, regional cooperation may be concentrated in different sectors: trade, industry, agriculture, service or labour. Orthodox functionalists tend to concentrate on trade creation and diversion, whereas neo-functionalists emphasise industrialisation, technology and capital-formation. Few regionalists advocate agricultural growth because of assumed lack of complementarity, although in fact regional food production is becoming an imperative. A balanced range of regional sectors may be desirable but that would have to be premised on a balanced set of regional advocates and resources, an unlikely situation. In general, regional schemes lay down a political framework and physical infrastructures of co-operation: who benefits depends on who can best exploit these facilities.

Fourth, the purposes of regionalism can differ from development to dominance. The peripheral participants would tend to favour the former orientation; semi-peripheral and core actors (state and non-state), the latter, despite their relative disinterest in regionalism because of the global reach of their interests. Clearly, the direction of any regional institution depends on which advocates, functions and sectors are dominant. In the ECOWAS case, is regionalism (1) to help the majority of poor states and citizens to develop, and/or (2) to help the minority of middling rich (for example, state and non-state interests in Cote d'Ivoire and Nigeria) to grow, and/or (3) to advance the interests of metropolitan countries and corporations (for instance, those most closely associated with EurAfrica, a collective and contemporary form of 'neo-colonialism' in an essentially post-neocolonial world)? Likewise, is SADCC intended to reduce dependence on South African and/or global capitalisms?

And finally, what results might be expected from these alternative variants of regionalism? An orthodox, semi-peripheral perspective would favour the development of underdevelopment, because its advocates can benefit thereby. However, a more radical peripheral position would prefer the reduction of dependence and the encouragement of development through collective self-reliance. But, because the latter position threatens established metropolitan and semi-peripheral interests, its prospects are circumscribed. On the other hand, if protectionism on a world scale leads to trade wars, then regions as well as states may be forced to look inwards rather than outwards, as noted in the penultimate paragraph below.

In any event, the outcome of the orthodox versus radical competition overlaps with the periphery versus semi-periphery tension as well as with Pan- versus EurAfrican conception; both of these respective modes of analysis and modes of production are preferred by antagonistic national, regional and global social formations, with their respective transnational coalitions. The future of ECOWAS depends essentially on the outcome of these complex confrontations which, in turn, are functions of changes in national political economies within the world system.

Finally, the environment for regionalism in Africa depends not only on regional, continental and global conditions in general but also on the outcome of the struggle in southern African in particular: will uneventful (reformist) or eventful (revolutionary) scenarios materialise there? For, just as political and economic relations among regions have affected the character and potential of ECOWAS (that is, North-South linkages with EEC and South-South linkages with ASEAN, CARICOM, and so forth), so the prospects for regionalism in southern Africa constitute, on the one hand an intriguing model for West Africa and, on the other, a potential resource base.

In the past African continental unity has been facilitated by collective opposition to colonialism and racism in southern Africa. In the future African regional unity may, as suggested above, be encouraged by the model and resources of southern Africa, with implications for the ability to resist EurAfrican pressures. The 'pariah' middle power of that region — South Africa — has made a series of largely unsuccessful attempts since World War II to widen patterns of regional co-operation in the southern part of the continent to enhance its own economic growth and military security. However, the execution of successful wars of liberation in Angola, Mozambique and Zimbabwe has not only increased opposition to South Africa's schemes but has provided the foundation for counter-dominance institutions like SADCC and PTA, despite the former's relentless pressure for bilateral strategic understandings.

If SADCC or PTA regionalism works, it will constitute a challenge not only to South African 'sub-imperialism' but also to more orthodox patterns of regionalism elsewhere on the continent. The appearance of more radical regimes in southern Africa because of the protracted liberation struggle there has already upset the continental dominance of more conservative (often semi-peripheral) states. The further transformation of these state socialist regimes into a viable radical regional political economy would pose another challenge to more benign forms of regionalism as in ECOWAS, as well as to prevailing axes of EurAfricanism.

In which case, by both example and resources, southern Africa might come to affect the orthodox versus radical political and analytical balances in West Africa. In turn, this would serve to reinforce the pressures towards more progressive and self-reliant Pan-African strategies already apparent because of the protectionist mood in the advanced industrialised states: the problematic character of EurAfrica in a disinterested Europe. The international division of labour between centre, semi-periphery and periphery would be further undermined as mercantilism in the North and disengagement in southern Africa came to produce alternative patterns of exchange and accumulation. Langdon and Mytelka have put such change in southern Africa into the context of shifts within global and continental political economies:

> Armed conflict in Southern Africa, though, is likely to be no more than the most dramatic form of confrontation between dependence and self-reliance in the 1980s. We expect the contradictions of periphery capitalism in Africa to become more acute in countries on the continent in the next decade, and we expect the struggles for change in such countries to become more bitter as a result. We are confident, however, that out of such conflict can come more equitable and self-reliant development strategies that benefit the great majority of Africans.[49]

In which case, the future for unity and development at continental and regional levels in Africa may be rather brighter but no more certain than already suggested.

ECOWAS and other Pan-African regionalist designs on the continent can only be explained and projected in the context of such pressures — national, regional, continental and global — in the international division of labour. Hence the continuing dialectic with EurAfrican conceptions, unless protectionism and recession so undermine extroverted fractions among Europe's bourgeoisies that the EEC comes to pull away from the ACP rather than vice versa. In a post-neo-colonial world, ACP advocates of Lomé may yet be abandoned by a combination of (1) introversion and isolation in Europe[50] and (2) Africa's Fourth World, leaving the semi-periphery functionless between a protectionist centre and a self-reliant periphery. In which case, Pan-African conceptions of regionalism would no longer have to compete with residual EurAfrican definitions, and Pan-Africanism could re-establish its primacy over EurAfricanism; a prerequisite for the redefinition of regionalism as self-reliance (see adjacent chapters). In this as in other ways, economic as well as political liberation in Africa could yet start in the South(ern) African revolution. As Sonny Ramphal has argued already 'The SADCC approach has made a contribution to the rethinking on regional integration movements among developing countries by its radical departures from both the common market and the integrated community approaches'.[51]

NOTES

1. An earlier version of this chapter appears as 'Regionalism and the African crisis: towards a political economy of ECOWAS and SADCC' in Julius E. Okollo and Stephen Wright (eds), *West Africa: regional cooperation and development* (Boulder: Westview, 1988).
2. Shridath S. Ramphal, 'Economic Cooperation and Collective Self-Reliance in Africa: retrospect and prospect' in Bernard Chidzero and Altaf Gauhar (eds), *Linking the South: the route to economic cooperation* (London: Third World Foundation, 1986) 3.
3. Adebayo Adedeji, 'Inter-African Economic Cooperation in Light of the Final Act of Lagos' in Adebayo Adedeji and Timothy M. Shaw (eds), *Economic Crisis in Africa: African perspectives on development problems and potentials* (Boulder: Lynne Rienner, 1985) 77.
4. See David Fashole Luke and Timothy M. Shaw (eds), *Continental Crisis: the Lagos Plan of Action and Africa's future* (Washington: University Press of America, 1984).
5. S. K. B. Asante, 'Development and Regional Integration since 1980' in Adedeji and Shaw (eds), *Economic Crisis in Africa*, 82. See also David Fashole Luke, 'Regionalism in Africa: a short study of the record', *International Journal* 41(4) (Autumn 1986) 853–68.
6. See Timothy M. Shaw, *Towards a Political Economy for Africa: the dialectics of dependence*, (London: Macmillan, 1985); Richard Sandbrook, *The Politics of Africa's Economic Stagnation* (Cambridge: Cambridge University Press, 1985); and Eboe Hutchful, 'The Crisis of the New International Division of Labour, Authoritarianism and the Transition to Free-Market Economics in Africa', *International Sociological Association* (New Delhi, August 1986).
7. For invaluable insights into debt in Africa see Alwyn B. Taylor, 'The changing international financial environment and Africa's external indebtedness'; and Philip Ndegwa, 'The deteriorating debt problem in Africa' in Chidzero and Gauhar (eds), *Linking the South*, 39–104.
8. Adedeji, 'Inter-African Economic Cooperation in Light of the Final Act of Lagos', 66.
9. Ibid., 74–5.
10. See John Ravenhill (ed.), *Africa in Economic Crisis* (London: Macmillan, 1986), Robert J. Berg and Jennifer Seymour Whitacker (eds), *Strategies for African Development* (Los Angeles: University of California Press, 1986); and Gerald K. Helleiner, 'Economic Crisis in Sub-Saharan Africa: the international dimension', *International Journal* 41(4) (Autumn 1986) 748–67.

11. See Timothy M. Shaw, 'Towards a Political Economy of the African Crisis: diplomacy, debates and dialectics', in Michael H. Glantz (ed.), *Drought and Hunger in Africa: denying famine a future* (Cambridge: University Press, 1986) 127–47.
12. See Leon Gordenker, 'The OAU and the UN: can they live together?' in Ali A. Mazrui and Hasu H. Patel (eds), *Africa in World Affairs: the next thirty years* (New York: Third Press, 1973) 105–19.
13. See Timothy M. Shaw (ed.), *Alternative Futures for Africa* (Boulder: Westview, 1982) and, with Olajide Aluko (eds), *Africa Projected: from recession to renaissance by the year 2000?* (London: Macmillan, 1985).
14. For an overview of these in relation to the work of Leon Gordenker see Timothy M. Shaw, 'The UN Economic Commission for Africa: continental development and self-reliance' in David Forsythe (ed.), *The United Nations in the World Political Economy* (London: Macmillan, 1988).
15. See Timothy M. Shaw, 'Inequalities and Interdependence in Africa and Latin America: sub-imperialism and semi-industrialism in the semi-periphery', *Cultures et Développement* 10(2) (1978) 231–63.
16. I. William Zartman, 'Africa as a Subordinate State System in International Relations', *International Organization* 2(3) (Summer 1967) 571.
17. Ibid., 574.
18. See, for instance, Timothy M. Shaw, 'Kenya and South Africa: sub-imperialist states', *Orbis* 21(2) (Summer 1977) 375–94; and 'International Stratification in Africa: sub-imperialism in eastern and southern Africa'. *Journal of Southern African Affairs* 2(2) (April 1977) 145–65.
19. See Immanuel Wallerstein, 'Dependence in an Interdependent World: the limited possibilities of transformation within the capitalist world economy', *African Studies Review* 17(1) (April 1974) 1–26.
20. Steven Langdon and Lynn K. Mytelka, 'Africa in the Changing World Economy', in Colin Legum *et al.*, *Africa in the 1960's: a continent in crisis* (New York: McGraw-Hill, 1979, Council on Foreign Relations 1980s Project) 204.
21. See ECA, OAU and UNIDO, *A Program for the Industrial Development Decade for Africa* (New York, 1982); and George M. Kimani 'Industry in Africa: continental cooperation and the industrial development decade'; and D. Babatunde Thomas, 'Technology and Industrial Development in Africa' in Adedeji and Shaw (eds), *Economic Crisis in Africa*, 219–65.
22. See Craig Murphy, *The Emergence of the NIEO Ideology* (Boulder: Westview, 1984).
23. See Timothy M. Shaw and Olajide Aluko (eds), (*The Political Economy of African Foreign Policy: comparative analysis* (New York: St. Martins, 1984), especially 1–24.
24. Zartman, 'Africa as a Subordinate State System in International Relations', 581.
25. For a review of these see Timothy M. Shaw, 'Peripheral Social Formations in the New International Division of Labour: African states in the mid-1980s', *Journal of Modern African Studies* 24(3) (September 1986) 489–508; and Bahgat Korany, 'The take-off of Third World Studies:

the case of foreign policy', *World Politics* 35(3) (April 1983) 465–87.

26. See Donald Rothchild and Robert L. Curry, *Scarcity, Choice and Public Policy in Middle Africa* (Berkeley: University of California Press, 1978) 48–91 and 301–35.
27. See Micah S. Tsomondo, 'From Pan-Africanism to Socialism: the modernization of an African liberation ideology', *Issue* 5(4) (Winter 1975) 39–46; and Teti A. Kofi 'Principles of a Pan-Africa Economic Ideology', *Review of Black Political Economy* 6(3) (Spring 1976) 306–30.
28. See Ravenhill (ed.), *Africa in Economic Crisis*.
29. James Mayall, 'The OAU and the African Crisis', *Optima* 27(2) (1977) 86.
30. See I. William Zartman and Yassin El-Ayouty (eds), *The OAU after Twenty Years* (New York: Praeger, 1983).
31. See Elenga M'buyinga, *Pan-Africanism or Neo-Colonialism: the bankruptcy of the OAU* (London: Zed, 1982).
32. Zartman, 'Africa as a Subordinate State System in International Relations', 390.
33. See Jerker Carlsson and Timothy M. Shaw (eds), *Newly Industrializing Countries and the Political Economy of South-South Relations* (London: Macmillan, 1987).
34. See Timothy M. Shaw, 'Debates about Africa's future: the Brandt, World Bank and Lagos Plan blueprints', *Third World Quarterly* 5(2) (April 1983) 330–44.
35. See Robert Boardman, Panayotis Soldatos and Timothy M. Shaw (eds), *The EEC, Africa and Lomé III*, Dalhousie African Studies Series Number 3 (Washington: University Press of America, 1984).
36. See Julius Nyang'oro and Timothy M. Shaw (eds), *Corporatism in Africa: comparative analysis and practise* (Boulder: Westview, 1989).
37. See *ECA and the Development of Africa 1983–2008: preliminary perspective study* (Addis Ababa, April 1983); and OAU *Africa's Priority Programme for Economic Recovery 1986–1990* (Addis Ababa, July 1985); see also Shaw 'The UN Economic Commission for Africa'.
38. *Biennial Report of the Executive Secretary of the United Nations Economic Commission for Africa 1977–1978* (Addis Ababa, February 1979, E/CN.14/695) 12.
39. See S.K.B. Asante, *The Political Economy of Regionalism in Africa: a decade of ECOWAS* (New York: Praeger, 1986), 'ECOWAS/CEAO: conflict and cooperation in West Africa' in Onwuka and Sesay (eds), *The Future of Regionalism in Africa* 74–95, and 'ECOWAS, the EEC and the Lomé Convention' in Domenico Mazzeo (ed.), *African Regional Organizations* (Cambridge: Cambridge University Press, 1984) 171–95.
40. See Olatunde J. B. Ojo, 'Nigeria and the Formation of ECOWAS', *International Organization* 34(4) (Autumn 1980) 571–604.
41. John P. Renninger, 'The Future of Economic Cooperation Schemes in Africa, with Special Reference to ECOWAS' in Shaw (ed.), *Alternative Futures for Africa*, 162–73.
42. Ibid., 170. See also John P. Renninger, *Multinational Cooperation for*

Development in West Africa (Elmsford, New York: Pergamon, 1979).
43. James A. Sackey, 'The Structure and Performance of CARICOM: lessons for the development of ECOWAS', *Canadian Journal of African Studies* 12(2) (1978) 272.
44. Ibid., 273.
45. Idem.
46. See Peter Meyns, 'SADCC and regional cooperation in Southern Africa' in Mazzeo (ed.), *African Regional Organizations* 198–224; Douglas G. Anglin, 'Economic Liberation and Regional Cooperation in Southern Africa: SADCC and PTA', *International Organization* 37(4) (Autumn 1983) 681–711; and essays by L. Adele Jinadu, Thandika Mkandawire, Yash Tandon and Ibbo Mandaza in Timothy M. Shaw and Yash Tandon (eds), *Regional Development at the International Level, Volume 2, African and Canadian Perspectives* (Washington: UPA, 1985) 41–53, 93–144.
47. See Joseph Hanlon, *Beggar Your Neighbours: apartheid power in southern Africa* (London: James Currey, 1986), especially 17–90; Reginald H. Green and Carol B. Thompson, 'Political Economies in Conflict: SADCC, South Africa and sanctions'; Robert Davies, 'Review article: the military and foreign policy in South Africa', *Journal of Southern African Studies* 12(2) (April 1986) 308–15; and Phyllis Johnson and David Martin (eds), *Destructive Engagement: Southern Africa at war* (Harare: Zimbabwe Publishing House, 1986) 145–280.
48. See Adebayo Adedeji, 'Inter-African Economic Cooperation in the Light of the Final Act of Lagos'; and S.K.B. Asante, 'Development and Regional Integration since 1980' in Adedeji and Shaw (eds), *Economic Crisis in Africa*, 59–99.
49. Langdon and Mytelka, 'Africa in the Changing World Economy', 104.
50. See Boardman, Soldatos and Shaw (eds), *The EEC, Africa and Lomé III*.
51. Ramphal, 'Economic Co-operation and Collective Self-Reliance in Africa', 11–12.

6 ECOWAS: Towards Autonomy or Neo-Colonialism?

S.K.B. Asante

Today, countries often group together in an effort to expand their economic space. The phenomenon is occurring among rich and poor countries alike, in both socialist and capitalist systems. This world-wide trend has not arisen capriciously. It is in response to economic and political realities. The challenge is especially urgent for countries in the developing world with small populations and limited internal markets. Their situation is aggravated by their historical and involuntary integration into an international capitalist system of market relations within which they occupy a subordinate position. This structurally induced inequality continues to be reflected in the adverse and degenerating terms of trade between themselves as primary producers and their industrialised trading partners.

It was in response to this trend to the challenges and opportunities of the last 25 years of this century that 15 heads of state and government of West African countries signed the treaty establishing the Economic Community of West African States (ECOWAS for English-speaking and CEDEAO for French-speaking) on 28 May 1975 in Lagos; Cape Verde has since joined as the community's 16th member. This event represented the culmination of many years of effort by these states to increase the economic mass, and therefore the bargaining base, of their economies through a pooling of economic sovereignty; to transform their economies so as to improve the living standards of their peoples and to extend the struggle for political decolonisation into one for economic decolonisation. The creation of ECOWAS was also a response to the recognition by the West African countries that the fragmentation of the subregion — the product of colonial balkanisation into narrow domestic markets — renders a shift in the pattern of production, designed to reduce dependence, both difficult and costly. History in the last century and a half indicates that only very large national units have a sufficient resource base, climatic diversity and population size to realise what

E. Oteiza and F. Sercovich have termed 'an autarchic self-reliant model'.[1]

In brief, therefore, the inauguration of ECOWAS must be seen as an attempt by the West African states to enhance their economic opportunity and to reduce external dependency; thereby they hope to overcome the existing structures of neo-colonialism and underdevelopment. The lessening of the high degree of external dependence is a precondition for achieving basic structural development goals. Viewed within the context of the New International Economic Order (NIEO), ECOWAS must also be regarded as an integral part of a wider desire of the poor nations of the subregion to eliminate, or at least to reduce, the inequalities inherent in the present international economic system. However, these effects cannot be attained automatically. Without a well-conceived and intensive effort and without adequate planning, ECOWAS could lead to the perpetuation of neo-colonialism, underdevelopment and inequality: to increased rather than decreased external dependence (see previous chapter). For, as Osvaldo Sunkel rightly remarked in the case of Latin America, 'integration, in fact, can be either a basic instrument of national realisation in Latin America; or it can be the instrument of accelerated dependence (*sucursalizacion*) of the region'.[2]

It is in light of this that I attempt in this chapter a critical evaluation of the extent to which ECOWAS as an institution is sufficiently equipped in terms of resources and power to disengage, even if partially, the peripheral West African countries (1) from inherited dependency on the former metropolitan powers and by extension (2) from existing patterns of asymmetrical economic and political relationships prevailing in the international system. The objective of dependency reduction would necessitate, firstly, the alteration of traditional trade and investment relationships with a view to making it possible for the West African countries to secure fuller control of their economic and political destinies. It would necessitate, secondly, among other things, a deliberate restructuring of the present mode of production and adoption of regional policies to regulate external linkages in the interest of domestic development.

The chapter is divided into six sections. In the first I examine key concepts and set out a hypothesis and approach to the subject. The second seeks to analyse the nature of economic neo-colonialism and dependency in West Africa, highlighting the major crucial issues and constraints. In the third and fourth sections the relevant ECOWAS treaty provisions are critically assessed in relation to the problems posed in the second section. The fifth section focuses attention on the political economy of regulation, the sixth on resistance to regionalism, while the final section attempts an overview and conclusion.

KEY CONCEPTS

In recent years the concepts 'autonomy', 'self-reliance' and/or 'collective self-reliance' have been used rather interchangeably in relation to the developmental strategies and objectives of the developing countries. These concepts tend to denote or emphasise the developmental goals of political and development planners of these countries. They also sometimes tend to take the form of an exhortation for political and motivational force.

Thomas Biersteker has recently observed that self-reliance as a 'logical prescription of Latin American dependency writers' who identify 'specific policies designed to eliminate dependence and exploitation'.[3] Therefore, self-reliance has become an essential component of 'alternative' strategies for the elimination of dependence and exploitation which are responsible for the distortion of development throughout much of the Third World.

The restructuring of basic international relationships of developing countries away from their traditional ties to industrial countries is generally described as 'collective self-reliance'. Collective self-reliance calls upon developing countries to intensify co-operation among themselves in order to exploit existing complementarities. The result should be accelerated, autonomous development and lessened dependence on the industrialised world.

While national and/or collective self-reliance may be regarded as a process or deliberate strategy for obtaining a set of objectives, 'autonomy' tends to reflect an 'end state'; that is, the creation of a highly integrated economy and society capable of substantialy providing for the basic needs of the masses of the people. As used in this chapter, therefore, 'autonomy' reflects the capability of ECOWAS to break the inherited links of dependency with the former metropolitan powers and the international economic system for the benefit of expanding horizontal links within the West African subregion to achieve a higher degree of integration in the subregional market. ECOWAS is therefore expected eventually to be self-managing or free from outside control. 'Autonomy' is indeed one possible consequence. It is freedom from control by others; hence, it rests on the idea of self-control.

My other concept — 'neo-colonialism' — came into general use in Africa in the early 1960s to describe the 'humiliating limitations of formal independence'. As Richard Vengroff recently put it, 'At the core of the question of neo-colonialism is the concept of dependence'.[4] Thus, while, as noted above, the concept of self-reliance reflects an opposition to all forms of dependency, neo-colonialism — which is the 'greatest threat' to African countries today — is an integral part of the dependency system. As used in this chapter, neo-colonialism is the process by which colonial patterns of dependency are sustained after the granting of formal political independence. Neo-colonialism thus describes a threat by the former colonial powers to establish 'backdoor colonialism'. Hence, it reflects the frustrated aspirations of most Africans for a significantly better life after achieving formal political independence.

A significant aspect of the neo-colonialism nexus — one which seems to possess the potential for sustaining the phenomenon for many years to come — is the role played by indigenous classes. Colin Leys sees this as absolutely central to the concept of neo-colonialism; it is 'the formation of classes, or strata, within a colony, which are closely allied to and dependent on foreign capital, and which form the real basis of support for the regime which succeeds the colonial administration'.[5] The neo-colonial relationship is thus the product of the transfer of formal political power to a class created by, and dependent upon, Western capitalism. To sum up, then, at minimum the neo-colonial approach postulates a relationship between an economy penetrated by international capital and a society and polity marked by the emergence of a pliable indigenous 'bourgeoisie'.

Since my subject-matter is West Africa, it seems essential to explain further and to identify briefly two very distinct strategies for maintaining neo-colonial relationships in this subregion. First, there is the older, more 'parochial' form of neo-colonialism. In this form influence is directed through the metropolitan government and a limited number of metropolitan-based corporations. The metropolitan military, which maintains direct relations with the ex-colonies' military establishments, provides the necessary protection of interests. The distinction between this type of neo-colonialism and the traditional forms of colonialism is quite small. As is made evident in the subsequent section, France practises this type of neo-colonialism in its relations with its former West African colonies.

There is, secondly, the more modern form of neo-colonialism in which direct metropolitan control is limited. Pierre Jalée explains that in this stage of neo-colonialism, 'imperialist exploitation tends to become depersonalised and multilateral; it is less often operated through the medium of national capitalist groups and more often through the operation of international, cosmopolitan monopolies'.[6] The metropole exerts its economic influence through large multinational corporations and their subsidiaries. In this case the 'internationalisation' of neo-colonial ties allows for the continued extraction of resources for the benefit of the developed capitalist nations, without the need for the costly use of overt national power. This latter type of neo-colonialism is what Britain employs in its ex-colonies in Africa.

The two operative concepts of this chapter — 'autonomy' and 'neo-colonialism' — are very much connected with, and can hardly be understood outside of, the dependency framework for interpreting the underdevelopment phenomenon. As a particular explanation of underdevelopment, 'dependency' theory is a relatively recent phenomenon. It seeks to explain the most pressing problems of the less developed world in terms of the relations between the developing and developed areas. Briefly, dependency is conceived as a particular structure of peripheral formation and relation in the world system through which former colonies and other underdeveloped countries are exploited economically, and their backwardness is maintained over time. It thus involves a situation where effective control over the economy of a country is external. Ownership and control of the productive elements of the 'national' economy are by transnational corporations (MNCs), which do not act in the primary interests of the local country or region.

This process has shaped the political economies of the peripheral countries in such a way as to subject their development to the needs of the capitalist countries at the centre. The result of such dependence for any country is continued uneven development, stagnation, unemployment, income inequality, regional disequilibria and low integration among economic sectors. This marginalisation and exploitation are effected through an apparatus of domination which, in dependent countries, takes the form of an alliance between internally privileged groups and external interests and forces all of which benefit from the *status quo*.

We can understand both the elusiveness of development and the complexity of neo-colonial structures in Africa through a dependency approach. It brings into focus the inter-relationship of external and internal factors which enables us to enrich our understanding of the extent to which the dynamics of the international politico-economic system affect the continued underdevelopment of the continent.

Given the pervasiveness of neo-colonial structures in Africa and the nature of external and internal linkages between the élites of the continent and their international and domestic constituencies, it is not surprising that most writing is pessimistic about the future of integration schemes which are designed to advance disengagement from the global economy. Timothy Shaw and Malcolm Grieve, for example, have recently observed that regional integration in Africa is 'unlikely to produce either self-reliance or integrated economies when some of its major advocates are foreign actors or collaborationist groups'. Further, these groups are likely to resist any radical change that may lead to a restructuring of 'their political economies and external linkages away from inherited, external orientation'.[7] Similarly, Abdul Jalloh concludes that regional organisations in Africa acquiesce, if not actually assist, in the 'perpetuation of neo-colonialism, serve the interests of those who benefit from neo-colonialism, and promote the values associated with neo-colonialism'.[8] Any attempt to promote autonomous development of 'integrated economies' may provoke a simultaneous confrontation of international and internal linkages of exploitation. Hence, for Shaw at least, regionalism in Africa 'remains largely an aspiration . . . and is often no more than a declaration of intent and an indication of continental alignment'.[9]

Ironically, however, despite this disillusioning record, the fervour with which regional cooperation has been proposed as a response to the problems of Africa has increased tremendously in recent years.[10] It has been given a new lease on life with the adoption of the *Lagos Plan of Action* (LPA) by African leaders in April 1980. Regionalism, which is discussed in virtually every chapter of the Plan, constitutes an integral condition of its implementation. This trend was reinforced at the November 1984 Organisation of African Unity (OAU) Addis Ababa summit where the African leaders reaffirmed, in an important resolution, their solemn commitment to a collective effort to implement the *Lagos Plan* through the process of regional economic co-operation and integration.[11]

Despite the renewed emphasis on regionalism, I remain sceptical about the capability of ECOWAS in helping to fundamentally restructure both national and regional political economies as the prerequisite for integration and development in the West African subregion. Put in another way: has ECOWAS the capability to help to alter the mode of production in most established West African socio-economic arrangements? Can it help break the age-old dependence of the West African countries on the former metropolitan powers as the crucial first step towards making their economies self-sustaining? And to what extent can ECOWAS initiate efforts towards intra-regional trade or horizontal exchange in order to overcome an inheritance of vertical integration with former metropoles, leading towards greater self-reliance at both national and collective levels?

My basic working hypothesis, therefore, is that though ECOWAS might not be an ideal instrument for the achievement of collective self-reliance and self-sustaining growth in the West African subregion, it does, nevertheless, represent a viable vehicle to set in motion a process that may result in the achievement of *some* measure of autonomy. The fulfillment of this goal would, however, require some more fundamental economic changes which should result in the transformation of existing productive structures. Only in this way can autonomous, self-sustaining growth become a reality.

WEST AFRICA: PORTRAIT OF A NEO-COLONIAL ECONOMY[12]

The economies of the West African countries since independence have exhibited a variety of structural characteristics which reflect and reinforce the subregion's dependency on the capitalist world system. As these economies have been structured to meet the needs of that system, their performance since the early 1960s must be evaluated within this context. Salient aspects of the structural characteristics of the economies are reviewed in this section, though the discussion is by no means exhaustive.

A significant aspect of this structural dependence is that all the West African countries do not only belong to one or other of the various currency and trading groups; they also exhibit the continuity of the presence of the metropole in most sectors. Thus, though 'Independence in Africa meant a change of the *dramatis personae* in the state, it did not involve the general re-establishment of national control over the economy or society . . . The new ruling classes, especially in the more dependent countries, were able to rule only through collaboration with external interests'.[13] This trend has effectively conditioned the development of the West African countries and consequently delayed the emergence in many of any signs of enhanced developmental capacity for autonomous decision-making. Since the ex-colonial powers in West Africa employ different methods to maintain neo-colonial control, it is useful to group the ECOWAS countries according to the metropolitan power with which they are linked. France and Britain, being the dominant ex-colonial powers in West Africa, the analysis will concentrate mostly on them and on their former colonies.

One of the ECOWAS groups — and perhaps the one whose dependence on the former metropole is most pervasive — is composed of the former French colonies whose monetary systems, with the exception of that of Guinea, are very closely linked to the French franc. Their membership of the franc zone[14] is central to the whole issue of France's relations with its ex-colonies. It is this link which has so far given Paris almost total economic, financial and, ultimately, political control. The surrender by these states to monetary control from France in effect deprives them of the right to exercise an essential component of their sovereignty. Not only has this placed serious constraints on their monetary independence — by favouring French and other foreign capital; it has also created the conditions for (1) establishing and furthering privileged (albeit centre-dominated) trading ties; (2) reinforcing the relative power of the French enterprises already in existence; and (3) ensuring continued dependence on export commodities bound for the international market.[15]

One noticeable result of this control from Paris is that movements in the exchange rate of the French franc — as occurred in late 1969 and early 1974 — or any French devaluation — which is decided exclusively by Paris — automatically affect the trading balance and the balance of payments of these African countries by increasing their already considerable external debts. On the other hand, these states can neither revalue nor devalue their currencies independently. Furthermore, as a consequence of the existence of a fixed parity with the CFA franc, the franc zone has created an avenue for the free transfer of capital. There is no control over the repatriation of capital abroad and this is a basic impediment to any accumulation of capital domestically. It has enhanced the position of foreign capital in the banking system and has naturally left an open path for French capital into the country.[16] Given the structure of foreign capital present in all the embryonic industrial sectors of francophone Africa, this free transfer has encouraged the investment of MNCs based in France through local subsidiaries; this has exacerbated the outflow of capital.

Besides, the structure of these countries is characterised by the paucity of indigenous control over key sectors of the economy. Countries like Senegal and the Ivory Coast have a very high proportion of foreign firms and technical assistants. In the case of the former, a critical Senegalese has observed that industrialisation remains largely in foreign hands, which has meant retaining overseas linkages rather than generating domestic ones.[17] Similarly, the much-heralded boom, which the Ivory Coast has enjoyed since the 1950s, has been superficially propelled for the benefit of the expatriate population which dominates the entire economy. Moreover, both development efforts and investment decisions are largely determined by the interests of metropolitan investors as well as those of the Westernised élites — the so-called 'comprador class' or 'auxiliary bourgeoisie', who control the political machinery and collaborate with the foreign capitalists to deplete the resources of the territory.[18] As Samir Amin has argued in a revealing study, the type of growth that the Ivory Coast has experienced over the years 'does not automatically result in an economic "take-off", but in an increased external dependency and the blocking of growth'. He has characterised the Ivory Coast example as 'growth without development'.[19] In other words, there has been negligible 'spillover' from growth to development.

The second ECOWAS group of countries comprises the four anglophone states of the Gambia, Sierra Leone, Ghana and Nigeria which were members of the sterling block, and still share membership in the Commonwealth. On the eve of independence each of these countries acquired independent currencies issued by their respective central banks. Although the strength of the economy of each depends on levels of foreign exchange reserves and balance of payments, each country still maintains a sterling link.

Unlike France, Britain is more thoroughly integrated into the growing world imperialist system. The British have not chosen the technique of continued direct involvement in their former colonies; instead they have allowed for a concentration of effort by MNCs. Resources are extracted and employed for the benefit of Britain in particular and international capitalism in general without the more overt use of direct national power over the internal affairs of dependencies. Consequently the former colonies of Britain give the appearance of having greater control over their own destinies than do those of France. This illusion is quickly dispelled, however, by the realisation that the economic dependence of both groups on externally-based capitalism is roughly equivalent. For example, while French monopolies control 95.7 per cent of Niger's economy, 87.4 per cent of Senegal's and 80 per cent of the Ivory Coast's according to 1974 UN sources on transnational corporations, British monopolies control 87 per cent of the Gambia's economy and 84.4 per cent of Sierra Leone's. In Nigeria, foreign monopolies continue to control 65 per cent of all industrial investment and a similar percentage holds true for Ghana as well.[20]

Of considerable significance is the trade pattern of the ECOWAS subregion.[21] For if trade dependence is a characteristic feature of developing countries as a group, such dependence is chronic in the ECOWAS countries. As Table 5.1 shows, trade of the subregion with developed countries for the period 1968–74, for example, averaged about 87.0 per cent of total trade while intra-subregional exchange for the same period was on the average about 3.4 per cent only. The channels of the ECOWAS countries are thus geared towards enhancing trade with former colonial powers in particular and with the industrial countries in general. The direction of trade between them follows the lines and patterns of dependence. As Kwame Nkrumah painfully remarked, 'Our trade . . . is not between ourselves. It is turned towards Europe and embraces us as providers of low-priced primary materials in exchange for the more expensive finished goods we import'.[22]

On the whole, therefore, it can be said with justification that the destiny of the ECOWAS countries is still in large measure shaped (1) outside the subregion and (2) within the subregion by foreign forces. Even the much-heralded Lomé Convention of February 1975 between the European Economic Community (EEC) and the African, Caribbean and Pacific (ACP) countries has not, in the last resort, created a qualitatively new relationship between industrial Europe and the developing ECOWAS countries. Lomé has reinforced the one-sided dependence and vulnerability that had existed between the (ECOWAS) ACP states and Europe. It is thus a means to 'preserve certain elements of the old international division of labour'.[23]

The central problem for the subregion, therefore, has always been how can the ECOWAS countries break free from the historical

TABLE 5.1 *Share of Intra-West African Trade* in Total External Trade, 1968–74*

Description of Trade	*Amount in US $ million*							*Average for the period (%)*
	1968	*1969*	*1970*	*1971*	*1972*	*1973*	*1974*	
(1) Total trade with all countries of the world	3 846.6	4 546.6	5 683.4	6 684.5	7 503.5	10 548.5	21 435.3	
(2) Intra-regional trade (ECOWAS)	144.8	133.9	162.3	236.4	241.9	248.3	795.3	
(3) (2) as percentage of (1)	3.8	2.9	2.9	3.5	3.2	4.1	3.7	3.4
(4) Exports to all countries of the world	2 017.6	2 392.2	2 954.3	3 397.2	4 126.4	6 094.5	13 902.3	
(5) Exports to countries in the subregion (ECOWAS)	75.1	66.1	86.2	140.4	127.1	231.1	411.3	
(6) (5) as percentage of (4)	3.7	2.8	2.9	4.1	3.1	3.8	3.0	3.3
(7) Imports from all countries of the world	1 829.1	2 154.5	2 728.5	3 287.3	3 377.1	4 454.0	7 533.0	
(8) Imports from countries within the subregion (ECOWAS)	69.7	67.8	76.1	96.0	114.8	197.1	384.0	
(9) (8) as percentage of (7)	3.8	3.1	2.8	2.9	3.4	4.4	5.1	3.6

* Excludes Guinea-Bissau.

SOURCES: IMF, IBRD, Direction of Trade 1968–72, 1969–73 and 1970–74.

conditions in which they find themselves. For since all social systems seek to ensure their continued existence, it follows that dominant countries will try to retain the bases of their dominance over others and thus see to it that dependent countries do not follow their 'dream of independence'. This, then, is the crux of the matter. By the early 1970s, when dislocations in the international economy revealed the extreme vulnerability of almost all the countries in the sub-region, the West African governments were faced with a choice between continuing to support the inherited structure of dependence or beginning to build an integrated economy. By creating ECOWAS in May 1975, the West African countries appeared to have opted for the latter strategy. But whether ECOWAS as an institution can really transform the West African economies from a dependent structure responsive to the external demands of the world market into an integrated economy responsive to domestic needs and resources is the subject of the next section.

ECOWAS AND THE NEO-COLONIAL MESH

As noted above, although the countries of the West African subregion have been 'independent' for at least two decades now, the basic structure of their economies and the welfare of the majority of their people have remained almost unchanged. None of the countries is, as yet, within striking distance of self-sustaining growth and economic independence. Yet the creation and maintenance of meaningful political independence requires the attainment of national political economies. A state whose economy is characterised by concentrated external dependence can hope to have neither a significant degree of control over the rate of growth and nature of allocation of domestic resources nor a high level of external credibility from which to bargain. The establishment of ECOWAS with seven principal objectives[24] is a reflection of the determination of West African governments to change this situation. To attain these objectives the member-states are 'convinced' that the promotion of harmonious economic development of their states calls for effective economic co-operation largely through a determined and concerted policy of self-reliance.[25]

The declared objectives of ECOWAS are lofty enough but it will be necessary to see to what extent the treaty as well as the protocols adequately provide for their attainment. More significantly, much of the success of ECOWAS in implementing its declared objectives would depend upon the extent to which it tackles the complex problems posed by external actors in the integration process. For, as Joseph Nye has observed, although the original neo-functional formulation of regional integration paid insufficient attention to the role of external actors in the integration process,[26] it is now widely recognised that regional change processes are not autonomous or self-generated; rather they are responsive to a context of global interdependence and interaction. An integration process can involve various actors, including outside governments, international lending institutions, private foreign investors and non-governmental actors. Thus, no matter what their original intentions, it is difficult to isolate regional deliberations from their context of global economic and political dependence.

The actions of external actors, or, what Philippe Schmitter has termed 'external penetration', can have a profound effect on the direction of an integrative undertaking. For example, in both the Central American and the European common markets foreign investment has played a key role, even though in neither instance was that the original plan.[27] In the specific case of Africa, the analyses by Steven Langdon and Lynn Mytelka of UDEAC[28] and by Peter Robson of CEAO[29] provide excellent case studies of the way in which MNCs and other external interests derive benefits from African regional integration to the disadvantage of partner states.[30] Instances are not rare of offers of financial support to national projects from transnational enterprises which directly cut across agreed regional integration projects. This is what happened after the Kampala Agreement of April 1964 when a multinational enterprise offered to establish a tyre factory in Kenya after this industry had previously been allocated to Tanzania.[31]

Given this background, it is easy to envisage the kind of problems likely to confront ECOWAS in the area of external penetration. There is, for example, the problem of initiating measures effective enough to combat attempts by extra-regional powers to take advantage of the newly created regional opportunities and thus derive more benefit from integration than would the intraregional participants. Or, put specifically, there is the problem of extricating the member-states of ECOWAS from the existing dependency relationships with the metropolitan powers and of using national and regional institutions to bring about greater local control over resources. For the term integration implies the replacement of the existing ties with the metropolitan centres by a new pattern of economic and politcal interaction within the region.

Given the complexity of this problem, the question that arises, then, is: how adequate are the provisions made in the ECOWAS treaty? What institutions under the treaty have been specifically charged with what Schmitter has termed 'policy externalisation'?[32] To what extent can MNCs be prevented from getting the lion's share of the benefits accruing to ECOWAS integration processes while at best making rather limited contributions to the development of the West African countries and at worst preventing development?

ECOWAS AND THE ISSUE OF 'POLICY EXTERNALISATION'

To fulfil their integration process, ECOWAS countries would need considerable foreign capital. The main attraction of an MNC's direct investment is supposed to be its transfer of finance capital and provision of access to technology, foreign markets, and managerial and technical skills. Given the low organisational and technical level of the ECOWAS countries, these may indeed be indispensable elements in their development process. For, since emphasis is placed on 'production deepening', involving many completely new activities, the existing technological infrastructure of many member-states of the Community is quite inadequate to meet the requirements of integration. Hence, sizeable injections of foreign capital — especially direct investment — which brings with it technology and management, will be needed to put the large pools of unemployed labour and natural resources in the subregion to work.

Thus the fundamental dilemma facing the West African countries in their integration process concerns the reconciliation of their acknowledged need for foreign capital and technology and the evolution (or survival) of their own autonomous entrepreneurial class as well as the process of local private capital accumulation. The debate, therefore, is not on whether foreign firms will participate in the ECOWAS integration process or not, but rather on how, under what conditions, and in what mix: foreign direct investments in wholly-owned subsidiaries, joint ventures, licensing agreements or management contracts?

The ECOWAS protocol on the rules of origin anticipated the problems posed by external linkages and accepts that the promotion of trade in goods originating in member-states as well as the collective economic development of the Community requires indigenous ownership and participation.[33] Conditions which goods must satisfy to qualify as 'goods originating in the Community' are specified. While these ensure a reasonable measure of participation of local factor endowments it is clear that a lot of room is left for foreign participation and for the utilisation of foreign resources and capital.[34] Two provisions, however, allow for the alteration of the basis of determining ownership and participation as well as any conditions for determining origin. The Trade Commission is empowered by article 11 (2) to make proposals, on the basis of appropriate statistics, to the Council of Ministers to review periodically any conditions of acceptance of goods originating in member-states for Community trade. Article 11 (2), together with the provisions of article 11 (3), could be used to ensure that a foreign firm does not set up in a member-state simply to exploit the enlarged market and thus encourage greater involvement by Community members in their own process of economic development.

At the summit meeting at Lomé in May 1980, the Community took advantage of these two provisions (article 11, para. 2 and 3) and made some amendments to the protocol on the rules of origin. Furthermore, the Authority at its May 1983 meeting fixed the desirable level of national participation in the equity capital of industrial enterprises whose products should benefit from the preferential duty arrangements resulting from the trade liberalisation programme.

Although the objective is to ensure that governments or nationals of Community origin hold a reasonable percentage of equity capital, the amended provision does not effectively tackle the problem of foreign ownership and participation. For a long time to come most industrial enterprises in the subregion will continue to have foreign majority ownership. Even the 51 per cent of indigenous ownership and participation, which will take effect throughout ECOWAS countries as from 28 May 1989, merely gives a false sense of satisfaction because in practice, the management will probably still lie in the hands of the transnational enterprises who can continue to manipulate economic decisions in their own favour.

Briefly, ownership and participation by themselves do not necessarily ensure local control, especially when it is seen that great reliance is to be placed on foreign technology and know-how. Although it is intended that this reliance on external resources should be minimised by pooling their subregional resources, the tendency of the Community technocrats to look outside for forces of development may tend to lead to greater dependence, making the possibility of achieving self-reliance even more difficult. Thus, unless the role which foreign partners are allowed to play within the Community market is carefully circumscribed and progressively minimised, they may become a dominant force within the Community. If this happens, then we would have created an opportunity for undermining sustained economic development in the subregion.

And, moreover, although article 30 of the ECOWAS Treaty calls upon the member-states of the Community to 'harmonise their industrial policies so as to ensure a similarity of industrial climates' and to exchange certain types of industrial information, 'no institution or body of ECOWAS is given the power to allocate industries, or to ensure that industrial policies are indeed harmonized'. The Council of Ministers of the Community can make recommendations in this regard but unless the recommendations 'are accepted' by the Authority of Heads of State and Government, they would not in any way be binding.

Of considerable significance is the fact that although 'policy externalisation' can be initiated under article 32 which calls upon the Council of Ministers to 'take steps to reduce gradually the Community's economic dependence on the outside world and strengthen economic relations among themselves', there is no institution or machinery in ECOWAS 'empowered' to enter into negotiation with external actors on behalf of the Community. Similarly, the Community has no institution which would be responsible for controlling the importation of technology.[35] Neither has the treaty any specific provisions for a common regime on direct foreign investment and divestment. Specifically, no agreed upon modalities of collective response to the fully anticipated increase in external penetration has been suggested under the treaty. Thus, the redefinition of ECOWAS's economic relationships with the outside world, which are 'crucial if the reduction of dependence is a goal', are largely ignored by the Lagos treaty. Yet for economic integration to be meaningful and lead to collective self-reliance, very advanced forms of integration, such as control of new technology transfers, industrial location, and regulation of direct foreign investment are required.[36] Without such measures, the degree of success of West African economic integration will be sharply limited. I agree, therefore, with Langdon and Mytelka that in order to transform integration into an instrument of autonomous development, regional policies that regulate external linkages in the interest of domestic development must be enacted. In their view, the cornerstone of such an approach 'would be a set of measures through which direct foreign investment and technology transfer are collectively regulated'.[37] The following section, therefore, outlines briefly measures which may be adopted in order to reinforce the ECOWAS provisions aimed at reducing dependency relationships.

THE POLITICAL ECONOMY OF REGULATION

The position of ECOWAS with regard to the adoption of measures at the regional level designed to reduce dependence on the metropolitan countries, as initiated by the Andean Community,[38] is not yet crystallised. It is necessary, therefore, for the Community to take a leaf from the Andean Pact's example and, based on the West African domestic environments, establish a clearly defined long-term policy towards foreign capital and imported technology. The basic assumption of this policy should be, firstly, that foreign capital and technology have to be acquired selectively; secondly, that these inputs only become fully effective if they are eventually controlled domestically; and thirdly, that considerable information is required, on the one hand, to make proper choice regarding what, when, and under what conditions foreign direct investment is to be admitted, and on the other hand, to avoid irregularities by existing foreign affiliates in the subregion.

Based on these conditions, it is necessary that, in addition to the adoption of the protocol on regional companies designed to promote 'authentically regional enterprises', the Community should establish uniform rules governing foreign investment in the sectors which have attracted historically the most foreign capital. In the volatile area of natural resources member states can grant concessions to foreign companies within a specified period. Also, the Community can, under its investment code, prohibit establishment of new foreign-owned companies in such strategic sectors as public services, insurance, and banking and finance. In order to continue receiving local deposits, foreign banking institutions already operating in the subregion should be compelled, under the code, to sell a very high percentage of their capital to domestic sources within a specified period. These institutions may no longer be permitted to receive new direct foreign investments.

In the manufacturing sector, too, it is necessary for the Community to place restrictions on the transfer of profits out of the subregion. This is particularly important because of the ease with which profits are repatriated, especially in those ECOWAS countries belonging to the franc zone. Foreign investors can be limited to annual transfers of a specified percentage of their investment. Besides, the Community can adopt the principle of the 'phase-out' by which all investments of extra-subregional origin, whether present or future, are to be accommodated within what may be described as 'subregional company law'.

In sum, the main objective of the Community's investment code is to keep the MNCs at arm's length and to offer subregional entrepreneurs — whether private, state, or co-operative — a significant amount of protection against their ubiquitous transnational competitors that mere tariff barriers have failed to give in the past. The message of the code will reflect the general concern for evolution of the the countries' capitalisation, the promotion of authentically national enterprises, and the development of local technological and productive capabilities. If the code meets these objectives, it can offer an alternative to economic domination by foreign capital in the form of a sharing of investments and more domestic participation in and control over all facets of West African economies.

However, in considering these 'radical' proposals for the Community, full account must be taken of the 'social forces and vested interests', both internal and external, that are opposed to what would seem to them to be somewhat 'revolutionary' programmes 'because of attendant political and economic sacrifices'. In these circumstances, it may be not only naive but also dangerous to believe that the implementation of regional measures aimed at regulating external linkages in the interest of domestic development 'can be affected by good will'[39] expressed by the variety of actors in the West African integrative process. Would the former metropolitan countries, for instance, support measures designed to reduce their control over the economies of their ex-colonies? Also, would the emergent bourgeoisies in the West African countries abandon the symbiosis with international capital which has provided them so handsomely with the means for their own embourgeoisement, and to do so in the interest of promoting collective self-reliance, especially in regard to production?

RESISTANCE TO REGIONALISM

Perhaps the first major threat to the Community's measures would emanate from the metropolitan powers (see chapters 7 and 8). For it is unlikely that former colonialists would easily allow their areas of influence and their sources of raw materials to slip from their grasp. To continue to maintain age-old dependency relationships, these powers may apply several adaptive strategies. They may use openly obstructive measures such as, for example, refusing to recognise the authority of regionally-elaborated decisions, seeking to invoke global or universalistic international norms, making separate and differential appeals to individual members of the Community, or threatening reprisals.

Should these measures fail to achieve their objectives, these powers may by aiding, advising, subsidising, cajoling, or flattering subregional and national actors in West Africa, seek to influence the source of collaborative efforts and thereby to protect their essential interests. There is also a tendency that these metropolitan countries will unite and through such kinds of summit meetings as, for example, the annual conferences of France and the French-speaking African heads of state and government, the biennial meetings of the Commonwealth countries, or the Lomé Conventions — may gradually and systematically undermine the Community's policies directed towards disengagement from the international political and economic system.

Besides, within the Community itself the more developed member countries, particularly if they have embryonic national bourgeoisies, will probably be more willing than the less-developed states to support measures to restrict investment and technology transfer. The former countries, as 'poles of growth', will be more likely to have sources of local capital or to be confident of attracting foreign investment even under more restrictive conditions than the latter countries. On the other hand, the less developed member-states of the Community, with much less productive capacity to marshal in the effort to develop and with a desire amongst their comprador elements to attract investment under almost any conditions, will be quite reluctant to support any measures which might constitute even the slightest deterrent to foreign investment.[40]

The major hurdle, however, relates to the extent to which the new social and political forces at the centre of economic and political decision-making in the West African countries will be favourable to such a 'nationalistic' approach to industrialisation. Timothy Shaw has recently argued that the post-colonial ruling class in Africa 'has little interest in going beyond reform towards a more radical definition of regionalism'.[41] The most important of these new social and political forces in this context, Mytelka has stressed, is the 'national bourgeoisie'.[42] Hence, one condition for the adoption of measures calculated to reduce dependence 'is the extent to which there is an emerging, albeit very weak, national bourgeoisie' that is large enough to be in competition with the transnational sector, to enlist the help of the government in its effort, and has 'reached a critical mass'.

This type of national bourgeoisie does not as yet appear to be apparent in much of West Africa. The bourgeoisie in the various West African countries, since it is in a position to benefit immediately and directly from the expanded markets resulting from the freeing of trade, has become the advocate of measures to establish a free trade area. However, this group is not likely to support higher levels of integration involving a common investment policy. For the commitments of the national bourgeoisie to principles of *laissez faire* capitalism makes this class likely to oppose distributive policies, particularly corrective measures which require a large degree of state involvement. More significantly, since there are close ties between the fraction of the bourgeoisie in control of the state and the transnational sector, this dominant group will find its position influenced by its identification with the position of the external actor with which it is affiliated. In the circumstances, it is difficult for one to make a distinction between the national and the comprador fractions since the bourgeoisie in Africa is 'essentially a comprador class', which cannot disengage on the massive scale necessary to substantially reduce the exploitative relations without endangering its material base.[43] Thus, the structural integration of West African economies and national bourgeoisies into the international capitalist order has constituted, as Segun Osoba has remarked in the case of Nigeria, 'a major constraint on the ability of the bourgeoisie, even if it were willing, to change radically this structure of dependency'.[44]

The pattern of structural imbalance and dependence of the West African subregion on the metropolitan countries has been reinforced by the relationship of ECOWAS countries to the European Economic Community (EEC) through the Lomé Conventions since February 1975.[45] Closely studied, the implementation of some key provisions of the Lomé system would seem to constitute one of the most important constraints on the degree of economic co-operation attainable within ECOWAS. As Timothy Shaw has recently concluded, inter-regional North-South relations, like EurAfrican connections exemplified by the Lomé system, are 'counterproductive' to the goal of greater regional autonomy.[46] In brief, the Lomé system is, in many respects, the EEC's brand of neo-colonialism.

To this point in the analysis, it is clear that the ability of ECOWAS to control the West African regional economy in the interests of autonomously generated development remains limited. But if non-dependence through the adoption of measures regulating direct foreign investment and technology transfer is not achievable at least for the immediate future, does it follow that the ECOWAS countries must resign themselves to the inevitability of dependence and limited development?

OBSERVATIONS AND CONCLUSIONS

Since adoption of measures aimed at a very greatly diminished reliance on economic relationships with the rest of the world is at present out of the question for the small and poor West African countries, it may be necessary for the Community to adopt a pragmatic and flexible approach towards the problem of dependency and neo-colonialism; that is, the pursuit of objectives capable of early realisation.

In this regard, one salient possibility worth considering is the Community's attitude towards foreign direct investment (see chapter 3). A question worth asking here is this: would it not be possible for recipient ECOWAS countries to benefit from foreign investment (even when investment leads to a capital outflow) through the acquisition of technology? Through foreign investment the ECOWAS countries might acquire vital technology which would otherwise be more costly or might be unobtainable altogether. I accept therefore the premise of Gerald Helleiner that 'turning inward' or 'reducing dependence' *need* not mean diminishing external relationships so much as consciously *employing* them as one of several instruments for the pursuit of a truly *independent strategy*.[47] It is not, however, implied here that foreign investment is completely or invariably beneficial to the West African subregion.

Another option still available for ECOWAS in the effort to tackle the problem of dependency, especially on the former metropolitan countries of Western Europe, is the diversification of the Community's external economic relations — trading partners and sources of technology and capital. This approach has the potential for strengthening the bargaining position of the governments of the subregion by enabling them to play off one developed economy against another. As a further counter-strategy to exclusive dependence on Western Europe, the ECOWAS members might also develop closer economic relations with the industrialised countries of the socialist community. It must be added, however, that the reason for strengthening economic relations with the countries of the socialist community is not because the socialist countries seek to supplant the EEC or other such capitalist organisations as a market and supplier, but primarily because the socialist countries provide the essential political and material counterweight to the power of world capitalism.

Added to this, the Community may develop some South-South relations, as in, say, ECOWAS connections with CARICOM or ASEAN, which may be fruitful, even if difficult (see chapter 1). Considerable new markets could be established through establishment of economic links with these various groups.

The conclusion towards which this chapter tends then is that, ECOWAS, in its present stage of development, is not sufficiently equipped in terms of resources and power to bring into reality a process of autonomous, self-sustaining growth. Neo-colonialism has become so entrenched, exhibiting so many facets and impinging on so many aspects of life in most West African countries that a narrow focus may be chasing its shadows rather than its substance. Its forces can only be eliminated through a systematic restructuring of the existing modes of production. Since ECOWAS is at present not adequately equipped to bring this about, the only alternative open to the Community is to pursue objectives capable of more or less immediate realisation. In this regard, it will be necessary for the Community to promote industrialisation, increase the ratio of subregional to external trade, diversify its economic relations, shift exports towards the manufacturing sectors, and increase the bargaining power of the subregion. Taken together these efforts, perhaps, will reduce somewhat the continued vulnerability of West Africa to outside forces, with important implications for regional and continental development practice and policy.

NOTES

1. E. Oteiza and F. Sercovich, 'Collective self-reliance: selected issues', *International Social Science Journal*, vol. 28 (1976) no. 4, 666.
2. Osvaldo Sunkel, 'National development policy and external dependence in Latin America', in Yale Ferguson (ed.), *Contemporary Inter-American Relations* (Englewood Cliffs, New Jersey: Prentice-Hall, 1972) 478.
3. Thomas J. Biersteker, 'Self-reliance in theory and practice in Tanzanian trade relations', *International Organization*, vol. 34 (Spring 1980) no. 2, 229.
4. Richard Vengroff, 'Neo-colonialism and policy outputs in Africa', *Comparative Political Studies*, vol. 8 (July 1975) no. 2, 235.
5. Colin Leys, *Underdevelopment in Kenya: the political economy of neo-colonialism* (London: Heinemann, 1975) 26.
6 Pierre Jalée, *The Pillage of the Third World* (New York: Monthly Review, 1968) 105.
7. Timothy M. Shaw and Malcolm J. Grieve, 'Dependence as an approach to understanding continuing inequalities in Africa', *Journal of Developing Areas*, vol. 13 (April 1979) no. 3, 235, 243.
8. Abdul Jalloh, 'Regional integration in Africa: Lessons from the past and prospects for the future', *Africa Development*, vol. 1 (1976) no. 2, 49.
9. Timothy M. Shaw,'Regional Cooperation and Conflict in Africa', *International Journal*, vol. 30 (Autumn 1975) no. 4, 680.
10. For details see S.K.B. Asante, 'Development and Regional Integration since 1980' in Adebayo Adedeji and Timothy M. Shaw (eds.), *Economic Crisis in Africa: African Perspectives on Development Problems and Potentials* (Boulder: Lynne Rienner, 1985) 82–6.
11. Organisation of African Unity, *Resolution on Inter-African Economic Co-operation and Integration*, Addis Ababa, AHG/Res. 131 (20), November 1984.
12. An earlier version of this section appeared in S.K.B. Asante, *The Political Economy of Regionalism in Africa: a decade of ECOWAS* (New York: Praeger, 1986) 35–42.
13. Shaw and Grieve, 'Dependence as an approach to understanding continuing inequalities in Africa', 236.
14. For a recent discussion of the franc zone see Guy Martin, 'The Franc Zone, underdevelopment and dependency in francophone Africa', *Third World Quarterly*; vol. 8 (January 1986) no. 1, 205–35.
15. Alex Rondos, 'How independent is francophone Africa after twenty years?' *West Africa,* 1 September 1980.
16. Alex Rondos, 'Franc Zone and French Africa', *West Africa,* 8 September 1980.
17. Rita Cruise O'Brien, 'Factors of Dependence: Senegal and Kenya', in W.A. Morris-Jones and Georges Fischer (eds),*Decolonisation and After: the British and French experience* (London: Frank Cass, 1980) 287.

18. M.B. Akpan, 'Neo-colonialism: the political economy of combating dependent modernisation in West Africa', (paper presented at the Conference on the New International Economic Order, Lagos, Nigeria, September 1977).
19. Samir Amin, 'Capitalism and Development in the Ivory Coast', in I. L. Markovitz (ed.), *African Politics and Society* (New York: Free Press, 1970) 288.
20. John Kwadjo, 'Collective self-reliance . . . or collective neo-colonialism?', *West Africa*, 15 September 1980.
21. Details contained in 'The profiles and potentials of external trade of members of the Economic Community of West African States', in *ECOWAS Trade, Customs and Monetary Study Project* (Geneva: UNCTAD, December 1979).
22. Kwame Nkrumah, *Africa Must Unite* (London: Panaf, 1963) 160.
23. For an extended discussion see S.K.B. Asante, 'ECOWAS, the EEC and the Lomé Convention', in Domenico Mazzeo (ed.), *African Regional Organizations* (Cambridge: Cambridge University Press, 1984) 171–95, and 'Africa and Europe: collective dependence or interdependence?', in Amadu Sesay (ed.), *Africa and Europe: from partition to interdependence or dependence?* (London: Croom Helm, 1986) 183–-221.
24. The objectives of ECOWAS are detailed in article 2 of the treaty.
25. ECOWAS treaty, preamble, para. 2.
26. Joseph Nye, 'Comparing Common Markets: a revised neo-funtionalist model', *International Organization*, vol. 24 (Autumn 1970) no. 4, 811.
27. Raymond Vernon, 'The role of US enterprise abroad', *Daedalus,* vol. 98 (Winter 1969) no. 1, 123.
28. Steven Langdon and Lynn K. Mytelka, 'Africa in the Changing World Economy', in Colin Legum *et al., Africa in the 1980s: continent in crisis,* (New York: McGraw-Hill for Council on Foreign Relations 1980s Project, 1979) 177–80.
29. Peter Robson, *Integration, Development and Equity: economic integration in West Africa* (London: Allen & Unwin, 1983) 41.
30. For details see S.K.B. Asante, 'Expectations and Reality: transnational corporations and regional self-reliance objectives of the *Lagos Plan of Action*,' in R.I. Onwuka, Layi Abegunrin and D.N. Ghista (eds.), *African Development: the OAU/ECA Lagos Plan of Action and beyond*, (Lawrenceville, Virginia: Brunswick, 1985) 106–16.
31. *A Methodology for the Study of the Role of Transnational Corporations in the Present Stage of African Regional Co-operation*, Joint ECA/CTNC Unit on Transnational Corporations, Working Paper No. 12, 7 December 1979.
32. Philippe C. Schmitter, *Autonomy or Dependence as Regional Integration Outcomes: Central America* (Berkeley: Research Series No. 17, Institute of International Studies, University of California, 1972) 1.
33. Protocol Relating to the Definition of Concept of Products Originating from Member States of the Economic Community of West African States, articles ii, iv and v, 5 November 1976.
34. Osite C. Eze, 'ECOWAS: hopes and illusion' (paper presented at the

conference of African Association of Political Science, Rabat, Morocco, 1977).

35. John P. Renninger, *Multinational Cooperation for Development in West Africa* (New York: Pergamon, 1979) 64.
36. Ibid., 65.
37. Langdon and Mytelka, 'Africa in the Changing World Economy', 189.
38. For the regional integration experiment of the Andean Community see, for example, David E. Hojman, 'The Andean Pact: failure of a model of economic integration *Journal of Common Market Studies*, vol. 20 (December 1981) no. 2, 139–60.
39. P.E. Ollawa, 'On a dynamic model for rural development in Africa', *Journal of Modern African Studies*, vol. 15 (September 1977) no 3, 422.
40. Andrew W. Axline, *Caribbean Integration* (London: Frances Pinter, 1979) 48–9.
41. Timothy M. Shaw, 'The Dialectics of Regionalism: EurAfrica and West Africa', in Sesay (ed.), *Africa and Europe*, 235.
42. Lynn K. Mytelka, *Regional Development in a Global Economy: the multinational corporation, technology, and Andean integration* (New Haven, Conn: Yale University Press, 1979) 22.
43. Claude Ake, 'Explanatory notes on the political economy of Africa', *Journal of Modern African Studies*, vol. 14. (March 1976) no. 1, 22.
44. Segun Osoba, 'The deepening crisis of the Nigerian national bourgeoisie', *Review of African Political Economy*, vol. 13 (May-August 1978) 69.
45. For further details see S.K.B. Asante, 'ECOWAS, the EEC and the Lomé Conventions'; 'Africa and Europe'; 'The Experience of the EEC: relevant or impediment to ECOWAS regional self-reliance objective?', *Afrika Spectrum*, vol. 17 (1982) no. 3, 307–22; 'The Lomé Convention: towards perpetuation of dependence or promotion of interdependency?', *Third World Quarterly*, vol. 3 (October 1981) no. 4, 658–72; and 'Whither Africa? Euro-African integration or African regional co-operation', *Development and Cooperation* (1986) no. 5, 9–11.
46. Shaw, 'The Dialectics of Regionalism' and Adebayo Adedeji, 'Inter-African Economic Co-operation in Light of the Final Act of Lagos' in Adedeji and Shaw (eds.), *Economic Crisis in Africa*, 71–4.
47. Gerald Helleiner, 'Aid and Dependence in Africa: issues for recipients', in Timothy M. Shaw and Kenneth A. Heard (eds.), *The Politics of Africa: Dependence and Development* (London: Longman, 1979) 225–6.

7 Foreign Military Intervention in Africa: The New Co-operative-Competitive Imperialism

Ladun Anise

INTRODUCTION

It is not difficult to imagine all sorts of conditions that could bring foreign intervention in African affairs, especially if past and present trends are projected into the future. What is really difficult is to specify any combination of events and developments that would leave most African countries outside the orbit of foreign intrusions in the immediate decades to come. The purpose of this chapter is to analyse the structure of such past interventions with special emphasis on military intervention up to the time of the American raid on Libya in 1986. Emerging patterns are then discussed in terms of both co-operative and competitive foreign intervention in African affairs; the new imperialism is expected to last far into the African future.

Clarification of some general thought patterns and predispositions on the notion of foreign intervention in Africa is necessary at the outset. One of the general orientations in writing on the subject is to assume that foreign intervention in African affairs is unconditionally bad. Given the susceptibility of Africanists, African writers and African leaders to African nationalist sentiments, it is relatively easy to fall into the trap of viewing all foreign intrusions as being against African interests. But this is not always the case. The case of Cuban military involvement in Angola since 1975, and the multinational aid responses to starvation across Africa's drought belt suggest that it is possible for some foreign intervention to be in support of largely African interests and needs, even if there is no unanimity of opinion about the desirability or effectiveness of such intervention.

Each act of foreign intervention is usually based on (1) the diplomatic and national interest calculations of the intervening foreign power(s), (2) the configuration of foreign interests and strategic balances represented within the particular African region or country, and (3) the configuration of élite power groups in the African country and the dynamics of their economic, political and ideological confrontations as these provide the context for foreign powers and groups to take sides in what may be largely domestic disputes. On the whole, it is by the effects of intervention and not the simple fact of it that one must judge its efficacy.

There is also a tendency to perceive as intervention only those direct and indirect, overt and covert acts of subversion that foreign powers undertake in their dealings with Africa. There is no denying the seriousness of such clandestine or direct military interventions or their tendency to prop up bad, dictatorial, corrupt and tyrannical regimes in Africa. But these should not be viewed as the only types of intervention.

In general, a more elastic conception of foreign intervention is desirable in order to call attention to other forms of interstate interactions that may have the effects of causing internal changes that would otherwise not occur if the country in question were left entirely to its own internal processes in the determination of event-outcomes. What then are the kinds of intervention that would emerge from this elastic definition?

First, the structure and configuration of foreign penetration of domestic structures, institutions and patterns of exchange should now be viewed as aspects of external intervention with resulting value judgement placed on either the positive or negative consequences on the African societies involved. Economic penetration by multinational corporations (MNCs) may have more permanent consequences by rigidifying the structures of dependency while also distorting the patterns of allocations of resources and incomes nationally. The renewed urgency with which the problem of African dependency is being tackled analytically will suggest the desirability of viewing such processes of economic and structural penetration as forms of international interventionist hegemony.[1] What is quite conclusive about the growing body of writings on African political economy, is that the dependency which characterises all phases of African development today is the result of the historical chain of foreign penetration and incorporation of Africa that took place over the last three centuries. From this, it can be concluded that the impetus of penetration and incorporation is not yet spent. The further exploration of the interlocking structures of dependency resulting from the continuing incorporation of Africa into the global capitalist economy would show that a new stage of imperialism more subtle than the crude version of neo-colonialism is now apparent in the nexus of the unequal international exchange involving Africa. For lack of a better phrase to capture the essence of such foreign-determined mode of production, reproduction and distribution, this newer form of imperialism may be termed foreign intervention by remote control. Technological innovations and their rates of development, adaptation and application to new production, distribution and storage systems constitute the indubitable hinges of external control and determination of internal domestic outcomes in Africa. It is the very pervasiveness of these patterns and processes that complicate the evolution of authentic or genuinely indigenous and autonomous development in Africa.

Imperialism and foreign intervention in Africa have actually taken new forms over the years. At first only European powers competed for hegemony in Africa. Belgium, Britain, France, Germany, Portugal, Spain and other lesser European countries engaged in what was then competitive imperialism over Africa. Sometimes they had to wage war against each other in order to extend their respective zones of imperial influence. The modes of penetration included the slave trade, military conquest, colonisation, missionary-religious evangelism, colonialism and finally economic imperialism.

Later, after political independence, the United States of America joined the Europeans. The stage was set for linkage penetration through covert government activities, foreign aid programmes, private investments, pervasive growth and expansion of the octopus-tentacled multinational corporations, and controlling international banking and financial institutions.

The emergence of the Soviet Union as a rival superpower brought a new dimension to the nature of foreign penetration and imperialism in Africa. The ideological warfare between East and West is played out largely over the lands, resources and souls of Third World countries. The result has been a transformation of imperial procedures in Africa. European powers capitalised on their ideological unanimity to forge a new co-operative imperialism whereby they maintain a common imperial front and policy against the challenging socialist ideological bloc. The outcomes are the practice of co-operative imperialism among European and North American powers and the practice of belligerent, combative competitive imperialism between East and West in Africa.

The Sino-Soviet rift has also added a kind of socialist competitive imperialism, somewhat reminiscent of the earlier practice among the capitalist European powers. This new form notwithstanding, the dominant structure at the moment is the virulent effort to penetrate and incorporate Africa into either the global capitalist system or the globalising (Soviet) socialist system (see chapter 4).

SPEED OF AFRICAN EVENTS

This analysis focuses mainly on events up to the end of 1986. In general, Africa has been reinserted into the debates on the East-West geopolitical and geostrategic confrontations that have abandoned *détente* for a return to cold war rhetoric and traditional competitive imperialism, since the Reagan presidency in the United States. Generally, political changes occur with bewildering rapidity in Africa.

But some things on the continent do not change that fast. One of these is foreign imperialism or intervention. Second is Africa's neocolonial dependency. A third is Africa's lack of unity. And finally there is the eternal problem of powerlessness in terms of (1) self-determination, especially in South Africa and the Horn of Africa, and (2) competitive international exchanges, linkages and influence. In fact it is this condition that provides the environment for disunity, and the exercise of arrogance by foreign powers in their competition over what the choices must be in the African geopolitical nexus. This is the background for understanding the concern in Western Europe and North America for the continuing Cuban and Soviet presence in Africa, which has been used to justify Western opposition to the independence of Namibia from illegal occupation and control by South Africa.

The specific purpose here is to review the record of foreign intervention in Africa since the 1960s and to determine who is doing what to whom and for what reasons. This is followed by an examination of the African states' role in the enthronement of their own dependency and disunity. The chapter concludes with an analysis of the renewed Soviet-American proxy wars in Africa, their rationale and possible outcomes (see chapter 9).

DECOLONISATION AND COLONIAL LEGACIES

Foreign intervention is Africa's chief inheritance from its encounter with Europe. From the days of European adventurism and voyages of discovery, through the periods of European commercial traffic in black slaves, to the era of neo-colonialism following incomplete decolonisation, foreign, chiefly European, intervention in Africa has been continuous. All forms of intervention have taken place, the latest being overt and covert military action. The European powers have always conducted competitive imperialism in Africa, mostly against the economic, political, social, cultural and psychological health of the African peoples. The differences between the old and the new forms of intervention are essentially two-fold.

First, the older competitive forms had been the monopoly of European powers until the late 1950s when the Americans came into the African picture. The exhaustion of Britain and France at the end of World War II created a 'power vacuum' in the eyes and minds of world imperialist powers. America's ascendancy to global supremacy at the same time required that it become the natural heir to European colonial bankruptcies in Africa and Asia. While Britain and France were liquidating their colonial administrative controls, Belgium, Spain and Portugal tried to hang on to theirs. Portugal, the first European power to encroach on Africa, became the last major colonialist to liquidate control — through blood, tears and destruction that nearly ruined Portugal itself at home.[2]

At present in Angola and Mozambique the struggle against imperialism goes on because the forced departure of the Portuguese created a new set of problems in Southern Africa where these two militant African states face severe challenges, including recurrent sabotage and destabilisation by the racist, white, apartheid regime in South Africa. Between 1975 and 1980, white Rhodesian forces violated the territorial integrity of Mozambique and Zambia repeatedly, without much concern in the Western world. Since 1975 South Africa has been invading Angola, Mozambique, Zambia, Zimbabwe, Lesotho, Botswana and Swaziland at will with continuing clandestine support from Western governments. Both Belgian and French troops attempted to mount search and destroy operations across the Zambian and Angolan borders in June 1978 even though their publicly announced mission was to rescue foreign hostages in Zaire's Shaba Province. All these occurred with direct and indirect support from America and Western European countries.

The presence of the Soviet Union, Cuba and China in Africa represents only an extension of this old competitive imperialism, although with some new twists. The Western powers now tend towards co-operative imperialism among themselves while maintaining a posture of competitive imperialism with the Eastern bloc.

Second, the old competitive imperialism and penetration had no regard for African opinion. It took place largely in the face of a militarily subdued Africa. Thus, the old intervention was fully backed by force. The new co-operative competitive imperialism on the other hand involves African leaders directly as participating agents of choice. These days no foreign power intervenes in Africa without an 'invitation' to do so by some African head of state or some nationalist group. If the old competitive imperialism was blatant in its complete disregard for African interests and desires, the new imperialism is bound up with duplicity on the part of African leaders. This is why the new imperialism cannot be fought with the old rhetoric of Pan-Africanism. The political and geostrategic context of the new imperialism therefore makes for chronic division, jealousy and rivalry among African states themselves. It covers the entire ideological spectrum, thereby exposing black Africa's economic vulnerability, political opportunism, and the structural powerlessness of the Organisation of African Unity (OAU). In spite of this, it is not clear that, *a priori* all these forms of foreign intervention are detrimental to long-range African interests.

Because of the present unequal global arrangements, agitation has grown among developing countries for the transformation of prevailing allocative structures into an equilibrating structure of global interdependence without chronic dependency. In short, there is a persisting demand for a new international economic order (NIEO). In a way, then, the new wave of foreign intervention in Africa reflects the growing battle for and against the preservation of the existing world order. This battle involves a confrontation between the rich and poor nations, capitalist and socialist states of the world in general and between the racist and non-racist countries in Africa in particular. As I have argued elsehwere, Africa is situated uniquely in the path of a global strategic resource zone whose importance is accentuated by increasing resource scarcity and global desperation to assure areas of hegemonic control.

Thus foreign intervention in Africa, especially from the superpowers, focuses increasingly on six interrelated geopolitical considerations. These are: (1) the continuation of the pressure and armed struggle for complete decolonisation in Southern Africa, especially in Namibia and racist South Africa; (2) the turbulent crises and confrontations in the Horn of Africa; (3) the involvement of the North African Arab states in the Middle East crises; (4) the American-Soviet geopolitical confrontations in Africa, the Middle East, and the Indian Ocean; (5) the burgeoning, militant anti-capitalist, pro-socialist ideological stance of increasing numbers of African states (for example, Algeria, Ethiopia, Guinea, Guinea-Bissau, Libya, Mozambique, Namibia, Tanzania and Zimbabwe) which threatens the historical hegemonic domination of Western capitalist countries in Africa; and finally (6) the never-ending intra- and inter-state military, ethnic, religious, irredentist, boundary and hegemonic conflicts in Africa which do bring increasing 'invitations' to various foreign countries to intervene.[3]

The first four considerations are linked directly with superpower competition and hence involve competitive imperialism. The last two considerations are closely linked with internal upheavals and potentially disruptive confrontations which are endemic to African political, social and economic structures. Unfortunately there does not seem to be any way of resolving these problems without implicating extra-African interests. In fact, it is the combination of the last two sets of forces that triggered the injection of Africa into recent East-West confrontations. Since all indications are that these problems will not soon go away, the continent seems destined to the disconcerting continuation of more foreign intervention in the future.

As African leaders and governments face increasing challenges to their power and positions from rivals, both rulers and rivals are likely to escalate their 'invitations' to foreign powers to assist them in achieving their objectives. Those in power will often find support from the Western bloc nations to maintain the *status quo* provided they are not the radical, marxist or socialist regimes which are likely to find opposition from such quarters and support from the Eastern bloc nations. The challengers — usually in the name of 'self-determination' and 'national liberation' — will tend to find support from the East. But no matter how the competition for power and control shapes-up in circumstances like these, East-West ideological confrontations will get imported into African politics. Sometimes it may even be convenient for rivals deliberately to adopt the ideological preferences of their would-be supporters even when the leaders themselves may have no particular ideological convictions beyond the desire to capture power or retain control of power already gained.[4]

COLONIAL LINKAGES AND THE STRUCTURE OF INTERVENTION

One feature of some writings on African politics is Western analysts' tendency to overlook Western intervention while counting as intervention any involvement in African politics by China, Cuba, the Soviet Union or any other socialist state. This is a carry-over from the colonial connection. A related feature is the tendency to explain Western intervention in terms of preserving law and order (maintaining the *status quo*), political stability (in Southern Africa this is a synonym for preserving white racist minority domination), peaceful change (anti- and counter-revolutionary insurgency), and economic growth through private investment (preservation of Western investments and high profits made possible by the exploitation of black labour in Southern Africa, and the extraction of minerals in all of Africa). By contrast, such analysis tends to view Soviet, Cuban, Chinese and other Eastern bloc interventions in terms of (1) a new colonial domination, (2) exportation of communism, (3) imposition of alien ideologies on African countries and peoples either by force, subversion, or through lack of inherent ability on the part of African leaders and peoples to choose for themselves, and finally (4) as a conspiracy to overwhelm democratic processes and institutions in Africa.

Thus the impression is left that Western intervention is redemptive while Eastern intervention is subversive of African interests and needs. As Secretary of State Cyrus Vance once put it:

> The recent introduction of large quantities of Soviet arms and thousands of Cuban troops in certain parts of Africa raises serious concerns: the size and duration of their military presence jeopardises the independence of African states. It creates concerns on the part of African nations that outside weapons and troops will be used to determine the outcome of any dispute on the continent. And it renders more difficult the efforts of Africans to resolve these disputes through peaceful means . . . [American policy, on the other hand, is a strategy] based upon an affirmative and constructive approach to African issues: helping African nations meet their pressing human and economic needs; strengthening their ability to defend themselves; building closer ties throughout Africa; and assisting African nations to resolve their conflicts peacefully.[5]

In effect the Carter administration retained the Kissingerian global perspective. This was particularly significant because it captured the logic of colonial linkages. According to Kissinger's view of *détente* with the Soviet Union, the latter may not extend its influence beyond zones already recognised by the West. Thus, any Soviet effort in Africa is to be viewed as an attempt to extend its sphere of domination and hegemony over existing zones of peace, and, therefore, an effort to reduce Western influence.

It is impossible to present the argument in this form without seeing the world only as an area of competitive imperialism between East and West. This view unfortunately does not provide any room for African initiatives or foreign policies based on African national interests. The continent is viewed as being under the domination of either East or West. It is this arrogance of perception that has shaped the pattern of Western intervention since the early 1960s.[6]

Much of the analysis that follows in the rest of this section is based on the excellent compilation of crises and intervention data with synopses in Robert Butterworth's *Managing Interstate Conflict, 1945–74*.[7] In general,West European countries have, by virtue of their historical colonial domination always assumed the right of free passage when it comes to military intervention in African affairs. Both Britain and France signed military defence pacts with many of their colonies as part of the conditions under which political independence was negotiated. While the British have been forced to abandon such treaties, the French have maintained theirs in most of francophone Africa.

The British gave up Anglo-African defence pacts essentially because of the adverse effects the debates on one such pact had in Nigeria in 1959–61. The Anglo-Nigerian pact allowed unilateral British intervention in Nigerian internal affairs if Britain thought the country was in danger of external intervention or breakdown of law and order. It allowed construction of British military bases and use of Nigerian airspace and facilities for military manoeuvres by British forces. Of course, Nigeria ostensibly through the treaty's bilateral provisions enjoyed similar privileges in Britain, except that Nigeria had no ability or capability to utilise them. The pact was viewed by university students and progressive political parties in Nigeria as a symbol of neo-colonialism; massive opposition produced its abrogation in 1961. However, when there were military mutinies in 1964 in Uganda, Kenya and Tanzania the British promptly sent troops to restore law and order and to preserve existing regimes. This military intervention was received positively by most African countries.

While the British intervened quickly in East Africa in 1964, they failed to do so in 1965 over white Rhodesia's illegal 'Unilateral Declaration of Independence' (UDI). This failure resulted in the OAU calling for an immediate military intervention by Britain to put down what was clearly treason against Her Majesty's Government. However, UDI remained effective for almost 15 years until armed struggle forced Britain and white Rhodesia to negotiate the 1979 Lancaster agreement that resulted in true black majority rule with Robert Mugabe's unconditional victory in the 1980 elections. Most African analysts would suggest that the failure to intervene militarily in this case was motivated more by racism than anything else.[8] The same British government conspired with France and Israel in 1956 to invade Egypt because it nationalised the British-controlled Suez Canal; clearly in this instance other than racist considerations were involved. Only American and international pressures aborted this three-nation attack on the sovereignty of an African state.[9]

The pattern of French military intervention in Africa is quite extensive (see chapter 8). The joint expedition with Britain and Israel against Egypt has already been mentioned. The war with Algeria (1954–62) was intended to maintain colonial subjugation against the will of the Algerian people. This war followed on the heels of the French military disaster at Dien Bien Phu, Indochina, in 1954, and was largely responsible for the final collapse of the French Fourth Republic in 1958.[10] It paralleled Portugal's wars of colonial oppression in Guinea-Bissau, Angola and Mozambique (1961–75) in its savagery and destruction of human life.[11]

Between 1957 and 1963 France engaged in continual military interventions in Morocco and Tunisia, resulting from its determination to prevent any support for the Algerian Liberation Front, holding on to military bases in Tunisia. In February 1958 France was accused of acting as if it still exercised sovereignty over Tunisia. In April and May 1958 French forces killed over 300 Tunisians; and 12 000 French troops remained stationed at Bizerte while France finally agreed to evacuate all other bases in the country. In July 1961 'French forces killed several Tunisian demonstrators near the base . . . 610 Tunisians and five French casualties were officially reported . . . More than 1,000 Tunisians and 21 French were killed [at Bizerte] during July 21–22'.[12]

During a three-year period in the early 1960s the French carried out an infamous series of atomic tests in the Sahara over the ineffective protestations of African states. Since 1965 civil war situations in Niger and Chad have necessitated extensive French military intervention on behalf of the autocratic rulers of both countries. But the French military presence has prevented bloody military coups in neither. As in Mauritania, it is not clear whether the coups were, in fact, facilitated by the presence of the French. In Chad, in particular, the government's 'military operations against the insurgents were helped considerably by extensive French military assistance, which included troops'.[13]

The general French posture is that francophone African affairs constitute a 'family affair' in which the President of France plays the role of Big Papa. At present France maintains bilateral and multilateral defence agreements with Cameroon, Central African Republic, Chad, Congo-Brazzaville, Gabon, Cote d'Ivoire, Malagasy, Mauritania, Niger, Senegal, Burkina Fasso, Djibouti and the Indian Ocean Islands of Mayotte, Réunion, Comoros, Seychelles and Mauritius.[14] The French have a combined force of about 17 000 troops, 15–25, roving war ships and supportive military hardware in and around these countries. These pacts allow France the potentiality to establish military bases in all 17 African states and islands. Although such pacts with Benin, Mali, Togo and Tunisia have since been abrogated, there is no doubt about the ease with which France could intervene militarily in these other francophone states. The increased French military presence in Chad since 1985 has helped to preserve President Habré's retention of power there.

In addition to French military interventions in North and West Africa, France has also intervened in the Cameroons, and in Gabon where French paratroopers helped to crush a coup against President M'Ba's government. In fact, Dakar, the capital of Senegal and Libreville, the capital of Gabon, are generally known as the centres for 'French secret service operations throughout West and Central Africa'.[15] The French also keep a 20 000 strong paratroop unit ready in France for quick deployment anywhere in Africa within eight hours.

The most telling instance of the readiness of France to intervene militarily in Africa was 'Operation Barracuda' which dethroned the self-styled 'Emperor' Bokassa on 20 September 1979. Two events happened before this operation whose significance surfaced only afterwards.

The first of these was the reaction of Western countries to the 'invasions' of Zaire's Shaba Province by exile Katangese gendarmes in March 1977, and May and June 1978.[16] French involvement against these invasions was aimed at consolidating French economic interests in Zaire in competition against other Western interests while at the same time enabling France to maintain a posture of defending Western hegemony in Central Africa.[17]

The second was the French-sponsored and orchestrated plan to create a 'Pan-African Force' to be equipped and trained by Western powers with countries like Gabon, Cote d'Ivoire, Morocco, Senegal and Zaire contributing soldiers for the Force. This was to be a Western instrument for maintaining the *status quo* in favoured African countries, propping up repressive, corrupt and shaky regimes in others and destabilising unfriendly governments elsewhere. In the end the plan failed because too many African states angrily denounced the effort as a not-so-subtle form of neo-colonial intervention in the internal affairs of African states.

Thus, it was on the heels of these activities that France sent in four troop transport planes carrying at least 200 soldiers, light armoured vehicles and 'the man who would again become President of the Central African Republic, David Dako', into that country on 20 September 1979 to overthrow French-made Emperor Bokassa. Within 24 hours of the first landing, a dozen other French troop carriers arrived and unloaded another 500 members of the French paratroop regiments to secure the total success of 'Operation Barracuda' in the CAR.[18]

This blatant military intervention was justified on grounds of French defence of human rights in the CAR. The French government argued that it intervened to remove Bokassa because the emperor had been found guilty of murdering over 100 students who had protested against his murderous rule. That case notwithstanding, it was also clear at the time that Bokassa was becoming a troublesome and unreliable 'ally', so much so that his removal was planned and executed in Paris for a period of 18 months before its actualisaton. So President Dako of the CAR owes his presidency to an undisguised French military invasion, thus complicating the problem of legitimacy and underscoring Africa's powerlessness. In fact, in this particular case, no invitation was sent and the French did not even try to justify their actions under that pretence. In a 'real emergency' imperialist powers often move unrestrained by the niceties of international law, or democratic principles that are supposed to inform the behaviour of

Western 'democratic' states. 'Invitation', then, becomes a matter of convenience.

Why then is such an extensive French military presence all over Africa not considered a threat to continental security? Why is this not perceived by Western analysts as another form of imperialism or, more correctly, as a continuation of French neo-colonialism? First, because the French are there ostensibly at the pleasure and invitation of the governments concerned. Second, because the French presence is considered a strategic measure to preserve not just French but wider Western economic, political and security interests. The unilateral action to send paratroopers to Shaba Province in 1978 was interpreted both as a move to consolidate French influence in Zaire, thus displacing Belgian influence, and as an effort on behalf of all Western nations to counter Soviet-Cuban 'adventurism' in Africa:

> Not only did the penetration by the Soviet and Cuban influence spur on the French to safeguard the interests of the West in Africa. It also threatened the largely conservative and capitalist-oriented governments in French-speaking Africa. The practical considerations of defense and the desirability of stronger Western influence to counterbalance the Soviet threat became increasingly important.[19]

The West's disposition to consider Africa its geopolitical preserve underscores the way particular non-Western intervention is analysed as a 'threat', not only to Western security but also to 'African' interests. Of course, the fact that French intervention in Zaire was designed to challenge Belgian hegemony as well as American monopoly only confirms the continuation of competitive Western imperialism in Africa. If Soviet, Cuban and Chinese 'threats' were removed, this 'in-family' competitive imperialism would not only grow but might indeed turn nasty, recalling Lenin's theory of wars amongst imperialist forces for the domination of global markets.

AMERICAN INTERVENTION IN AFRICA

Belgian, British, French and Portuguese intervention in Africa may be explained as a continuation of old colonial relations in the form of hegemonic neo-colonialism. But American involvement is generally understood in terms of superpower global 'obligations', usually self-imposed. If West European influence declines in any part of the globe then American power is inclined to move into the 'vacuum' for no other reasons than the necessity to contain 'communism' or to make the world safe for democracy (read: capitalist exploitation and hegemony?). Direct American involvement in Africa began late, in 1958. It has been largely economic, with a substantial portion of US investment going to Southern Africa where corporate profits run between 16 and 27 per cent per year. In 1975, for the first time since 1958, American investment in the rest of Africa outside Southern Africa rose to more than 50 per cent of all US African investment.

But Southern Africa is a centre of racism and oppression. *Apartheid* continues to claim an indentification with Western democracy and anti-communist ideology. Also, this is the region where American and other NATO countries aided Portugal from 1961 to 1975 in a brutal war of colonial oppression. According to Dennis Brutus, Southern Africa is where 'the people ask not that their shackles be polished but that they be removed'.[20]

American military involvement in Africa centred largely on Ethiopia until 1974 and on Zaire since 1960. It included clandestine support for Portugal to continue colonial control in Angola, Guinea-Bissau and Mozambique until 1974, and since 1974 to the present, for 'pro-western' liberation groups — UNITA and the FNLA. The nature of this involvement is, of course, slightly different from Soviet-Cuban involvement. There are no American troops in Africa, at least not officially. There are only military advisors and instructors, principally in Zaire. The orientation of American military involvement, especially since the Vietnam disaster, has been to finance military operations through the CIA, through third party governments, Morocco, Saudi Arabia and Zaire, and throuugh direct and indirect financial support of factions like UNITA, the FNLA and the Cabinda Liberation Front in Angola.[21] For these purposes the US sends military equipment through clandestine sources. For example, the US Senate Foreign Relations Committee hearings on US involvement in Southern Africa revealed that the Nixon-Ford administrations provided about $60 million in clandestine and illegal support to anti-MPLA forces in Angola through the Zaire connection between 1974 and 1976 alone.[22]

Once it became clear that Portugal was going to fail in Southern Africa, the Nixon administration tried to install 'moderate' leaders and regimes in Angola and Mozambique. When this policy was shown to be bankrupt, too, a typical strategy of counter-insurgency was introduced. This called for the destabilisation of the so-called radical regimes and liberation movements through clandestine manoeuvres headquartered in Zaire and South Africa. The US and South Africa have been behind the financing of most of the mercenary operations designed to destabilise the radical movements in Southern Africa in the last ten years. The discovery through ex-CIA agents' disclosures of the continuation of destabilisation policies in Angola under the Carter administration and the painful realisation that Zaire would not be safe without some US concessions to the Angolan regime prompted the Carter administration's belated about-face overtures to the government of Angola in 1979. The move was aided by pressure from that administration's chief African interest advocates, most notably Andrew Young and Donald McHenry, among others. This slim policy change was reversed by the Reagan administration with the pressing of its 'Constructive Engagement' policy in 1980–86.

But what has been causing great concern in the US is the convergence of five essential geopolitical and geostrategic forces in southern Africa (see chapter 9). First was the sudden collapse of the Portuguese colonial empire in Southern Africa in 1974. This altered Western calculations about the pace of change in southern Africa and for the first time since the rise of African nationalism, exposed the bastions of apartheid and racism in Southern Africa, thus endangering Western capitalist investments and profits in the area.

Second was the escalation of the traditional support from Cuba, China and the Soviet Union for anti-colonial liberation movements in Southern Africa. The sudden and massive Soviet-Cuban involvement was not anticipated in the US. But once it came, it has to this point had a decisive impact on the outcome of factional rivalry, especially in Angola. The nature and extent of this intervention also nullified the role of the Chinese at the same time. It was this outcome that triggered the 'unholy alliance' between China, the US and South Africa in the abortive invasions of Angola with South Africa serving as standard bearer for the protection of Western interests against 'communist expansionism'. Once Marxism 'succeeded' in Mozambique, America and South Africa sought to prevent another 'communist takeover' in Angola. This effort also failed and the result was panic in US African policy.

Third was the exacerbation of pressures against the *status quo* by the rebellion of Black African youths in Soweto. This raised the level of violence and vicious and brutal counter-violence on the part of the South African racist regime that blatantly confounded Carter's human rights crusade and put the policy to a severe test.

Fourth was the dramatic geopolitical and geostrategic transformation occurring within the Southern African region as a result of the combination of the effects of the first three factors identified above. This transformation implies a dramatic shift in the balance of forces in the region. Because Africans had appeared to be powerless both in the economic and military senses, US strategic analysts had always felt that Southern Africa was not seriously in danger from this kind of dramatic shift in the balance of power. However, the shift came to threaten a racial war to end white domination and to undermine US corporate and strategic interests in the area. The full support for this shift in the balance of forces by the Soviet-Cuban military presence in a way that favours African interests and total regional decolonisation triggered Western counter-insurgency reactions throughout the continent.

Finally, the obvious success of Soviet-Cuban intervention in Ethiopia after the initial apparent success of Soviet penetration of Somalia, has had wide-ranging implications on geostrategic calculations involving the Horn of Africa, the Persian Gulf, the Indian Ocean and the Cape route. These five factors help to explain uncertainties and inconsistencies in recent US African policy. This combination of forces finally tilted the scale in favour of the Reagan administration's active collaboration with *apartheid* South Africa and enlarged sponsorship and financing of 'freedom fighters' in Angola, Mozambique, Chad and elsewhere.

President Reagan's aggressive anti-communism, his determination to re-establish the global prestige and power of the United States militarily, and the pressures imposed on his administration to demonstrate US power and policy successes against international terrorism, all combined to push the United States into its bombing raids on Libya in January and April 1986. The aim was partly to punish Gaddafi, the leader of Libya, for supporting terrorist organisations, and finally to overthrow or assassinate him because of his anti-American, pro-Soviet activities. Reagan was hoping thereby to install, if he could, a pro-American regime in Libya. These concrete cases of overt American military aggression failed to achieve the intended objectives.

Moreover, even before these attacks took place, the United States had made determined efforts secretly to persuade Egypt to serve as its proxy and declare war on Libya. The Egyptians were to do the actual fighting while the Reagan administration would have financed the entire war, including the supply of all weapons and logistics. This

American-sponsored Egyptian invasion was to have taken place early in 1986. The intent was the same: to overthrow Gaddafi on behalf of the United States. Of course, the President of Egypt refused this invitation to war as a proxy. The US military attack on Libya and the focus of that attack on Gaddafi's headquarters rather than on 'terrorist training camps' or on military barracks suggest that the April 1986 invasion was designed to murder the head of the government of Libya, even though doing so would have been a clear violation of the laws of the United States prohibiting the assassination of other countries' political leaders.

President Reagan had planned to use Egyptian troops to fight his war against Libya primarily so that the American public would be won over to support him as simply coming to the aid of an ally who was fighting against aggression and terrorism in Africa. Similarly the efforts to mobilise the European allies to do the same failed. In the end Reagan was not deterred. He invaded Libya directly only when no proxy could be motivated to do so. The limit imposed on the invasion of Libya was therefore determined by the calculus of potential human casualties that the United States would have suffered in a land invasion and the fear that there would be no public support for such magnitude of human losses among the American people. Had the President had his way, two African countries would have gone to war at America's instigation with little of Africa's national interests being at stake. Nevertheless, Egypt finally agreed to engage in a joint military exercise that was indeed very provocative to Libya before the actual American raid in April 1986.[23]

ANALYSIS OF IMPERIALISM BY PROXY

Imperialism by proxy is not a new phenomenon in world politics. Rather it is only a new facet of an old problem. Nowhere in the Third World has political independence been able to overcome economic imperialism in the form of neo-colonialism. This has institutionalised chronic dependency in the former colonies. Lenin thought that colonialism would be the last stage of Western imperialism, but by the time of the Nkrumahs of the Third World, neo-colonialism had grown into a full-fledged monster. Both are global in their structures and consequences. They involve total penetration of the economic, political, socio-cultural and psychological fabrics of dependent peoples in Africa and the Third World.

What was unique about imperialism in all its forms or stages in Africa was that it began as, and also remained, a totally European phenomenon. African economies have been patterned after Western models; they exist only within the context of the global capitalist system which largely determines their structures, possibilities and potentials. Western competitive imperialism remains pervasive in Africa, with its attendant dependency and control. Its presence is summed-up in the adoption of English or French (and now Portuguese) as Africa's legal, business and international languages.

This has enthroned the psychology of a Western hegemonic preserve. Within this preserve, various Europeans and North Americans may compete for strategic, economic and political penetration and consolidation without raising within their élites any fears of dominant rivalry or recolonisation. Moreover, the conduct of this post-political independence competitive imperialism is never viewed as posing any threat to African independence and self-determination.

More importantly, this new imperialism is not conceived to be a process that stands in the way of fundamental structural change. In its particulars the new Western imperialism is anti-change, although it is presented as being only against revolutionary changes. In South Africa, for example, it is said to be in favour of gradual, peaceful, non-violent change. But it is exactly this kind of change that the supremacist white minority regime has rejected through its laws, political and economic institutions and social practices. It is almost impossible to call the attention of the Western world to the fact that it is the whites and not the Africans who have made orderly non-violent change impossible in South Africa. The Portuguese did so in Angola and Mozambique; white Rhodesians did so in Zimbabwe; and *apartheid* white South Africans are doing so in Namibia as well as South Africa. What Africans are meant to accept in the name of peace, freedom and civilisation is a condition of slavery in perpetuity. Those who reject this slavery are forced to seek support from the non-Western world because the West is essentially the guarantor of their enslavement.

The West, with its political, economic, cultural and educational advantages in Africa, needs no external proxies to maintain the *status quo* or to carry out occasional military interventions. Much of the leadership of African bureaucracies, businesses and universities can be bought cheaply to accomplish that purpose.

When a number of African heads of state were named as paid CIA agents, when the military clique in a progressive African state could be paid up to $5 million to overthrow the government of their country; when Morocco, Senegal, Cote d' Ivoire and Gabon could be persuaded to supply 'African' troops to act on behalf of Western interests in Western Sahara or Shaba; when a Biafra could take military aid from *apartheid* South Africa and America, and Roberto and Savimbi of Angola could do the same in order to wage war against their own people, then it must be obvious that the West is definitely not in need of external proxies to advance its penetration. What the West needs, only the West can supply; covert financial support and covert military aid.

For instance, before 1973 when Israel confronted massive diplomatic setbacks in Africa, a great deal of US military aid reached Africa by way of Israel; now US and other Western military aid is reaching Africa by way of Egypt, Cote d' Ivoire, Morocco, Saudi Arabia and Senegal often for forwarding to other troubled destinations. Before his death, the President of Egypt, Anwar Sadat, charged that Soviet penetration of black Africa marked a return to the colonialist wave.[24] But Egypt has been making strenuous efforts since 1967 to extend its own influence throughout black Africa. What is more, Sadat did not see chronic Egyptian military and economic dependency on the US and France as a case of neo-colonialism that guaranteed Israel's military supremacy in the Middle East and perpetual Egyptian subordination to Israel.

Actually, though, there has been a substantial transformation in the operative styles of Western competitive imperialism in recent years. As long as Africa was exposed only to Western imperialism, Western powers could practice a kind of relatively unrestrained competitive imperialism among themselves. But the challenges posed by Cuban-Soviet and Chinese attempts to penetrate Africa have brought about a kind of united or co-operative imperialism among Western allies. Thus, since about 1975 the Western countries have been compelled to practice what can be called dualistic imperialism. Whenever and wherever they confronted Eastern bloc interests, they would attempt to practice co-operative imperialism amongst themselves, and competitive imperialism against the 'communist' threat in Africa. Wherever and whenever this threat is not active, Western states revert to competitive imperialism among themselves. In a simplified way this is how the dynamics of the new co-operative-competitive imperialism works not only in Africa but also throughout the rest of the Third World.

The Soviet Union and China have not been so strategically lucky in Africa. They may not have incurred the stigma of colonial imperialism in African history, but they have not been able to take advantage of established infrastructures either. It is this lack of natural historical hinges with Africa that impels the Soviet Union towards action only through military proxies. China is even worse situated; it does not have the capabilities to sponsor viable international proxy agents beyond South East Asia. Thus it can be seen that the Soviet Union has a decided advantage over China in sponsoring international proxies to intervene in Africa, South East Asia and Latiñ America.

Generally the Cubans have often found themselves acting as the unavoidable proxy of the Soviet Union in Latin America and Africa. But this is not because Cuba is such an incurable puppet of Moscow but because,

> as a leader of the Third World revolutionary movements since the 1960's, sometimes over Soviet opposition, *Cuba has stronger ties with some African political leaders than the Soviet Union. Castro is probably more genuinely committed to political involvement in the Third World than Russia. Cuban and Soviet joint operations in Africa are a product of converging interests,* not Soviet domination. The wildly voiced view that the Cubans are Soviet mercenaries or merely Soviet surrogates grossly exaggerated Soviet power and underrates Cuba's political commitments and initiatives.[25]

Cuba began a policy of ideological and material support for the armed liberation struggle in the Portuguese colonies as early as 1961, just two years after the success of the Cuban revolution. That support escalated into the deployment of Cuban troops in the form of military advisors and trainers in 1968, and full-fledged fighting forces in 1975. What cannot be denied is that Soviet military support for such intervention through the provision of large-scale military equipments and logistics during 1975–77 in Angola and 1977–80 in Ethiopia makes effective Cuban intervention possible. Otherwise, Cuba, with a total population of less than 15 million, could not really be expected to finance all the logistical support for, and maintenance of 40 000 troops in six or so African states. It is a similar convergence of interests that often allows Saudi Arabia and Egypt to 'front' for the United States in Africa.

Because of lack of viable economic and political springboards in Africa, Soviet and Chinese support has typically taken the form of military aid. This policy also constitutes a strategy of deliberate cultivation initially of disengagement by African states from their chronic Western dependency and later, whenever possible, of turning such states into permanent allies or dependencies of the Soviet bloc. Given the Sino-Soviet rift and consequent 'competitive socialist imperialism' in Africa, there now is opposition between Cuba and the USSR on the one hand and China on the other. But this is reflective of the pursuit of divergent national interests by these countries in Africa. Such national interests are not always intrinsically congruent with African interests.

What has made Soviet, Cuban and Chinese military support in Africa generally acceptable is the geopolitical situation of Southern Africa: Cuba, the USSR and China all identify their national interests in Africa ideologically and militarily with African self-determination. Given the overriding concern of African states about racism it is clear that whichever foreign power actively supports African aspirations in Southern Africa is likely to gain tremendous favour with many African states, including those that may have strong reservations about 'communism'.

It can be taken as a general foreign policy guide that no external power which finds itself on the wrong side of the racial and decolonisation questions in Southern Africa can gain much favour with most of Black Africa. This is the predicament of the US and other Western powers. Their public rhetoric and democratic posturing notwithstanding, they are all generally on the wrong side of these issues. Until these are resolved successfully, Western historical and traditional structural advantages in Africa are not likely to be sufficient to enable them to compete with a Soviet Union which is ready to provide military aid to liberation movements.

Given the Cuban commitment to liberation and genuine revolution in the Third World, the Soviets may not need to send Soviet troops at all. Provision of equipment with their logistical deployment is all that is needed. Whatever the Cubans could not supply, East Germans, North Koreans, Bulgarians, Czechs and even Libyans may be able and willing to supply as conduits for Soviet arms, military advisors and trainers. There is, therefore, nothing startling in the East-West use of proxies in their attempts to penetrate black Africa or to conduct competitive imperialism through military interventions.

On the Soviet side, the estimate of military support from 1971–75 is

$2 billion to 12 countries (Algeria, Angola, Egypt, Guinea-Bissau, Guinea, Libya, Mali, Mozambique, Nigeria, Somalia, Sudan and Uganda).[26] Between 1975 and 1977 an estimated $1 billion was spent on military installations and military base facilities in Somalia before the Soviets were suddenly and unceremoniously ejected in November 1977. From 1975 to mid-1979 the Soviet Union provided about $2 billion worth of aid, mostly military, to Ethiopia. What must be noted is that the Cubans, Russians and Chinese have very little direct investment in Africa. For instance, the Tanzam railway, built by the Chinese to link Zambia and Tanzania, was not carried out as a form of investment but rather in the form of aid. Thus, it is always relatively easy to dislodge the Chinese and the Russians as has happened in Egypt, Ghana, Guinea, Somalia and Sudan. Military aid alone does not achieve the same degree of deep-rooted penetration that years of interrelated economic, political and educational investment by the West have already achieved in Africa.

The situation in the Horn of Africa creates paradoxes of its own. Somalia's irredentism led to an invasion of Ethiopia's Ogaden Province in support of the self-determination or 'liberation' movement of the Somali people who live in Ogaden. Regardless of the historical claims of the Somalis to Greater Somalia, this was clearly a violation of international law, the UN charter and the OAU charter. The latter charter has declared all existing colonial boundaries in Africa inviolate; only mutually satisfactory, peaceful means may be used to adjust such boundaries.

This condition notwithstanding, Somalia invaded Ethiopia; and the West once again found itself on the wrong side. Soviet-Cuban support was on the side of territorial integrity and the national sovereignty of Ethiopia. The US even persuaded Egypt, Iran, Saudi Arabia and Sudan to send aid to Somalia. The American media spoke almost exclusively of a Soviet-Cuban threat to Somalia as if Ethiopia was the aggressor. Cuban troop participation in that war could not be flawed by any African government although the situation led to the increasing dependency of Ethiopia on Cuba and Russia. The West was more concerned about the geostrategic location of Ethiopia and Somalia in relation to the oil resources of the Persian Gulf and the energy needs of Western nations. So the Western definition of national interest overlooked international law and simple justice and hence failed to impress African states.

It is also this concern for Western geostrategic interests in Southern Africa that is producing the current flow of events in South Africa and Namibia. The Western solution in Zimbabwe was partly a product of panic diplomacy and partly of Western double-think. That solution was not seriously enforced on the white rebels in Zimbabwe but it had the effect of preventing the 'Cuban-Soviet army from gaining control' of the Patriotic Front. This not only bought time for Ian Smith and the betrayal called the internal settlement; it also paved the way for Smith's 'democratic elections' in December 1978, after which the 'democratic government of Rhodesia' was expected to be recognised promptly by Western countries. In the end, regardless of any decisions to carry on the armed struggle, the Patriotic Front could have been betrayed and left in the cold. A 'moderate government' dominated by a constitutionally entrenched white minority with military and economic control for not less than ten years, would then have helped to 'stabilise' the Southern African frontier against 'communist aggression'. In the end the strategy failed badly. Namibia faces a similar situation, and it appears that it may be muddled sufficiently to allow a combination of externally-sponsored factionalism within SWAPO, and new 'democratic' fronts sponsored by South Africa and Western penetration to entrench a non-revolutionary or non-socialist conservative regime in Namibia. Such clandestine manoeuvres led to the promotion of linkage policy by Western powers in Namibia: Namibian independence has been tied to withdrawal of Cuban forces from Angola. Finally, Western diplomatic strategy calls for the support of *apartheid* South Africa in implementing Western blueprints for freedom in Namibia. If South Africa granted such support to 'sacrifice' fellow whites in Zimbabwe one conjecture is that the price for that support would be Western agreement to prevent non-peaceful change in South Africa itself. Of course, peaceful change must be understood in this context to mean white supremacy forever and African dismemberment and slavery in perpetuity. These are the stakes that are enough to force African armed struggles into receiving military aid from the devil, if that is what it would take to reject slavery and racist oppression.

American policy to encourage increased Chinese activities in Africa is an extension of the logic of Western anti-Soviet strategies in Southern Africa. US policy-makers welcomed the visit of Chinese officials to Zaire immediately after the Shaba crisis in June 1978. The move was seen in the West as part of a transformed foreign policy orientation and perception among the new Chinese leadership. It was supposed to signal a broader, more open interaction with the rest of the world. Some saw it as an end to China's cultivated isolationism of the Mao era. This has led to increased co-operation between the Reagan administration and the reformist Chinese leadership since 1981.

But the Chinese outward venture, signified by the visits of the Chinese Communist Party Chairman, Hua Kuo-Feng to Warsaw Pact countries of Romania and Yugoslavia, and to Iran, along with the 'treaty of peace and friendship' with Japan in 1978, is clearly in China's anti-Soviet tradition. Peking's global strategy seems

> designed gradually to limit the political and military strength of the Warsaw Pact countries. Hua has made it clear that China is seeking new allies of any political colour who can help provide the technology needed to present a modern and effective challenge to Russia.[27]

This appeal went to Europe, Asia and Africa in China's attempt to wage an ideological campaign against Soviet global hegemony.

This is what is described as the 'China Card' among foreign policy strategists in the US. The encouragement of the Chinese anti-Soviet campaign in Africa is therefore conceived as a strategy to forge a possible encirclement and isolation of the USSR as a means of curbing the expansion of Soviet imperialism in Asia and Africa. Western policy strategists may have concluded that if this China Card could be played successfully against the Soviets in Africa, especially in Southern Africa, then the West could easily return to deal with the Chinese presence later. After all, China does not seem capable of backing its African friends with the same degree of committed support and massive military hardware. Even *apartheid* South Africa, the most anti-communist campaigner among the Western bloc, seems to be nonchalant about the 'Chinese threat' in Africa. This new posture, along with the unholy 'alliance' between China, South Africa and the US in the continuing destabilisation war against the Angolan government confirms the view that not only is morality seen as irrelevant to foreign policy but also that internal consistency in the application of general principles is of little account in the deadly game of global competitive imperialism. It may be that Chinese communism is preferable to Soviet communism in Africa. But to accuse the West of ideological inconsistency in the encouragement of increased Chinese influence in Africa not only ignores the single-mindedly anti-Soviet nature of the campaign, but exposes the moral posturing of African powerlessness as well.

Many have advocated a shift in US policy to a clear alignment with the forces of liberation in South Africa.[28] Only this kind of policy has any real chance of preventing continued Soviet penetration and influence in the region, while serving to enlarge those areas of shared interest between African and Western nations. However, it is almost impossible to imagine how Western countries could provide military aid to Africans in any fight against white racism in South Africa in sufficient magnitude to bring down the *apartheid* regime. Continuing military co-operation between South Africa and the West, including the development of nuclear reactors and research, suggests that the West may yet remain Africa's greatest oppressor into the 21st century.

It is within this context of international co-operative-competitive imperialism that African powerlessness and disunity must be viewed. The francophone states are, with a few exceptions, aligned with the West, with France as their 'moral' and diplomatic leader. They form the core of the conservative bloc with Egypt, Morocco, Sudan, Zaire and others. The radical states have socialist ideological orientations that push them towards the Soviet bloc. Included in this group are Angola, Algeria, Ethiopia, Guinea, Guinea-Bissau, Libya, Mozambique (Somalia until 1977) and Tanzania. The 'moderates', represented by Ghana, Nigeria, Zambia and so on, are in the middle. As the July 1978 Khartoum OAU conference indicated, the debate over foreign intervention has exposed the OAU's structural vulnerability, Africa's disunity, and the use of African states as agents of competitive foreign penetration of the continent.

Even before that OAU meeting, a conference of francophone African heads of states in Paris in June 1978 and the NATO conference earlier in the US all led to the bizarre suggestion that the West should sponsor a Pan-African Security Force to protect Africa from communist domination. The OAU as an organisation was not even consulted. The irony was pregnant with danger and African self-degradation: in 1885 Europe dismembered Africa at a Berlin Conference; in 1978 Europe and America meeting in Paris, agreed to sponsor an all-African force that could go anywhere to deter aggression in Africa. This is a legacy of the Shaba conflicts of 1977 and 1978.

If a Western-sponsored All-African Force or Military Alliance is considered the 'height of arrogance', as President Nyerere termed it, then the effective military participation of Cuba in protecting African states can also be viewed as a source of embarrassment to African dignity and self-identity. Angola has nearly 20 million people, Cuba has less than 15 million. Ethiopia has over 35 million people, Egypt has at least 40 million and Nigeria had about 100 million people in 1987. Nigeria alone has close to 200 000 troops. Moreover, most African states achieved independence only a few years after the Cuban revolution. Yet Cuban soldiers are needed to fight imperialism in Angola and Ethiopia. Nigeria alone has eight times more people than Cuba. What then explains this paralysing powerlessness and lack of commitment among Africans towards their own liberation? Whatever the explanation, it remains a fact of African weakness and vulnerability that such a small country as Cuba should have to be relied upon to give Africa a little sense of military competence to engage the forces of continued domination and exploitation.

This pattern of events must be disconcerting to all who believe that ultimately Africans are the only people who can, through their own commitments, assure Africa's final decolonisation and independence. As the phenomenon of unrelenting revolutionary rebellion by the black youths of South Africa shows, the drive for African freedom and self-determination must never be allowed to remain perilously in the hands of external forces to supply the commitment to die in order for Africans to assert their human rights. In the same spirit, African and Soviet-Cuban national interests cannot always remain in convergence. In the end Africa must justify its right to freedom and independence through its own children's commitment to blood and tears, and, if necessary, to the efficacy of death, in order that racial enslavement be finally terminated. This is the inescapable challenge for Africa and African leaders as they journey into the 21st century.

NOTES

1. See Peter C. W. Gutkind and Immanuel Wallerstein (eds), *The Political Economy of Contemporary Africa* (Beverly Hills: Sage, 1976); Dennis L. Cohen and John Daniel (eds), *Political Economy of Africa* (New York: Longman, 1981); Timothy M. Shaw, *Towards a Political Economy for Africa* (New York: St. Martin's Press, 1985).
2. See Ladun Anise, 'The Collapse of Portugal's Illusive African Empire', *Black World*, August 1974.
3. Ladun Anise, 'Prospects for Future Superpower Intervention in Africa', *Issue*, 8(4) (Winter 1978) 35–9. See also Gerard Chaliand, *The Struggle for Africa* (New York, St. Martin's Press, 1982); A.T. Asiwaju, *Partitioned Africans* (New York, St. Martin's Press, 1985);

D. F. Luke and T. M. Shaw (eds), *Continental Crisis* (Washington: University of America Press, 1984).

4. Consider the role of Jonas Savimbi in Angola and the war of destabilisation funded first by South Africa and finally by the United States in 1986. A similar role is played in Chad by France, the United States and Libya, each having a different leader to support in one of Africa's longest civil wars.
5. Cyrus Vance, 'Elements of US Policy Toward the Soviet Union', 19 June 1978, Bureau of Public Affairs, Washington D.C., 3.
6. One can compare President Reagan's support for Savimbi in Angola as a 'freedom fighter' with his opposition to the African National Congress (ANC) of South Africa as a 'terrorist, communist organisation'. Even the meeting with Oliver Tambo by the US Secretary of State George Shultz in February 1987 did not earn open endorsement from the President, nor did the President criticise the harsh conservative denunciation of the meeting and Shultz's role in promoting it.
7. Robert L. Butterworth, *Managing Interstate Conflict, 1945–1974* (Pittsburgh: University Center for International Studies, 1976).
8. Ibid., 369–71.
9. Ibid., 156–8, 219–21.
10. Ibid., 187–90; Mohamed Alwan, *Algeria Before the United Nations* (New York: Speller, 1959); A.S. Heggoy, *Insurgency and Counter Insurgency in Algeria* (Bloomington: Indiana University Press, 1972).
11. See Arthur J. Klinghoffer, *The Angolan War* (Boulder: Westview, 1980); Fola Soremekun, *Angola: Road to Independence* (Ile-Ife: University of Ife Press, 1985).
12. Butterworth, *Managing Interstate Conflict*, 234–5, 314–16.
13. Ibid., 392.
14. See *New Africa*, November 1979, 33–45. The French support for Habré in Chad made all the difference in his defeat of Weddeye and subsequent control of the Presidency. Early in January 1987 it was reported that French troops stationed in Chad had launched an attack on Libyan troop positions in the north of Chad.
15. *To the Point International*, 2 June 1978, 10.
16. See Oye Ogunbadejo, 'Conflict in Africa: A Case Study of the Shaba Crisis, 1977', *World Affairs*, 141(3) (Winter 1979) 219–34.
17. This can be illustrated by the rivalry between France, Belgium and the United States over controlling economic and political influences in Zaire from 1965 to 1977 when United States influence became predominant.
18. *Africa*, no. 99 (November 1979) 17–18; *New Africa* (December 1979) 28–9.
19. *To the Point International*, 2 June 1978, 10. For more detailed exposition of such security problems see J. Rohr (ed.), *Problems of Africa: Opposing Viewpoints* (St. Paul, Minnesota: Greenhaven Press, 1986); Leslie Macfarlen, *Violence and the State* (London: Thomas Nelson, 1974); M. T. Klare and C. Arnson, *Supplying Repression: U. S. Support for Authoritarian Regimes Abroad* (Washington, D. C. : Institute for Policy Studies, 1981); Abdul-Monem M. Al-Mashat,

National Security in the Third World (Boulder: Westview, 1985); Bruce E. Arlinghaus, *Military Development in Africa* (Boulder: Westview, 1984); and Bruce E. Arlinghaus, (ed.), *African Security Issues* (Boulder: Westview, 1984).

20. *The Advocate*, 3 August 1978.
21. A case in point is the pledge of $15 million to Savimbi on his visit to the White House in 1986, as part of President Reagan's global sponsorship of 'freedom fighters'. The US also tried but failed to use Egypt as a proxy to declare war on Libya in 1986. *CBS 60 Minutes*, 22 February 1987.
22. United States Senate, 'US Corporate Interests in South Africa: Report of the Committee on Foreign Relations', Washington, D.C. (January 1978) 173–87. The United States Congress finally passed a sanctions bill against South Africa over President Reagan's veto in 1986.
23. See *Newsweek*, 20 January 1986, 14–21; *Time Magazine*, 21 April 1986, 18–27; *CBS 60 Minutes*, 22 February 1987.
24. *Newsweek*, 31 July 1978, 32.
25. Cole Blasier, 'Cubans in Africa: A Time for Quiet Diplomacy', *Washington Post*, 20 June 1978.
26. Africa Freedom Foundation, *Africa Freedom Annual, 1977*, 65–80.
27. *To the Point International*, 25 August 1978, 14.
28. Perhaps Secretary of State Shultz's meeting with ANC President Oliver Tambo is a small beginning towards such a policy shift.

8 France's Africa: A Struggle between Exclusivity and Interdependence

Emeka Nwokedi

The complexion and the complexity of France's relations with Sub-Saharan African states are controversial subjects both within and outside the political framework of the Hexagon itself. The left-wing coalition in the French political spectrum has often criticised these relationships as being paternalistic and neo-colonialist.[1] For their part, the right-wing parties consider them to be nothing to have a guilty complex about and, in fact, congratulate themselves for having granted independence to the African states in an atmosphere of 'friendship and mutual respect'.[2]

This disagreement notwithstanding, the two sides to this essentially electoral debate accept the fact that for historical, economic, cultural and geo-strategic reasons, Africa remains a critical factor in the definition and determination of France's global foreign policy. The importance of Africa to France and the latter's perception of its role in the former, find common, albeit, disquieting expression in the words of former French Minister of Foreign Affairs, the late Louis de Guiringaud, who submitted that:

> Africa is too close to us [Europeans] and its populations too marked by European colonisation that we cannot but look after its future.[3]

As patronising and global as this assertion is, the concept of Africa to French foreign policy-makers has, until recently, had a narrow definition and a restrictive application. Africa was synonymous with black Africa and referred specifically to Sub-Saharan francophone states. These were carefully distinguished from the Anglophone states especially and also, from the states of the Maghreb. The implication of this conception was that although France maintained economic relations with other Sub-Saharan African states, it was only within the black francophone states (with few exceptions) that it strove strenuously to maintain its incontestable position of influence and dominance.

The objective of this chapter, therefore, is to discern and to analyse the varying patterns and dimensions of France's high profile in Africa against the background of its interests and motivations. It will be argued that although France's quest for exclusive relationships with Sub-Saharan francophone states reinforces its influence in these states and bolsters its confidence in dealings with both African and extra-African powers, this posture is at once a limitation to and tends somewhat to contradict its ambition of projecting itself in the continent as an *interlocuteur valable* within a EuroAfrican framework of interdependence. It will equally be argued that this contemporary stance is as much self-interested as it is reflective of France's increasing perception of Africa through a Cold War ideological prism. The first part of this essay will examine the exclusive links, while the second will concern itself with analysing the forms and substance of the interdependent drive. The essay terminates with a look at the likely future course of French African policy.

PATTERNS OF EXCLUSIVITY

The independence of the French-speaking African states in 1960 (Guinea became independent in 1958) signalled the collapse of the ephemeral French community which, as a constitutional arrangement, had been designed to conciliate at once the demand of the African states for independence and the reluctance of France to supervise, as it were, the loss of its erstwhile African possessions. The dissatisfaction of the African states over the working of this compromise arrangement was to lead inevitably to their attainment of full, formal political sovereignty in 1960.

The counterpart of this independence, however, was the French insistence that the African states enter into a series of bilateral and multilateral co-operation accords with it before acceding to full sovereignty. As has been pointed out by several analysts,[4] independence and the co-operation accords were interwoven; the acceptance of the latter by these states was a precondition for their attainment of the former. Although the co-operation accords were designed to serve as a new legal framework for Franco-African relations after independence, the circumstances under which these were signed as well as their operation have clearly made a mockery of this independence. The accords covered such areas as Franco-African monetary relations, military co-operation agreements including defence treaties, economic, cultural and political relations as well as other forms of technical assistance agreements.

The underlining motivations for these co-operation accords have received the attention of analysts and commentators.[5] Most reject the altruistic image often painted by French authorities of their actions. There is, to begin with, the factor of exercising political as well as economic control over the territorial expanse that constitutes France's privileged zone of influence in Africa. The Sub-Saharan francophone states are 'privileged' markets for, on the one hand, the supply of primary raw materials to the metropole and, on the other, for the absorption of French-manufactured exports and capital investments. It has been estimated that France's dependence on the African states for the supply of certain minerals and commodities is 100 per cent for cobalt, 87 to 100 per cent for uranium, 83 per cent for phosphate, 68 per cent for bauxite, 100 per cent for groundnut oil, 50 per cent for coffee and 35 per cent for cocoa.[6]

Moreover, the French have had a standing tradition under colonialism of cultural, political and economic protectionism. The adoption of the co-operation accords, therefore, conforms to this practice in so far as it seeks to continue attaching these states to the apron-strings of the metropole by 'protecting' them from cultural 'dilution' and political penetration by its rivals. This phenomenon is more poignantly illustrated by examining aspects of Franco-African monetary, economic, politico-military and cultural relations.

THE FRANC ZONE: PERPETUATION OF NEO-COLONIALISM

The importance of money both as a symbol and a concrete manifestation of national sovereignty can hardly be over-stressed. French transactions with Sub-Saharan francophone states (excepting Guinea and laterly Mauritania) come under the framework of the Franc zone monetary arrangement. The Franc zone is a multilateral monetary co-operation agreement which links France with, besides the overseas departments (DOM-TOM), the West African francophone states on the one hand, and with the Central African French-speaking states on the other. In other words, the Sub-Saharan francophone states emit through their separate issuing authorities and utilise a common currency — the CFA (*Communauté Financière Africaine* franc — which is tied to the metropolitan franc.

Although the Franc zone had its origins in French colonial practice, the post-independent transformation of the *Colonies Francaises Africaines* to Communauté Financière Africaine was supposed to have marked the beginning of a new era in Franco-African monetary relations. This was only a symbolic gesture, however, because the objective of protectionism is still assured by this arrangement, as was the case in the past. The principles which govern the operation of this monetary arrangement attest to this. First, there is a fixed parity between the metropolitan Franc and the CFA Franc and this is unaffected by the tribulation to which the former has been subjected ever since it floated in the early 1970s. Second, there is free convertibility and unlimited monetary transfers between member-states of the Franc zone. Third, member-states operate a common external reserve and France guarantees foreign payments made by members of the zone even when the accounts of the two African central banks lodged with the French Treasury are in deficit. Finally, there is a commitment to co-ordinate monetary and financial policies.

However, before the 1973–74 revision of the Franc zone arrangement, and ever since, it was and still is recognised that the system put the participating African states in a situation of inequality and dependence on France.[7] The French guarantee of the CFA Franc was not without its counterpart; France has the right to control the monetary policy of its African partners in order to avoid having to cover the deficits which result from their deliberate pursuit of inflationary policies.[8] Factors such as these have led Tchundjang Pouemi to comment sarcastically that France has succeeded as the only country in the world to 'realise the extraordinary feat of getting its money, and nothing else but its money in use in otherwise independent countries'.[9]

This has meant that the French do not worry unnecessarily about payments in their transactions with the African states since these do not involve the use of foreign exchange. The 1973–74 reform of the West and Central African components of the Franc zone has permitted the Central banks of the West (BCEAO) and of the Central (BCEAC) African states to place respectively 35 per cent and 20 per cent of their external assets in currencies other than the French Franc. Even then, there is a proviso that in the event of a foreign exchange squeeze on these states, they must first exhaust the reserves denominated in other currencies before addressing themselves to the French Treasury.

On balance, it is more convincing to argue that these reforms were cosmetic since the fundamental issues of fixed parity and unlimited convertibility and transfers were never called into question. The transfer of the headquarters of the two Central Banks to African capitals (Dakar and Yaounde, respectively) and the increase in African membership within their separate *Conseil d'Administration* are symbolic concessions because France still wields a decisive influence in formulating monetary policies within the Franc zone as a whole.

Furthermore, the African states are not totally protected from the adverse consequences arising from the devaluation of the French Franc, which has suffered four such devaluations in the period 1981–87. Although the external reserves of the African states denominated in French Francs are cushioned from such devaluations through a system of calculation based on the value of the Special Drawing Rights and the European Unit of Account, the foreign debt as well as payments on goods and services (especially petrol) denominated in currencies other than the metropolitan Franc (US dollar) suffer from such devaluations, which increase indebtedness. Here, the only obligation on France is merely to *consult* with its African partners before taking any decision which would 're-align' its currency within the European Monetary System.[10] The African states can neither block such devaluations nor seek compensation thereafter.

In the light of this, Ondo-Ossa and Lapiquonne lament what they describe as the

> distortion which exists between money and economy in the Franc zone (where) monetary power is in the hands of France which has interests and objectives different from and antagonistic to those of the African member-states. [Thus, the African states] lose an essential attribute of their sovereignty and certainly, the cornerstone for a self-reliant development.[11]

It is the control exercised by the French in these monetary matters, as well as the extra risks coverage granted to metropolitan exporters by the *Compagnie Francaise d'Assurance de Commerce Extérieur* (COFACE) — the equivalent of the British Export Credit Guarantee

Department — which has made the Franc zone the basic field (*pré carré*) for French economic investments.

Within the framework of the comprehensive co-operation accords, French public agencies, parastatals, and private industrial, commercial and banking multinationals virtually dominated and still dominate the commanding heights of the economies of many of the French-speaking Sub-Saharan states. Before the revision of the co-operation accords in the 1970s, the French monopolised, through their Atomic Energy Agency, the mining of strategic minerals located within the francophone states and could stop their export to rival countries. In Niger Republic, for instance, it was Hamani Diori's insistence on reviewing upwards the price fixed and paid for Niger's uranium by the French that contributed to his overthrow in 1974.[12] Even under the present circumstances, the French can still have their way by virtue of the top priority accorded them by these African states under the framework of their special relationship and do enter into long-term procurement contracts with this same group of states in order to control price increases on materials imported from them.

It is a reflection of the huge economic interests at stake in these African states that France has always been willing to meet shortfalls in the budgetary provisions of some of these states. More importantly, it has continued to channel public assistance in addition to encouraging the flow of private investments from the centre to the African periphery as a means of, at least, shoring up favourite regimes among the francophone states.[13] The degree of French commitment to some of the African governments has tended to vary slightly between the successive presidencies but this is more a matter of form than of substance. Whatever differences there are always get straightened out as a result of the over-riding economic interests and, for the African leaders, of the regime interests at stake.

In summary, the over-arching framework provided by the Franc zone arrangement as well as the various other aspects of the co-operation accords, 'softens' the ground for further French penetration and control of the economies of the francophone states. It is doubtful whether the French would exercise the same degree of control without these arrangements. In spite of the successes which the French have recorded in economic links with other parts of Africa (Nigeria, for example), the major stumbling block for them in such places is the absence of comparative political, economic, financial and cultural control as in the francophone states. The quest for control which, essentially, is neo-colonialist, is tied up with the quest for exclusivity and this is most evident in the area of political and military relations.

POLITICO-MILITARY RELATIONS

Political and military relations between France and the Sub-Saharan francophone states complement and, indeed, constitute the protective shell for the wide-range of economic and cultural links between these partners. Military relations in particular have been covered either by the technical co-operation agreements or by the mutual defence treaties between France and these states. These relations serve diverse functions (see previous chapter).

First, they are used to prop up regimes or African leaders who are the 'trusted allies' of France on the continent. This is an insurance for the African states against domestic political instability. French military actions in Cameroon against the guerrillas of the *Union des Populations du Cameroun* (UPC) between the late 1950s and the early 1960s and also its military intervention in Gabon in 1964 to restore Leon Mba to power come within this category. Conversely, France has used the military dimensions of its African relations to oust leaders whose stay in office has become increasingly perceived by this European power as a threat to its economic and strategic interests. The *coups d'état* which removed Modibo Keita of Mali (1968), Hamani Diori of Niger (1974), Maurien Ngouabi of Congo Republic (1977), Moktar Ould Daddah of Mauritania (1978) and Jean-Bedel Bokassa of Central African Republic (1979) from power belong to this caterogy.[14]

Furthermore, military interventions or even the mere stationing of French troops within the territories of some of the French-speaking African states serve to guarantee France's widely-dispersed interests on the continent.[15] The military bases in Senegal, Cote d'Ivoire, Gabon and Central African Republic protect French economic interests especially in the first three states, but also in the neighbouring francophone states, while the bases in Djibouti, Comoro Islands (Mayette) and Réunion respond more to other strategic considerations and to great power rivalry in both the Indian Ocean and the Red Sea.

But, considerably more reprehensible have been the interventions which have supposedly sought to arrest the threat of generalised destabilisation within the continent. French interventions in Mauritania against the Polisario Front and in Chad against Libyan-backed opponents of the central government in N'djamena are eloquent examples.[16] While such interventions have often raised more problems than they have solved, it is clear that the underlying motive is France's self-interest. Apart from the desire to maintain either the territorial integrity of such states or to provide protection for one or other favoured regime, such interventions send signals to other francophone states to the effect that the metropole is both willing and able to come to their aid whenever they are threatened, in conformity with obligations arising from the military agreements between them.

On other occasions intervention has responded to the wider issue of East-West, NATO-Warsaw Pact rivalry, as was the case in Chad to some extent, but also in France's decision to intervene in the Shaba uprisings in Zaire.[17] Although France's declared objective, especially when it intervened directly in Shaba in 1978, was to 'safeguard French and foreign [mainly European] residents of Kolwezi', this was a mere camouflage and was not quite the interpretation given to its actions by some African states. The Zairean Head of State, Mobutu Sese Seko, for example, was to declare that while the rest of the West had shied away from its responsibilities, 'France alone dared to stand up against the Cubans and the Russians'[18] who were said to have trained and armed the dissidents normally harboured by Angola.

While many African states openly voiced their opposition to French interventions in Zaire, especially as these had received the tacit and active support of, respectively, some European NATO member-countries and of the United States, the then Senegalese Prime Minister, Abdou Diouf, was stupefied by these criticisms. In an interview which he granted to the influential French independent daily, *Le Monde*, during the 1977 annual Franco-African summit he said:

> We do not understand the protestations generated by the French decision to give logistic support to the Moroccans engaged in action in Zaire. Indifference constitutes a dangerous attitude for the West and it is necessary to end this wait-and-see attitude or see the whole of Africa run the risk of becoming communist.[19]

Abdou Diouf's position is hardly surprising. French interventions in Chad in particular have been openly solicited and endorsed by the so-called 'moderate' French-speaking African states such as Senegal,

Cote d'Ivoire, and Gabon which, with Cameroon,[20] constitute the core of French economic investments in Sub-Saharan Africa. The interventions in Zaire and Chad (Operation Manta) betray a growing tendency by France to view such conflicts as arising from ideological polarisation.

These military interventions have not always been based on a solid legal foundation. There is no defence co-operation agreement linking France with Zaire, neither is there any between it and Chad.[21] This does not, however, rule out the existence of secret defence treaties between France and these countries. While France has responded to such situations at the supposedly express request of the governments concerned, the scale of these operations constitutes in the absence of a formal agreement, an interference in the domestic political processes of these states. But these interventions come generally within the overall French ambition of safeguarding France's 'sphere of influence' on the continent, and in this way it portrays itself as a fire-fighting interlocuteur between the Western alliance and the rest of the continent. The quest for exclusivity has its cultural dimensions, too.

CULTURE AS AN INSTRUMENT OF DOMINANCE

The power of culture in international relations is not just acknowledged by the French but effectively utilised, perhaps more than by any other ex-colonial power, in fostering its economic objectives and in foisting upon the global arena its identity and world view. Although the French have since abandoned the cultural policy of assimilation conceived for the colonised peoples, its contemporary cultural policy aims at spreading and perpetuating the French language and culture in the world, educating (African) élites in French institutions and, through these, aiding the process of expansion of French international trade.[22]

The centrality of culture in Franco-African relations is greatly emphasised. Indeed, that there are privileged or close relations at all between these partners is a reflection of the cultural affinity which colonialism achieved through the French language. The francophone African states including Guinea under Sékou Touré use the French language exclusively or in conjunction with another, as their official or working language, but most certainly as their language of instruction. Most of these African states are involved with France within the framework of the *Agence de Coopération Culturelle et Technique* (ACCT) which oversees among other functions, administrative and technical training of cadres from these states.

For most of these African states, the primary to tertiary education syllabuses are patterned after that of the metropole and, in fact, African students still write the same final examinations as their French High School counterparts. Their legal, financial and administrative systems reflect the traditions well-established in the metropole itself. These incidences of cultural affinity are no doubt instrumental in the decision of the worldwide French-speaking states to inaugurate, after several postponements, the francophone summit in February 1986. While it is still too early to determine the overall impact of this organisation, the wish by African participants, as expressed by Senegal, to conceive it as a 'conscious realisation of our solidarity and our fraternity'[23] portrays both its exclusive thrust and its long-term economic and political undertones. It met for a second time in Quebec City in Canada in September 1987.

The pursuit by France of 'privileged' and exclusive relations with its Sub-Saharan francophone partners has served, as has already been analysed, to maintain these areas as its zone of influence or *chasse gardée*. While this policy has favoured some African leaders, it has generally placed limitations on the independence of decision and action of some African states over economic (financial) and defence policies in particular. Moreover, France's resort to either political manipulation through an expansive network of personal links or to military intervention as the major instruments of pursuing this policy has not always gone down well with every African state; neither has the ideological coloration subsumed under such actions.

In another vein, this policy would appear to have impeded the development of French policy (or non-policy), at least before the emergence of Georges Pompidou as French president, towards non-francophone African states. Part of De Gaulle's hostility towards Nigeria, for example, was seen in his determination to dismantle the 'giant' federation in order to check its eventual emergence as a rival to France in the smaller and weaker francophone states which surround it.[24]

Be that as it may, the fact that the Sub-Saharan francophone states themselves clamoured for a revision of the co-operation accords in the 1970s, is proof that the utility to them of the policy of exclusivity itself is doubtful. As the late Hamani Diori of Niger put it:

> If, as the official thesis affirms, the goal of Co-operation is to enable our states one day to forego external assistance, quite honestly, this objective will be very difficult to achieve within the framework of the present system of development assistance. This, no doubt, permits us to keep our head above the water but cannot give us the necessary strength to arrive at the shore . . .[25]

But even with these revisions settled, the modalities of Franco-African relations which still leave France with a high profile on the continent induce one to agree with Albert Bourgi that 'Co-operation appears as the pursuit of colonialism by other methods'.[26] It would appear, therefore, that in order to overcome self-imposed limitations the French have since 1972 consistently sought to widen their field of operation within the continent.

DIMENSIONS AND PROBLEMS OF INTERDEPENDENCE

The overtures towards non-francophone African states were initiated by Georges Pompidou and have been carried forward by his successors. The underlying motivation was economic. In an increasingly competitive international environment, especially that between the industrial countries, the French can only ignore to their commercial detriment the vast markets which exist outside France's traditional sphere of influence on the continent. The thrust of this interdependence can be analysed under four broad categories: (1) France's relations with Anglophone states, particularly with Nigeria; (2) the incremental absorption into the francophone fold of countries where Belgian and Spanish influence had higherto predominated; (3) to a lesser degree, its relations with apartheid South Africa; and (4) finally, France's continental posturing both as the intermediary between the West and the rest of Africa and as the champion of Third World causes.

France's political relations with Nigeria have, in the past, always been difficult. It was part of the former's exclusive francophone policy which led it, we have noted, to adopt a hostile attitude towards Nigeria during the Biafran drama. The fear of Nigerian intrusion into, and indeed domination of, the francophone states was to induce France to oppose, at least initially, the establishment of the Economic Community of West African States (ECOWAS), co-sponsored by Nigeria and Togo.

Beginning in 1973, Nigeria was to emerge as an important African oil producing and exporting country. Neither the francophone states which surround it nor France itself could ignore the potentialities and, for the latter, the opportunities for investments and export-markets which Nigeria represents. The Arab oil boycott of 1973–74 but also the generally tense political situation in the Middle East was to make Nigeria an important supplier of petroleum to France. By 1976 the value and the volume of Franco-Nigerian commercial exchanges (petroleum for consumer durables and non-durables) surpassed those of France's exchanges with any of the Sub-Saharan francophone states. With about 130 French firms currently active in diverse sectors of the Nigerian economy and either having executed or still executing multi-million dollar construction contracts, France has emerged, since the 1980s, as Nigeria's second supplier after Britain and its second customer after the United States.[27]

It is a mark of recognition of Nigeria's stabilising role in Africa and, particularly within the West African subregion, that France has tried to involve it in the process of resolving the Chadian conflict. While fears remain within some French circles over Nigeria's long-term regional ambitions, France would want to see Nigeria act more decisively as a counterweight to Libya's Sub-Saharan ambitions which directly threaten its interests in the francophone states.

All the same, while the new thrust in French African policy is notionally designed neither to contradict nor to dilute established exclusive relations with francophone states, this cannot altogether be avoided. On this point both French leaders and particularly the leaders of the francophone states appear to be in agreement. Alarmed at the phenomenal growth of Franco-Nigerian exchanges, Sedar Senghor, then President of Senegal, was to complain that France was becoming 'more dynamic in Nigeria than in the black francophone countries'.[28] French leaders have since reaffirmed that co-operation with non-francophone African states can never assume the same level of closeness as that between their country and the francophone states and that, in any event, the latter group of states has *absolute* priority in the disbursement of French aid to African states.[29]

If France's thrust towards the anglophone states is somehow problematic for the francophone states, the same cannot be said for its overtures towards Zaire, Burundi and Rwanda — all French-speaking states — and Equatorial Guinea. The task of 'absorbing' the first group of states into the francophone fold has been facilitated by cultural affinity which the French language permits. Also, this has been aided by the fact that for both groups of states, their ex-colonial powers — Belgium and Spain respectively, — have relatively weaker and isolated capability credentials on the continent and this is further compounded by the turbulant relations which have existed or exist between these and the African states.

For France, the vast mineral resources in both Zaire and Equatorial Guinea (petroleum, fishing and so on) and the market potentials of Zaire were determinant factors in extending the co-operation arrangement to these states. French military interventions in Zaire in both 1977 and 1978 might not have had immediate economic justifications[30] but they do have long-term economic implications. While it is yet too early to assess adequately the overall significance of Equatorial Guinea's adhesion to the Franc zone monetary arrangement through its membership of the Central Bank of the Central African States (BCEAC), there is no doubt that the foundation for eventual French supremacy in that country has been laid.[31]

The thrust to extend its field of action as in the foregoing instance seems to belie the contention that France acts in Africa with the acquiescence of the Western Alliance. What is clear is that some members of this Alliance approve French actions (the United States provided logistical support for the intervention in Zaire), especially when other European states appear hesitant to adopt the same line of action. But this in no way effaces France's considerable self-interest in such actions and, by this fact, the 'justified' indignation of a country like Belgium whose former Foreign Minister, Renaat Van Eslanade, charged in the aftermath of the Shaba intervention that 'France is particularly interested in Zaire's natural resources and Belgium resents this as international rivalry'.[32]

While interdependence as has been discussed so far is designed to win new African friends for France and to open new markets for its exports, the same cannot be said for its relations with the Republic of South Africa. To be sure, France's relations with South Africa are of long standing and do not fit neatly into this framework. It is, however, convenient for us to employ this term in the sense that the acute rivalry and competition between the Western industrial countries and Japan, especially the rivalry between France and the Anglo-Saxons for the South African market,[33] induces France to build an increasing network of interdependence between itself and South Africa, and this at the risk of offending some Sub-Saharan African states. Whereas such key francophone African countries as Cote d'Ivoire,

Senegal, Gabon and Zaire were in the forefront in the proposition of a policy of dialogue with South Africa, Nigeria in particular had been prepared to reconsider its growing links with France if the latter did not stem its South African connections. Although France was not alone, as has already been indicated, in maintaining significant commercial dealings with the *apartheid* regime in South Africa, its military and nuclear co-operation with Pretoria lacked subtlety, at least before it decided officially in 1977 to join the arms embargo against the latter; a decision that was more symbolic than real.

All the same, the toughening in France's attitude towards Pretoria, especially under the presidency of François Mitterand, has been used to woo African opinion and, particularly, that of the Front Line States for a more positive appreciation of French African policy. On the political front, President Mitterand has been highly critical of the *apartheid* policy. South Africa's obstinacy over independence for Namibia led France to terminate its active membership of the 'contact group' in 1983 as demanded by its black African partners.[34]

On another level, both the Front Line States and several non-francophone states now participate in the annual Franco-African summit which was established in 1973 as a forum between France and its African partners. Although it has always been the desire of French authorities to see this forum enlarged to encompass as many African states as are willing to participate, the closed-door sessions with some Heads of State still distinguish it as a privileged francophone assembly.[35] Moreover, some francophone states have openly expressed the fear that enlarged participation will lead inevitably to a loss of francophone identity.[36] Nevertheless, this gathering is in keeping with the wish expressed by Valery Giscard D'Estaing, former French President, for EurAfrican solidarity on issues of mutual interest such as the North-South dialogue.

In spite of all this, the French authorities should be satisfied with the knowledge that the Franco-African summit attracts increasing participation even when the Organisation of African Unity (OAU) finds it difficult, as was the case in 1982, to attain the quorum for its meeting. The relevance of this annual summit to the African states remains doubtful but there is no gainsaying the fact that France has utilised it most adroitly to project itself as the privileged interlocuteur between the West and the continent and as a sounding board for its Third World propositions. These Third World stances which are peculiar to the socialist government have, however, suffered reverses as a result of pressures from the francophone Africa lobby in Paris.[37]

Considered in its broadest perspective, though interdependence has opened up wider horizons for France it has equally encouraged other challenges to French African policy. It has induced its rivals, for example, to seek to penetrate its traditional zone of influence on the continent. In fact, the expanding economies of such states as Cote d'Ivoire, Togo, Cameroon and Gabon have been increasingly and successfully penetrated by US business interests.[38] This has been, in part, a result of the deliberate policies pursued by the governments of these states, who find the United States, West Germany, Canada and Britain alternative sources of finance and aid, and have used these connections as a leverage in their dealings with France. The pertinent question to ask is whether France can meaningfully sustain the momentum of its diversifications in Africa, especially in the light of the right-wing swing in the metropole?

CONCLUDING REMARKS

One cannot, at present, give a categorical answer to the question posed above. But an examination of the pronouncements and actions of the right-wing government in France, under the leadership of the neo-Gaullist Jacques Chirac (until May 1988), can give some useful indications.[39] First, let it be understood that while the cohabitation arrangement left the French President with a lot of influence in the area of foreign policy, the pronouncements and actions of Chirac suggest that he intended to share the stage with the President in the so-called *domaine réservé* and, more importantly, to exercise considerable clout in Franco-African affairs.

First, the Chirac government restored the autonomy of the Ministry of Co-operation which its Socialist predecessor subordinated to the Ministry of External Affairs in its quest to adopt a Third World, instead of a Franco-francophone Africa approach to aid and development issues. It must be remembered that it was under the right-wing government of Général De Gaulle that the foundation of Franco-African co-operation was laid and that diversification of partners and policies of interdependence were equally initiated by his close associates who later succeeded him. In these circumstances the Ministry of Co-operation has been crucial in implementing French African policy. The new autonomy suggests the determination of the government to revert to the old tradition of ranking Franco-African relations above Third World concerns.

Second, the appointment of Jacques Foccart as a political Adviser to the Prime Minister was not without significance. An old Africa hand, it was Foccart who set up the network of informal penetration and manipulation of the political processes of the African states. While one does not exclude a return to the era of blatant interference and military intervention in African affairs, the signal may be for a more subtle control of intrusions into France's zone of influence.

It remains to be seen, however, how the post-Chirac government will reconcile its fervour with both the interdependent dimensions of its Africa heritage and, particularly, with its ideological (anti-Marxist) perception of the strategic situation in contemporary Africa, especially given the revival of right-wing racism in France in the late 1980s.[40] The French Ambassador to Pretoria, who was withdrawn in 1985 by the Socialist government in protest against South Africa's brutal repression of black protestors following the introduction of a state of emergency, did return to his post. Such actions undertaken by the Chirac government smacked of mercantilist determinism.

While France tries very hard to maintain its dominant role in African affairs, it is clear that it has to depend increasingly on the acquiescence and, at times, on the overt support of its Western allies in order to achieve this objective. Yet, part of France's strategy has been to step, as it were, on the economic and strategic toes of some of these very allies. If France has so far succeeded in exercising economic and cultural hegemony, over the francophone states particularly, this has been because the political leadership in such states 'co-operates' with it *de gré à gré*.

NOTES

1. Parti Socialiste, 'Le Parti Socialiste et l'Afrique sud- Saharienne', *Le Mois en Afrique* (Paris), (June-July 1981) nos. 186–7, 16–20; Jean-Pierre Cot, 'Pour une conception auto-gestionnaire de dévelopment', *Europe Outremer* (Paris), (May 1981) no. 616, 2; Richard Joseph, 'The Gaullist Legacy: Patterns of French Neo-Colonialism', *Review of African Political Economy* (May-August 1976) no. 6, 4–13.
2. RPR, 'La Nouvelle Politique de Coopération du RPR', *Le Mois en Afrique* (April-May 1986) nos. 243–4, 3.
3. Louis de Guiringaud, 'La Politique Africaine de la France', *Politique Etrangère* (Paris) (June 1982) no. 2, 443. My translation as elsewhere in this chapter.
4. See, for example, Albert Bourgi, *La Politique Française de Coopération en Afrique: le cas du Sénégal* (Paris: L.G.D.J., 1979) 3–5.

5. See Brigitte Nouaille-Degorce, *La Politique Française de Coopération avec les Etats Africains et Malgaches au Sud du Sahara 1958–1978* (Bordeaux: CEAN, 1982) 72–100; Bourgi *La Politique Française de coopération en Afrique*; CEAN and Institut Charles de Gaulle, *La Politique Africaine du Général De Gaulle 1958–1969* (Paris: Editions Pedone, 1980) 200–29.
6. Figures from Guy Martin, 'Les Fondements historiques, économiques et politiques de la politique Africaine de la France: du Colonialisme au Néo-colonialisme', *Genève-Afrique*, vol. XXI (1983) no. 2, 51–3; Robert Taton, 'Les Relations Franco-Africaines', *Europe Outremer* (November 1973) no. 526, 18–19.
7. Guy Feuer, 'La Révision des Accords de Coopération Franco-Africains et Franco-Malgache, *Annuaire Français de Droit International* vol. XIX (1973) 733.
8. Ibid.
9. Joseph Tchundjang Pouemi, *Monnaie, Servitude et Liberté; la répression monétaire de l'Afrique* (Paris: Editions Jeune Afrique, 1981) 27.
10. Jacques Alibert, 'La Zone Franc: Intelligence et Réalisme', *Afrique Contemporaine* (Paris) (April-May-June 1983) no. 126, 7.
11. A. Ondo-Ossa and A.T. Lapiquonne, 'Faut-il Réformer la Zone Franc?' *Le Mois en Afrique* (December-January 1984) nos. 215–16, 67.
12. Richard Higgot and Finn Fuglestad, 'The 1974 Coup d'Etat in Niger: Towards an Explanation', *The Journal of Modern African Studies*, vol. 13 (1975) no. 3, 383–98.
13. See Emeka Nwokedi, 'Franco-African Aid Relations', *Conference on Aid and Development in Africa*, University of Ife, May 1985.
14. Martin, 'Les Fondements historiques, économiques et politiques de la politique Africaine de la France', 47.
15. On this see the excellent piece by Robin Luckham, 'French Militarism in Africa', *Review of African Political Economy* (December 1982) no. 24, 55–84.
16. See Pierre Lellouche and Dominic Moisi, 'French Policy in Africa: A Lonely Battle Against Destabilisation', *International Security*, vol. 111 (Spring 1979) no. 4, 108–33; See also David S. Yost, 'French Policy in Chad and the Libyan Challenge', *Orbis*, vol. 26 (Winter 1983) no. 4, 996–7.
17. Bassey Eyo Ate, 'The Presence of France in West-Central Africa as a Fundamental Problem to Nigeria': *Millenium: Journal of International Studies*, vol. 12 (Summer 1983) no. 2, 117.
18. *Africa Research Bulletin*, Political Series, vol. 15 (15 June 1978) no. 5, 4858.
19. Reported in *Afrique Contemporaine*, (May-June 1977) no. 91, 21.
20. Officially, Cameroon denies being a francophone country owing to its bilingualism, but it is the usual practice to treat it as one.
21. President F. Mitterand admitted this much. See *Africa Research Bulletin*, Political Series, vol. 22 (15 January 1986) no. 12, 7884.
22. *Le Projet Cultural Extérieur de la France* (Paris: La Documentation Française for Ministry of External Relations, 1984) 9.

23. *Africa Research Bulletin*, Political Series, vol. 23 (15 March 1986) no. 2, 7960.
24. For details see, Emeka Nwokedi, 'Nigeria and France', in G.O. Olusanya and R.A. Akindele (eds), *Nigeria's External Relations: the first twenty-five years* (Ibadan: University Press for NIIA, 1986) 289.
25. Hamani Diori quoted in Robert Bourgi, *Le Général De Gaulle et l'Afrique Noire 1940–1969* (Paris: LGDJ, 1980) 452–3.
26. Bourgi, *La Politique Française de Coopération en Afrique*, 7.
27. Nwokedi, 'Nigeria and France' 288.
28. Quoted in *Afrique Contemporaine* (May-June 1984) no. 73, 3.
29. *Coopération au Développement* (Paris: La Documentation Française, 1983) 14.
30. See Daniel C. Bach, 'La Politique Africaine de Valery Giscard D'Estaing: Contraintes historiques et Nouveaux Espaces Economiques', *Conference on Africa and the Great Powers*, University of Ife (June 1983) 6.
31. On this process see Max Liniger-Goumaz, 'Guinée Equatoriale et Zone Franc: Réfléxions sur un système monétaire et une Récupération' *Genève-Afrique*, vol. XXIII (1985) no. 2, 57–78.
32. *Africa Research Bulletin*, Political Series; vol. 15 (15 June 1978) no. 5, 4858.
33. René Otayek, 'France-Afrique du sud: Le Compromis et ses limites', *mimeo*, 8–9.
34. Jean-Claude Gautron, 'La Politique Africaine de la France', *Colloquium organised by CHEAM, (Paris)* at the Centenary Celebration of the Berlin Treaty of 1885 at Berlin (March 1985) 19.
35. For details see Emeka Nwokedi, 'Franco-African Summits: a new instrument for France's African strategy?', *The World Today*, vol. 38 (December 1982) no. 12, 478–82.
36. *West Africa* (10 October 1983) no. 3482, 2332.
37. Jean-François Bayart, *Politique Africaine de Françcois Mitterand* (Paris: Editions Karthala, 1984) 125–40.
38. Howard Schissel, 'United States Companies Challenge the French', *African Business* (October 1982) 29–31; Peter Blackburn, 'US Firms Nibble at French Supremacy', *Africa Economic Digest*, vol. 3, (25 March 1982) no. 12, 2–3; 'Ivory Coast: France v. America', *Africa Confidential*, vol. 23, (17 February 1982) no. 4, 6–7.
39. See RPR 'La Nouvelle Politique de Coopération du RPR', *Le Mois en Afrique*, 3–33; Paul R. Michaud, 'Chirac's Africa Strategy', *West Africa*, (19 May 1986) 1040.
40. RPR, 'La Nouvelle Politique de Coopération du RPR', 4.

9 The Angolan Puzzle: Intervening Actors and Complex Issues[1]

Kenneth W. Grundy

Too frequently policy-makers in Washington or Moscow see local or regional issues in Southern Africa solely through their own, often distorted, lenses. And seen exclusively in ideological, which in this case means East-West or Cold War, terms they view their interests as inherently antagonistic. One is drawn to the old African maxim popular among non-aligned leaders in the early 1960s (and mentioned earlier): 'When the bull elephants fight, the grass gets trampled'. Yet, unlike two elephants contesting clashing claims to territory or sexual supremacy, Southern Africa is not the territory of either of the superpowers. Neither does Angola belong to other regional powers, notably South Africa. Although such states may have 'interests' there, Angola is not theirs to claim or shape.

One way of slicing into Angolan analysis is to try to appreciate the diversity of parties to the dispute. Angola is tremendously complicated. It is an issue that has metastasised in the sense that it has ramified or spread out to touch not only Angolans, but neighbouring peoples, and governments far beyond Southern Africa.[2] This is not new. During Angola's war for independence, Portugal's membership in the North Atlantic Treaty Organisation (NATO) provided support for its faltering colonial regime. It thus almost assured that Portugal's wars would be internationalised. To offset that external weight, the various national movements for independence turned for assistance and sanctuary to other states, other movements and interstate organisations.

Metastasis implies that a localised disease spreads as it grows. Angola also serves as a magnet, a lure attracting foreign interests that see in Angola an opportunity to expand their power and influence. By imposition as well as invitation external forces sought to exploit Angola's vulnerabilities. As a result, ten years ago Colin Legum titled one of his books *After Angola: the war over southern Africa*.[3] His implication was that Angola was the key to the subcontinent. In many respects it still is. For 25 years now, as John Marcum so well reviews, Angola has represented an issue of continual unrest.[4] Angola does not go away, and until its conflict is resolved other regional issues cannot be addressed directly.

Thus, Angola involves more than just geographical Angola. The Angola puzzle is at once an issue of domestic Angolan politics and one of international political economy, both regional and global. In that respect we might approach the question as a problem in the classic level-of-analysis dilemma.[5] Do we study Angola chiefly as a question of the international system? In that case issues of domestic interest are seen as instrumental to the larger interstate systemic issues. How do various state and non-state actors relate to one another and why? What is the larger balance of forces and interests or the correlation of forces in the world and in the region?

Or do we see international politics as just one component of the domestic Angolan political struggle? The interstate system level of analysis emphasises external determinants of state behaviour. The national or state level of analysis attributes such behaviour largely to internal characteristics: the political system, the economy and the social structure of Angola itself.

There is a third level of analysis that enables us to get an even sharper, more microscopic view of the Angolan question. I refer to the decision-making level. We might focus upon the policy-makers, the policy process and the decisions taken by individual governments and decision-making bodies of non-state actors and movements. How do policy-makers perceive the political arena in which they operate? Which elements, factions and interests prevail in the various actors involved and how do they relate to other actors and interests?

A chief consideration with regard to Angola is the tremendous complexity of the issue, a complexity reflected in several different ways. First, there are a large number of major actors involved: various Angolan parties, especially the Popular Movement for the Liberation of Angola (MPLA) and the National Union for the Total Independence of Angola (UNITA), diverse foreign forces and governments, and even national liberation movements against foreign regimes. Secondly, within many of the actors there is debate and disagreement on how best to deal with the issues at hand. We Americans have followed closely the pull and tug between various US parties, factions, offices and personalities over Southern African policy. No less a confusion of opinion exists, for example, in South Africa or within the Angolan government. This, in turn, contributes to the third element of complexity, the fact that official or stated positions are far from clear, firm and consistent. There is a good deal of flux and hence uncertainty in policy positions and tactics among actors. Because of this, it might be said of Angola what the *Financial Mail* said of Namibia, that it is in a state of 'chronic transition'.[6] Positions change because the ground on which they rest is a quicksand of risk and opportunity. This, in turn, holds out the prospect for the various involved parties that if they temporise, perhaps their own positions will improve. Why concede now, when conditions or bargaining power are less than ideal? Tomorrow it may be better. Many actors, for one reason or another, share the perception that time may be on their side.

Finally, complexity is a function of the tendency on the part of several of the actors to 'link' an Angolan settlement to concessions on equally contentious issues elsewhere or to 'link' settlement on extraneous issues to concessions over Angola. South Africa will not agree to withdraw from Namibia until Cuban forces are removed from Angola.[7] The MPLA government insists that a Namibian settlement according to the terms of UN Resolution 435 must first be arrived at before they will ask the Cubans to depart, and so forth. Each party, it seems, has either a hidden agenda or an open agenda that clashes frontally with the policy preferences of some other, equally significant actor, or both.

In short, what we call the Angola issue is actually a concatenation of several issues begging for progress, trade-off, or simultaneous resolution. No issue can be settled without spilling over into the other questions.

To begin with, there is the dispute over the very character and composition of the Angolan government, and the role, if any, for UNITA and the FNLA (Front for the National Liberation of Angola) in the central government. Crucial is the struggle between the MPLA government and UNITA, with the FNLA playing a supportive role. Each party is based in a different region of Angola. UNITA support is rooted in the Ovimbundu and other central-southern peasant societies. The FNLA is still largely Bakongo. The MPLA operates as a self-styled 'vanguard of the proletariat' with a nationwide ideologically-rooted appeal. In fact, however, it has failed to secure a following much beyond the urbanised intellectual élite, the urban working forces, and Luanda's Mbundu hinterland. The Ovimbundu and other southern peoples are not represented on the MPLA's political bureau. It is true that the eastern and southern regions of Angola are its least developed and hence are less likely to create the sorts of leaders that would gravitate to the MPLA. The MPLA argue that Portuguese colonial practices contributed to these divisions in Angolan society and to ethnic distrust, or worse. But the MPLA's insistence on centralised rule, and their refusal on principle to pander to ethnic and racial loyalties, provide little assurance to peoples fearful of 'outsiders'. When such ethnic elements are led, as they are, by one with the political acumen and salesmanship of Jonas Savimbi and are aided and supported by strong elements in Washington, and by the South African government, itself prepared to use the SWAPO (South West African People's Organisation) excuse to justify the direct use of force, then the MPLA is in deep trouble.

Clearly UNITA and the MPLA are at loggerheads as to the composition and character of the Angolan state. To expect them to reconcile their differences peacefully is naive, at best. One thinks back to Woodrow Wilson's expectations with regard to representation for Russia at the Versailles proceedings. He simply could not understand why the representatives of the warring factions in Russia could not resolve their disagreements. He even proposed that they be brought together on the Island of Prinkipo in order to negotiate a settlement. But what the Bolsheviks and their Russian opponents were interested in was one another's total destruction. There was no room for amicable discussion. The planned conference was never held.

Likewise, at present UNITA and the MPLA are not prepared to negotiate away their respective advantages. Partition has been suggested. So has the idea of creating a demilitarised zone straddling the Angola-Namibia border. So far, however, neither internal party has expressed a desire for partition. Perhaps the government in Pretoria might entertain such a prospect, but a territorially divided Angola would please few within the country.

It is not impossible that MPLA and UNITA elements can be brought together. The US and the USSR have held direct talks on a Namibia-Angola package. Certainly, compromise and ideological jugglery are not unknown to Jonas Savimbi. But the current constellation of powers does not seem to admit of half loaves.

Related to this is a second issue, the matter of when and how external military forces are to be withdrawn from Angola. The Cuban troops, presently numbering some 30 000 and representing a major financial drain on the Angolan state treasury, are regarded by Luanda as indispensible to the maintenance of the integrity of the Angolan state and its MPLA government. But SADF (South African

Defence Forces) units, regulars and specialised reconnaissance groups and a battalion of Portuguese speakers (32 battalion), have directly intervened or assisted UNITA forces since the Angolan state gained independence in 1975. These external actors are reluctant to surrender their principal leverage and the Angolan elements that each supports are even less inclined to see their military backers depart.

Thus, the third issue is external involvement and meddling in Angolan affairs. The South Africans back UNITA and the FLNA. Cuba, the Soviet Union and other members of the socialist bloc are committed to the Luanda government.[8] The United States has its candidate and is involved with military assistance and diplomatic pressure.[9] Even SWAPO gains support in Angola and beyond. The Front Line States are also deeply interested in the outcome. Parties to the diverse facets of what is known collectively here as Angola are being used by other parties, and are using others.

Angola's future is also tied to a Namibian settlement, with most of the same actors involved, and some new ones — the United Nations, the Western Contact Group, SWAPO, a cacophony of indigenous Namibian parties and coalitions and, of course, Pretoria in all its guises.[10] All want a hand in the determination of government and the transfer of power.

Tied into these vexing issues are Cold War considerations, particularly the status of socialist construction and capitalist penetration in Africa. Western powers fear the strategic isolation and vulnerability of Zaire, Botswana and Zambia. They are concerned about the security of their private investments and the continued supply of key minerals.

The socialist states likewise see Angola, Mozambique and Zimbabwe as models for the transition to socialism and as exemplars of socialist bloc commitment to fraternal allies. Should their economies fail or their governments falter in resisting destabilisation from South Africa, the prestige and stature of the USSR and its allies would be perceived to suffer. Ideological, personal and national egos are at stake among governments not noted for their reserve and humility.

We have a multifaceted issue, involving many actors, many of which have the capacity to unsettle Angola. Not one, single-handedly, has the capacity to resolve the Angolan puzzle. It is as if we have a complex tumbler lock. Each party has a part of the key. Somehow these parties, few of which trust one another, must insert and turn their keys, all at the same time. And finally, each expects that the door they unlock will provide benefits commensurate with the risk. That might not be impossible. Yet one gets the further impression that some actors really want no settlement, certainly not with the present alignments of power in the region. States and movements with ostensibly irreconcilable interests are in constant flux as they jockey for favour and control.

Several actors are, themselves, riddled with division in their ranks. I shall examine in some detail the foreign/strategic policy-making process in one state, South Africa, as it applies to Angola.

Since the first large-scale South African incursion into Angola in 1975–76, it has been apparent that the regime in Pretoria is not of a single mind on how best to deal with neighbouring states. Likewise, analysts of South African regional policy do not agree on its objectives, its strategic choices, or the tactics employed. There seems to be enough ambiguity in Pretoria's positions, enough vascillation over time, and sufficient internal dispute to lead analysts to wonder if there is a clear and fully rationalised direction in regional policy.

South Africa's decision to intervene in Angola before and immediately after that country's independence in November 1975 was hotly debated in high places.[11] Prior to the determination to intervene, General Hendrick van den Bergh of the Bureau of State Security (BOSS) had provided much of the impetus for John Vorster's efforts at detente.[12] Hilgard Muller had proven to be a lacklustre foreign minister and certainly not one influential in the party or the government. He was not the sort to be a strong and effective advocate of departmental policy and growth in NP (National Party) counsels, not in comparison to van den Bergh, P.W. Botha (then Minister of Defence) or Connie Mulder (Minister of Information), each in his way headstrong and manipulative.

When government was faced with some very difficult decisions regarding policy in the unfolding Angolan civil war leading to independence, Muller took a back seat and more forceful personalities contested the wheel. At one point the Foreign Ministry did not even learn of the SADF's first major offensive into Angola until a Portuguese note of protest was handed to the South African Ambassador in Lisbon.[13] Insofar as the policy dispute can be characterised as one between hawks and doves, it was Defence arrayed against BOSS and Foreign Affairs (DFA), with Information playing a supportive role. As conditions shifted in the field, the coalition of voices for or against deeper involvement or withdrawal shifted. In this instance field conditions refer not only to the military situation in Angola itself, but also to the global diplomatic picture, and particularly the indecisive American position (especially a result of the interplay among diverse US branches and organs of government), the appeals of black states in Africa, the ebb and flow of independence movement support, OAU activities, and other foreign military and diplomatic dabblings.

Pretoria wavered largely because no clear-cut policy direction had been established. The same South Africans were not in control, to the same degree, at every stage of the decision process. Contestants for power realised that their domestic bases for support rested on shifting foundations.

Although Defence and the SADF were identified with a hawkish orientation, they were somewhat restrained in their policy advocacy. Apparently Military Intelligence, after approaching indirectly each of the Angolan liberation movements, concluded that an MPLA government in Luanda might threaten South Africa's security interests in Namibia. In June 1975 the SADF submitted to Defence Minister P.W. Botha a policy paper setting out South Africa's options and the implications of each. It then went from the Minister of Defence to the Prime Minister. It took Vorster months to arrive at a decision on the issue. In the meantime, the South African forces were engaged in southern Angola in a vacuum of policy direction. P.W. Botha, after consultations with Vorster, reportedly provided the SADF with interim guidance — if attacked by MPLA forces, drive them off decisively. According to Geldenhuys, '. . . a political decision opening the door to offensive military operations in Angola had been taken, and the two principal (if not the only) political decision-makers who were to control South Africa's military involvement in the Angolan war . . . identified'.[14]

Perhaps the decision-makers were too inclined to believe their intelligence about MPLA weaknesses and UNITA-FNLA strengths. Perhaps they overestimated American commitment and underestimated Soviet aims. For whatever reasons, they did advocate deeper involvement and more direct and unambiguous orders. But in planning a military invasion, they were temperate. Their initial large-scale strikes, Operations 'Zulu' and 'Foxbat', demonstrated restraint in the number of South African troops deployed and the composition of the forces, consisting of a San battalion, a black FNLA battalion, and about 300 'advisors/instructors' and SADF officers and NCOs. Perhaps this reflected the compromise character of the decision and the conduct of the intervention, by which hawks carried the decision provided the doves were mollified by a less intensive and extensive

SADF deployment. The escalation of South African involvement came after Angola's November 11th independence. The later cross-border operations were more overtly South African exercises in terms of personnel, with up to 2000 SADF members eventually engaged.

Throughout that period, however, there were few if any doves among the South African military strategists. At least they appreciated that little could be gained by sending in more South African troops without more tangible Western support. And when they came to realise that Western support would not be forthcoming, and that what had been a free-wheeling bush war had become more like a conventional war with long logistical lines, larger troop concentrations, rapidly deployed vehicle columns with heavier artillery and projectiles, and when the SADF thinkers realised that their Angolan allies and clients, UNITA and FNLA, especially the latter, were ill-prepared for that kind of protracted struggle, the SADF leaders were forced, reluctantly, to pull back to more defensible positions (militarily and diplomatically).

The decision to retreat, that is, to abandon the SADF's optional plan that included the capture of Luanda and to withdraw all forces except for border protection, was taken over the 1975 Christmas holiday during which the Cabinet was unable to meet. The military hierarchy wanted to continue their support for the FNLA and UNITA. The doves in BOSS and DFA argued that this military intervention was being used against South Africa and alienating many African and Western governments that earlier had been critical of the MPLA and a Cuban presence in Africa.

Throughout the intervention, top military men felt tethered to a foreign policy that made their jobs difficult. During the crisis it was BOSS, not DFA, that kept communications open with black governments in Africa and it was BOSS that was able to elicit discrete appeals from these governments to intervene and to stay in Angola.[15] It was BOSS as well that argued for withdrawal and eventually BOSS got its way. There are stories of other major confrontations between P.W. Botha and van den Bergh that contribute to this atmosphere of competition at the center.[16] The SADF took the initiative in Angola. It unsettled the civilian politicians. Out of the crisis emerged BOSS and Information as Prime Minister Vorster's 'second Department of Foreign Affairs' to offset the weight of Defence.

Interestingly, it was the Angolan issue with Defence arrayed against BOSS and DFA that probably led P.W. Botha to want to reorganise the entire foreign policy decision-making apparatus. South Africa lacked clear policy objectives in Angola and thus it was awkward for the SADF to carry out policy and plan operations, the purposes of which were fuzzy or worse. This did not deter SADF from elaborate operational planning of 'its' Angolan responsibility, but without political guidelines it must have been frustrating. When the information scandal broke and BOSS and Vorster plummetted from power, P.W. Botha was able to establish his new, more rationalised policy machinery.[17]

The machinery in place for policy-making on the early Angolan issue did not work well. It was *ad hoc* and idiosyncratic. In the end Vorster and Botha dominated. Parliament had virtually no role to play. Even the full Cabinet met only after the vital decisions were taken. The State Security Council was conspicuously silent. Foreign Affairs frequently was excluded from the groups that made decisions. Intelligence, at least on the matter of the United States and on Cuban and MPLA policy, was unreliable. The National Party caucus was not consulted. It was the Vorster and P.W. Botha show with van den Bergh providing periodic relief and tension. Such an arrangement could not be reliably counted upon the next time crisis decision-making was required. The process for regional and security decision-making had to be more structured and systematised.

South Africa's defence forces captured the foreign policy initiative, or at least through tactical activism framed policy or strategy by default. In May 1978 a massive strike against SWAPO bases in southern Angola, code-named Operation 'Reindeer', was the first large-scale military strike into Angola after the 1975–76 incursions. The 'Reindeer' decision was P.W. Botha's revenge on the non-military voices in the Party. Others in the SSC and in Cabinet warned of international repercussions, possibly even UN-sponsored sanctions. Defence carried the day. The raid was a military success and the diplomatic liabilities were contained. Operation 'Reindeer' strengthened the security establishment in foreign policy councils. Its success led directly to a series of massive pre-emptive raids into Angola.[18] The Namibian conflict added to the authoritative role of SADF in foreign policy.

There is some evidence that the SADF sought to sabotage the 1982–83 Cape Verde Islands talks between DFA and Angola. Even after Foreign Minister Pik Botha returned with agreements for a preliminary package that included South African military withdrawal, military voices in the SSC rebuked him. In addition, top SADF brass often participate directly in the negotiation process.

Military Intelligence is usually included. Although there would appear to be subtlely different orientations within the military, they do share a common professional military perspective.

Those in position to shape the outcome in Namibia, the military men, would appear to favour the view that the Republic can best be defended from forward positions. Although they have stressed that it is for government, not the SADF, to decide, they insist that South Africa should not 'rush into a settlement' for Namibia. They feel capable of maintaining the military situation for a long time. Hidden in their vague generalities is a hard-line view that the military still has a key role to play in Namibia, strategically and politically, and by implication in Angola, and that SADF thinkers are extremely sceptical of any concessions to other negotiating actors. Apparently confident that it has the security situation in the field well in hand, SADF leaders are portentously signalling the politicians that they had better not do anything impetuous or irresolute. From this vantage, the SADF would seem to want to deny, as much as practical, a settlement that might lead to a SWAPO government in Windhoek. To the hawks in Pretoria a SWAPO regime would, whether for ideology, strategy or a sense of obligation, invite in the Soviets and Cubans, given sanctuary to the ANC (African National Congress) and thereby endanger the Republic directly. Just as importantly, the SADF is in an immediate position to engage in cross-border strikes, to undermine a cease-fire should an agreement be reached, or to torpedo the transitional process to independence. Initiative, it would seem, lies with Defence Headquarters and particularly its Intelligence section, not with Foreign Affairs.[19]

But there are costs associated with no settlement and with the delays. Direct security expenses, plus costs of administration, total around $1.5 billion per year. Moreover, South African control in Namibia has diplomatic disadvantages, and risks the imposition of sanctions. The trade-offs must be constantly recalculated. By hanging tough militarily, South Africa appears to have achieved some success, at least in terms of its chief goal, South African security. It has not undermined the negotiating process altogether. A dual strategy of keeping channels of negotiation open while trying to destroy SWAPO would seem to be preferable to Pretoria. South Africa's continuous and deep operations in Angola, so far, have not enmeshed it in a war it has been unable to manage, at least not until the strategic setbacks and diplomatic re-engagements of mid-1988. For the military leaders, the war in Angola is not a bad thing.

It has been said of the SADF that it has no policy to pull together its tactics, that a series of strikes to destabilise neighbouring governments do not constitute a larger design. By and large this is an unfair criticism. Strategic thinkers in the SADF and people in the secretariat of the SSC have devoted great energy to devising a winning strategy for South Africa. One might want to dispute the wisdom of it, the intelligence on which strategy is based, or its insensitivity to black peoples' aspirations in South Africa and in the region, but one cannot in fairness to security specialists deny that they have tried to look at the big picture.

They might, in a form of *ex post facto* reasoning, seek to convince outsiders that the 1983–84 success of Pretoria's 'peace' offensive was tangible proof that a consistent policy of firmness (less generous analysts call it destabilisation) would contribute directly to better relations in the region. It has, in other words, been destabilisation with a purpose.[20]

I cannot at this juncture outline the extent of the destabilisation policy in order to examine the intentions of the security establishment. The military actions against Angola, ostensibly to negate pre-emptively the SWAPO incursions, have been described. South Africa's Angolan policy is an extension of its Namibian policy. Once Pretoria realised the benefits of military forcefulness, it followed that being able to manipulate the domestic Angolan situation, especially to impose a UNITA role in government and a diminished role if not an end to the Cuban presence, was not only desirable but within its grasp. Angola has never denied SWAPO infiltrations from Angola. In fact, Angola provided SWAPO's military arm with bases and training facilities. This presents a rationale for cross-border strikes. Once embarked on a course of aggressive defence, the case for South African military operations elsewhere in the region became easier.

When it comes to intervention further afield one might attempt to justify intervention as the exercise of the traditional right of self-defence. Alternatively, it might be rationalised as a form of counter-intervention — that is, intervention to redress a balance of force that has been disrupted by another's outside intervention. In this case, the incursions into Angola might so qualify, but only in a contorted fashion, since the Cuban forces have the blessing, indeed, have been invited in by the Luanda government. Nonetheless, the Cuban 'threat' serves as a standing alibi for Pretoria, enabling it to vindicate South Africa's refusal to come to terms with the MPLA or with SWAPO or to abandon UNITA. Recent Cuban actions and statements imply that Cuba intends to stay on in Angola for quite some time, that is, until '*apartheid* is ended'. Moreover, the Soviet-Cuban presence is seen to temper hostile pressure on South Africa from the West, especially during the Reagan-Thatcher-Kohl tenures. The presence of socialist bloc forces is trumpeted as testimony that South Africa's struggle with the ANC and SWAPO is part of a global resistance to Soviet expansion and communist revolution. Ironic it is that Pretoria counters the Marxist menace by contributing to a continued Soviet-Cuban involvement in Angola.[21] Pretoria needs the Marxists from abroad to discredit its own indigenous revolutionaries.

South Africa's regional policy is reminiscent of the old 'good guy, bad guy' ploy. It is a Pavlovian technique allegedly popular with police interrogators. One interrogator pretends to be the helpful, reasonable partner. The second member of the team is violent, uncontrollable and unreasonable. The 'good guy' can thereby appear to be the detainee's friend, protecting him from his fearsome partner and thereby gaining the confidence of the one being grilled. It is to the 'good guy' that the detainee confesses or provides the intelligence.

The SADF and its proxies in this case play the bully, destabilising governments in the region and exposing their vulnerabilities. 'Pik' Botha and the South African diplomatic and economic operatives are supposedly the 'good guys'. They offer to repair the damage if only the black governments will co-operate — that is, sign pacts of non-aggression, solidify economic ties and 'normalise' relations, and expel the ANC or SWAPO forces from their territories.

Some writers have referred to an ambiguity in South African foreign policy.[22] The stick and the carrot; wavering from one pole to another. We might profitably ask — why does South Africa seem to vascillate in its policy towards various black states? Is Pretoria simply unsure of what it wants? Are there really deep divisions in the South African élites? First one group gains prominence and then another. Does this account for two or more foreign policies? Is Pretoria consciously playing the 'good guy/bad guy' routine? Does it honestly change its mind from time to time as the context of policy changes? If so, why? Moreover, there may be other explanations worthy of our examination.[23]

For South Africa, policy towards Angola cannot be divorced from the domestically politically volatile issue of Namibia. In both Angola and Namibia the SADF does appear to have a surprisingly free hand. But the Pretoria government is playing several games at once. By far their main concern is holding power in the Republic of South Africa itself. So Pretoria prevaricates, trying to keep as many options open as it can, in a world where its options are shrinking by the year.[24]

Similar analyses might be rendered of politics within the MPLA, of US policy in Southern Africa, of divisions within SWAPO, or of the other actors on the Angola stage. There are elements of continuity in various policy lines, and these must be identified. And there are factions and strategic and tactical disputes, too.[25]

It is hoped that for Angola, with every one wanting a piece of the action, chronic transition does not become terminal.

NOTES

1. This essay appeared originally in *Issue* 15, 1987, 35–41 and is reprinted here by permission of the author and the US African Studies Association.
2. James S. Coleman and Richard L. Sklar, 'Introduction', in Gerald J. Bender *et al.* (eds), *African Crisis Areas and U.S. Foreign Policy* (Berkeley: University of California Press, 1985) 7–12. On the internationalisation of the region, see: Kenneth W. Grundy, *Confrontation and Accommodation in Southern Africa: The Limits of Independence* (Berkeley: University of California Press, 1973) 191–227.
3. Colin Legum, *After Angola: the war over southern Africa* (New York: Africana, 1976).
4. John A. Marcum, 'Angola: Twenty-five Years of War', *Current History*, vol. 85 (May 1986) no. 511, 193–6 and 229–31.
5. J. David Singer, 'The Level-of-Analysis Problem in International Relations', in Klaus Knorr and Sidney Verba (eds), *The International System* (Princeton: Princeton University Press, 1961) 77–92.
6. 'Namibia: Chronic Transition', *Financial Mail* (Johannesburg), vol. 98, (3 January 1986) no. 14, 27.
7. There is evidence that this particular linkage idea originated with the US. See Robert S. Jaster, *South Africa in Namibia: The Botha Strategy* (Lanham: University Press of America, 1985) 86.
8. The earlier period is covered in Arthur Jay Klinghoffer, *The Angolan War: A Study in Soviet Policy in the Third World* (Boulder.: Westview, 1980) and William M. LeoGrande, *Cuba's Policy in Africa, 1959–1980* (Berkeley: Institute of International Studies, 1980). Later material appears in: David E. Albright, *The USSR and Sub-Saharan Africa in the 1980s* (New York: Praeger, 1983) and Albright, 'New Trends in Soviet Policy toward Africa', *CSIS Africa Notes* (29 April 1984) no. 27.
9. Gerald J. Bender, 'American Policy toward Angola: A History of Linkage', in Bender *et al.* (eds), *African Crisis Areas*, 110–28; Herbert Howe, 'United States Policy in Southern Africa', *Current History*, vol. 85 (May 1986) no. 511, 206–08 and 232–4; and John A. Marcum, 'U.S. Options in Angola', *CSIS Africa Notes* (20 December 1985) no. 52.
10. Jaster, *South Africa in Namibia*.

11. An early and somewhat speculative account is Robin Hallett, 'The South African Intervention in Angola, 1975–76', *African Affairs*, vol 77 (July 1978) no. 308, 347–86. More recent data can be found in Deon Geldenhuys, *The Diplomacy of Isolation: South African Foreign Policy Making* (Johannesburg: Macmillan, 1984) 75–84.
12. See Chris Vermaak, 'The BOSS Man Speaks', *Scope*, (29 June 1979) 16–23, esp. 21–2.
13. Geldenhuys, *The Diplomacy of Isolation*, 79.
14. Ibid.
15. Ibid., 82–3; and Hallett, 'South African Intervention', 370.
16. See *Guardian* (London) (8 August 1979) 6.
17. Kenneth W. Grundy, *The Militarization of South African Politics* (Bloomington: Indiana University Press, 1986) 19–57.
18. Willem Steenkamp, *Borderstrike!: South Africa into Angola* (Durban: Butterworth, 1983). See also Geldenhuys, *The Diplomacy of Isolation*, 83.
19. Grundy, *The Militarization*, 1–57. See the substantive evidence from the Vaz diary in 'Counting on Colonel Charlie', *Africa News*, vol. 25 (4 November 1985) no. 9, 8–12; 'Hawks Ascendant', *Financial Mail*, vol. 97 (27 September 1985) no. 13, 36–41; and John S. Saul, 'Mozambique Socialism and South African Aggression', paper read at the annual meeting of the African Studies Association, New Orleans, November 1985.
20. Richard Weisfelder, '"Peace" from the Barrel of a Gun: Nonaggression Pacts and State Terrorism in Southern Africa', in Michael Stohl and George Lopez (eds), *Foreign Policy and State Terror* (Westport, Conn.: Greenwood Press, 1986). South African statements can be found in R.K. Campbell, 'Support for Cross-Border Strikes', *Paratus* (Pretoria), vol. 34 (April 1983) no. 4, 10–11; and Republic of South Africa, Department of Defence, *White Paper on Defence and Armaments Supply, 1984* (Cape Town: 1984) 3.
21. Robert M. Price, 'Creating New Political Realities: Pretoria's Drive for Regional Hegemony', in Bender *et al.* (eds), *African Crisis Areas*, 64–94; and Jaster, *South Africa in Namibia*, 110–11.
22. For example: Jaster, *South Africa in Namibia*, 76.
23. A more complete treatment of this theme can be found in: Kenneth W. Grundy, 'Regional Coercion and Domestic Domination: South Africa's Militarization at Home and Abroad', a paper presented at the conference on 'Militarization in the Third World: The Caribbean Basin and Southern Africa'. Queen's University, Kingston, Ontario, January 1987.
24. Robert S. Jaster, *South Africa in Namibia*, 62.
25. Robert S. Jaster, *South Africa's Narrowing Security Options*, (London: International Institute for Strategic Studies, Spring 1980) Adelphi Paper No. 159.

Conclusion: The Political Economy of Africa in the World System, 1960–85[1]

Timothy M. Shaw

> If the study of the foreign policies of underdeveloped countries is underdeveloped, the systematic analysis of their foreign policy decisions is not. It is simply nonexistent.[2]

The first half of the 1980s has posed new challenges for African foreign policy in practice and analysis symbolised by the Ethiopian drought and Southern African conflict but generalised in the continental crisis of negative growth. The halcyon days of the 1960s — the innocence and optimism of early African nationalism — have long since disappeared, obliterated by the global and regional shocks of the 1970s. The continent's first independence decade coincided with a period of gradual economic expansion; as it turned out, the continent's last. The decade since the mid-1970s — the end of the postwar Bretton Woods era — has been characterised by slow growth at best, for a minority of states, and no growth for the majority of countries and peoples. Thus the African agenda has shifted dramatically from nation-building to salvaging and from import-substitution to deindustrialisation. Somewhat fanciful notions of regional and continental integration have been replaced by pragmatic imperatives of food aid and debt relief.

At the same time as Africa's external preoccupations changed the world economy shifted from expansion to contraction, so analysis of its foreign policy in particular and of the world system as a whole underwent a minor revolution: transnational economic relations came to balance interstate political interactions. This coincidence of African development priorities and global economic analysis is reflected in a new genre of work now appearing: the political economy of African foreign policy. Ironically, as economics was being recognised as a legitimate issue area in international relations, the cold war was renewed, thus reviving another set of strategic factors, again reflected in the African as well as in the general literature. The conjuncture of the mid-1980s thus challenges established assumptions, assertions and prescriptions for both policy-makers and analysts concerned with the African condition.

Despite the somewhat melancholy circumstances of drought and degradation, the juxtaposition of African development crisis and global economic uncertainty has induced something of a revival in African foreign policy studies. The first 15 years were characterised by rather unsophisticated studies of leaders, ideologies, diplomacy and conflicts. A second stage produced some debate about orientation, consistency and contradiction. But the real second generation work began to appear as Africa's crisis commenced: comparative foreign policy and political economy typified by Ali Mazrui's *Africa's International Relations* and Okwudiba Nnoli's *Self-Reliance and Foreign Policy in Tanzania.*[3] The integration of economic crisis and perspective has come together in the second wave of books symbolised by the seminal collection from Bahgat Korany and Ali E. Hillal Dessouki *et al.*, *The Foreign Policies of Arab States* (Boulder: Westview 1984), signifying Africa's analytic maturation along with its economic marginalisation. Despite the developmental difficulties of the continent, its place in foreign policy studies is now established and assured: a relatively sophisticated and comparable sub-field.

As African international relations moved beyond politics to economics and strategy towards the new mainstream of the discipline an important debate developed within the sub-field: over the definition of *political economy*. This paralleled and reinforced two related debates: first, that over approaches to comparative politics within Africa — modernisation versus materialism — and second, that over approaches to international politics in general — realism versus radicalism. These strands have come together in the mid-1980s African literature typified by Bill Freund, *The Making of Contemporary Africa*, Claude Ake, *A Political Economy for Africa* and Crawford Young, *Ideology and Development in Africa.*[4] Perhaps it most celebrated exponent is Basil Davidson, whose magnificent TV series on Africa has challenged myths and popularised critiques.[5]

Whilst the recognition and refinement of this mode is not yet universal — time-lag in espousing new theoretical trends is one indicator of dependence in both academe and regime at the periphery — the new 'paradigm' of political economy is already generating another debate inside and around Africa: more or less materialist definitions and conceptions. This continental debate parallels the global one over the salience of economic rather than diplomatic, strategic and political forces and has generated an increasingly nuanced literature well beyond the simplistic *dependencia* of the 1970s. As it becomes indisputable that most of Africa is increasingly marginal to global economic growth so nationalist assumptions of neo-colonialism can no longer be contained; only a few African states, resources and markets are relevant in a world (1) of high-tech security and communication and (2) of foreign exchange scarcity and conditionality. But Leninist assumptions die hard and strategic competitions perpetuate selective external attentions.

This review chapter seeks, then, to situate current African(ist) analyses of foreign and development policies in the context of changing international relations and intellectual responses, with particular emphasis on the articulation between 'internal' social formations and the 'international' division of labour. In addition to being concerned about the embryonic dialogue between more and less materialist conceptions of political economy and ways these relate to 'foreign policy', I am interested in the innovative 'development strategies' advanced by African institutions for the escalating continental crisis. These strategies are not mere reflections of continental diplomacy but constitute significant responses to (1) the elusiveness of development over the past decade and (2) the inappropriateness of explanation and prescription.[6] In short, the accelerating transition in the prevailing 'African studies' paradigm away from post-colonial orthodoxy has begun to be both recognised and advanced by indigenous institutions[7] as well as by African(ist) academics.

This intellectual-cum-political response is a recognition of and reaction to not only disappointments about development but also apparent changes in the global economy. The economic as well as analytic climate has been transformed over the last decade as assumptions about Africa's place in the world system have been undermined. The seeming certainties of 'neo-colonialism' — unequal exchange of commodities for manufactures buttressed by dependant leaders and forces — have been superseded by the glaring uncertainties of 'post-neocolonialism' — the marginalisation of African products and markets in a post-industrial system of microchips and lasers. The problematic character of the remainder of the 20th century for Africa has compelled a re-evaluation of assumptions, expectations and projections: will the 'dark continent' be any less gloomy after the centenary of the Treaty of Berlin which formalised its balkanisation and extrovertion? And how will discarded regimes respond to their further peripheralisation? In the sections which follow, I move from more global to more parochial levels and from more theoretical to political concerns.

BEYOND DIPLOMACY

The new 'African diplomacy' is distinct from the 'old' (that is, pre- and post-colonial protocols) because of its emphasis on (1) economic as well as political factors, and (2) developmental as well as diplomatic issues. First, then, radical studies typified by the Korany, Dessouki *et al.* volume locate the causes of foreign policy in political economy rather than in ideology or leadership or institution: the external dimension of 'peripheral social formations'. And second, they treat issues of development — Basic Human Needs (BHN) of food, health, infrastructure and so on — as integral aspects of foreign relations: the external aspect of changes in relations and patterns of production, distribution and accumulation.

Thus, juxtaposition of foreign policy with political economy and development strategy makes its definition both broader and more reflective of African imperatives; that is, survival and self-containment as well as sovereignty or status. On the one hand, this permits the African case to be compared with the external links of other social formations, particularly those in the North (OECD) and South (Non-Aligned). And on the other hand, it enables development dilemmas to be contrasted with other external — or rather transnational — constraints and opportunities. It helps to capture the essence of Africa's contradictory position in the emerging international division of labour. A final, third but not so central, reformulations of African diplomacy has been in the area of 'strategic studies' as indicated in Bruce E. Arlinghaus' several works, especially his *Military Development in Africa: the political and economic roles of arms transfers* (Boulder: Westview, 1984): 'military development' and regional 'military-industrial complexes' rather than simply military regimes and interventions.

ECONOMIC AND ANALYTIC STATUS

One poignant symbol of the African condition of both painful reconsideration and potential renaissance is the dialectic already noted between economic *marginality* and diplomatic-cum-analytic *maturity*. The world's most fragmented region — the OAU at its coming-of-age in 1984 had 51 member states — is still influential in UN and Non-Aligned circles even if the material basis of the 'reformist' coalition is eroding. As reflections of both marginality and maturity, analyses of African diplomacy are increasingly sophisticated and sustained, unlike the rather superficial and ephemeral descriptions of the initial post-independence period. The continuing crisis has concentrated the minds of statespersons and scholars alike.

Further, both indigenous and expatriate analysts are beginning to go beyond *superstructure* to examine *substructure*: modes and relations of production, distribution and accumulation. As symbolised by the long-awaited appearance of the Korany, Dessouki *et al.* collection 'on Arab states' foreign policies, they have begun to transcend the established assumption, common to students of 'old' and 'new' states alike, that foreign relations consist only of policy, diplomacy and strategy or even of dependency.[8] Instead, particularly for dependent and vulnerable states, there is a new recognition that economic relations are central and that indigenous social forces are integral to both external interests and foreign policy: the reconsideration and reconceptualisation of 'national interest'. In short, 'foreign policy' and 'development policy' have been redefined to take into account social forces in peripheral formations: a veritable African intellectual 'revolution'.

TOWARDS A POLITICAL ECONOMY OF FOREIGN POLICY

Nowhere is this analytic transformation and potential — the conjuncture of the last decade — marked better than by the innovative, comprehensive yet sensitive collection by Korany and Dessouki on *The Foreign Policies of Arab States*. In both overviews and cases they and their six collaborators go beyond tired formulations for foreign policy as protocol, politics, idiosyncracy and ideology to examine its social roots and roles: the causes, contexts and contradictions of external connections and ambitions. In an informed, balanced and readable volume they transform Arab (and African) foreign policy studies from an obscure and obscurantist sub-field not only into the mainstream but the very vanguard: comparative foreign policy cannot be the same now that the periphery is being treated appropriately as well as the centre. As with other Third World regions, the Arab literature had hitherto been both unsophisticated and uncritical: 'Our field has been plagued by inadequate conceptualization, overemphasis on historicism and the uniqueness of the Islamic-Arab situation, and neglect of a truly comparative outlook'.[9] Yet in identifying three major common dilemmas confronting new states — aid/ independence, resources/objectives, and security/development — Dessouki and Korany, particularly in their own seminal case studies on Algeria, Egypt and Saudi Arabia, go well beyond even contemporary behavioural formulations to idetify (1) various bases of foreign policy forces, particularly bureaucratic, military, technocratic and religious fractions within indigenous bourgeoisies; and (2) kaleidoscopic coalitions amongst these fractions and between them and external actors, individual and institutional. Their rich descriptions of formidable 'foreign policy' fractions in major Arab states — their contradicting coalitions and constraints — constitute a significant contribution and advance: the periphery (and semi-periphery) illuminating the system as a whole; an irony, perhaps, but characteristic of responses to unsatisfactory inherited assumptions and prescriptions.

Dessouki and Korany also go beyond not only several layers of analysis — the interaction among as well as separation of national, regional and global levels — but also point to the salience of treating Third World social formations as more than mere 'dependent' peripheries, but rather as complex and contradictory political economies. In their conclusion, they call for 'more comparative and cumulative studies on the foreign policies of developing countries, either within one region (Africa, Asia, or Latin America) or interregional'.[10]

Such a direction points not only towards case studies of countries, policies, decisions and institutions, but also towards consideration of the characteristics and dialectics of peripheral (and semi-peripheral) political economies: social connections and contradictions. In particular, it suggests two types of comparative analyses: (1) comparisons among similar *social forces* in different states (for example, technocratic, military, comprador or national bourgeois fractions in several peripheral political economies) and (2) comparisons between similar *state actors* in different periods (for instance, before, during and after the successive 'oil shocks' of the early and late 1970s). The informed and nuanced chapters by Bahgat Korany on Algeria and Saudi Arabia are particularly suggestive of the emergence of distinctive indigenous fractions which exist in different patterns and combinations under successive regimes, in part determined by the cyclical condition — expansion or contraction — of the global economy; that is, the dialectic of change produced by the juxtaposition of 'external' and 'internal' forces in their essentially 'transnational' mode.

The balance of political, technocratic, military and religious forces in both these particular Arab OPEC states is quite comparable, for example, to that in Indonesia and Nigeria, as well as in Mexico and Venezuela.[11] Such novel varieties of social coalitions or 'triple alliances'[12] in oil-rich states in the post-OPEC order have led to distinctive diplomatic postures and initiatives; for instance, Algeria over NIEO and Saudi Arabia over Israel (see the nice descriptions in Korany's chapters).[13] These proposals were far more than reflections of individual psyches or national values: they reflected real social contradictions within as well as between states. In short, the particular expressions of 'national interests' in Arab and Sub-Saharan Africa are not aberrations — the assumption of distinctive 'African' mores and laws — but rather reflections of constraints and contradictions at the (semi-) periphery in a changing global order.

Korany and Dessouki help to abstract and advance a new agenda for such (redefined and reformulated) 'foreign policy' studies continuing into the 1990s. To their considerable credit they go beyond simplistic, ahistoric analyses of contemporary conflict, so prevalent in Middle East as well as African studies, and instead treat military relations as but one product and factor of peripheral national and regional political economies; the military aspect or correlate of underdevelopment. Nevertheless, the rediscovery and redefinition of strategic issues in African studies are a related, albeit secondary, trend worthy of attention; rather than being treated as separate relations they are instead concerned at aspects of underdevelopment which often coincide with ecological and economic difficulties.

FROM STRATEGIC STUDIES TO MILITARY DEVELOPMENT AND SELF-RELIANCE

Finally, then, an additional third transition in the field serves to both reinforce and undermine the old mode: the (re)new(ed) emphasis on strategic, rather than either diplomatic or economic, issues. This reinforces because of its emphasis on peripheral states and metropolitan powers[14]; yet simultaneously it undermines because of a new concern with the interrelations of security and economy: regional military industrial complexes and hegemonies.

Happily, the new guard in this long-established strategic studies subfield has gone beyond previous preoccupations with global strategy, foreign assistance, and local interventions to situate the military as institution and issue-area in the context of distinctive and interrelated international and national political economies. The major author and animateur in this reformist genre is surely Bruce Arlinghaus with his continuing series of personal or collected volumes on the new strategic studies for Africa: from arms transfers to the cluster of questions around technological and skills transfers and appropriate policies and technologies.[15]

Issues of strategic response and technological self-reliance are situated by Arlinghaus within broader contexts of development directions and debates: the political economy of military priority and practice. In so doing, he exposes several prevailing myths about military development on the continent[16] and projects a plausible short-term strategic scenario in terms of the balance between goals, forces, economies, technologies, suppliers and financiers concluding, as does William Thom in a recent overview of 'Sub-Saharan Africa's changing military environment' that

> The military situation in Sub-Saharan Africa is dynamic, and change will continue. Stereotypes about the African military are in many cases becoming obsolete . . . Military capability in Africa south of the Sahara is increasing, as is the propensity to use it . . . The imbalance of military power in Africa is becoming more precarious; regional military powers are emerging and will be significant factors in local conflicts and regional security.[17]

Yet while such new emphases apparent in 'African strategic studies' are to be welcomed — political economy, technology transfers, regional powers, local military industrial complexes, new Third World suppliers, and so on — the genre still remains essentially uncritical: the material bases of inter- and intra-state conflicts are not probed and military-civilian class and fractional coalitions are not treated.[18] In short, while the focus is broader and more relevant it still eschews radical concerns and conclusions: the class as well as corporate and country interests of officers, soldiers, suppliers and opponents. And the field is still marked by a prevalence, however misplaced and outmoded, of optimism: military development rather than social underdevelopment, security rather than instability and continued relevance rather than marginalisation. Nevertheless, the present heurism and potential utility of the new strategic studies for any political economy of foreign policy is significantly higher than that of the old formulations in Africa as elsewhere.

BEYOND NEO-COLONIALISM

The prerequisites for any critical and convincing analysis of African states befitting the 'post-neo-colonial' order of the current decade onwards are, then, to go beyond not only strategic conflicts and national interests but also (1) the artificial internal-international divide; (2) the diversion of dependence; (3) the assumption that leaders are 'compradors'; and (4) the over-concentration on super- rather than sub-structure. In other words, to situate peripheral (and semi-peripheral) social formations in the context of a changing international division of labour in which a cluster of transnational 'bourgeois' relations over technology and ideology have begun to effect new patterns of articulation. This means building on the recent positive evaluation of Korany which appeared ironically enough in that bastion of orthodox comparative studies, *World Politics*:

> . . . a political economy approach to foreign policy analysis is maturing . . . The link between comparative politics and international relations is . . . what we have been insisting upon since the 1960s. Nowhere are these two fields more organically connected than in the permeable societies of the Third World. If the 1980s witness the application of this linkage, we will be able to maintain the momentum of the take-off . .[19]

Reflective of the salience of this new juxtaposition — with its emphasis on inequalities within and between African states rather than further repetition of the old shibboleth about Africa's homogeneity and equality — is a remarkably non-dogmatic collection of East European Africanist scholarship assembled by Anatoly Gromyko of Moscow's Institute of African Studies on *African Countries' Foreign Policy* (Moscow: Progress, 1983). This volume emphasises sub- rather than super-structure, whilst appreciating the limits of economic determination and the resilience of politics on the continent: 'Differentiation — on a class not a national basis — is becoming increasingly typical of African foreign policy'.[20]

It also nicely situates the dialectic between continental integration and global marginalisation as Africa confronts the changing international division of labour:

> Any analysis of the foreign policy pursued by independent African countries should take into consideration two simultaneous processes in inter-African affairs. First, the trend toward unity, concerted action and comprehensive cooperation on the continental scale. Second, the socio-economic and political polarization of these countries . . . These centrifugal and centripetal trends affect the policies of each independent African country . . . The dialectical contradiction between consolidation and differentiation . . .[21]

Such divergencies or contrasts constitute the stuff of the new African diplomacy both practically and intellectually. They also constitute the heart of the new orthodoxy in African (historical) studies as a whole as reflected in Bill Freund's masterful work of radical synthesis — *The Making of Contemporary Africa* — which, as already noted, is characteristic, possibly classic, of current innovation. This general critical text redefines and relocates African history for the more troubled world — existential and intellectual — of the 1980s, thus providing a relevant and poignant context for current relations and investigations:

> . . . Africanist history can no longer seriously be taken as read: the synthesis envisioned by petty bourgeois nationalists in Africa and their would-be managers in the West is in disarray.
>
> This book therefore does not start with the old arguments about Africa having or loosing a history, with hypotheses about 'enlargement of scale' or balance sheets of good and bad in 'contact' with the West. It tries to adhere to the new critical tendencies emerging in Africa and elsewhere. The central themes which dominate the modern history of Africa are the penetration of capital with its relationship to political and economic imperialism and the resultant transformation of class and class struggle.[22]

BEYOND INEQUALITY

Differentiation in Africa can be seen to be increasing from the perspective of international political economy in at least four often interrelated ways: between states, between classes, within classes and between genders. The first division is based on very uneven and exponential patterns of growth: the minority of *Third* and majority of *Fourth* World countries, or the NICs versus the LLDCs.[23] The second contradiction is founded on different relations to the means of production (and decision): more versus less bourgeois. The third tension exists within such classes: national, bureaucratic-technocratic, comprador or military fractions within the indigenous bourgeoisie; more versus less aristocratic within the proleteriat; and big or small fractions within the peasantry. And finally, the 'gender gap' is both growing and increasingly recognised as women's role in agriculture as well as in the household becomes crucial in a period of economic decline. Taken together, these distinctions throw up a variety of new challenges for both African scholars and statespersons: how to go beyond established assumptions about inequalities and ideologies.[24]

Novel patterns of differentiation have produced, then, a variety of new relationships and *problématiques* for Africa at the levels of analysis and *praxis*, which exist below or beyond those of orthodox state centrism. Amongst the more central and controversial as articulated *en passant* in the new wave of books and by the underlying questions posed are: (1) the definition of the *post-neo-colonial state* in both theory and diplomacy; (2) the prospects for *African capitalism* based on the national fraction of the indigenous bourgeosie; (3) the potentials for *class coalitions* as well as contradictions in a period of economic contraction; (4) the possibilities for redefinitions of *gender relations* given the imperatives of agricultural revival and population control; and (5) the identification of alternative development strategies — self-reliance or reincorporation, informal sectors or reindustrialisation based on new international, national and sexual divisions of labour. Each of these issues has generated academic and political debates, with particular relevance for foreign policy, as reflected in the Gromyko volume:

> For a number of historical and socio-economic reasons, especially the weakness of the nascent working class, intellectuals and civil servants, including army officers, have today emerged as an influential force in many African countries. However, differentiation is under way among the people in this category too. Some . . . forge links with the indigenous businessman and form a group described as the 'bureaucratic bourgeoisie.' This differentiation is especially pronouced in foreign policy.

The analysis in this book also leads to the calculation that foreign policy factors exert a growing influence in the overall development of independent African countries.[25]

Gromyko *et al*, proceed to identify some of these foreign and development policy interconnections, which have intra- as well as inter-class and country implications:

> Pursuing primarily its purely self-serving class interests, the indigenous bourgeoisie in some developing countries often encourages closer political and economic relations with the more reactionary regimes . . . .[26]
>
> Today, social orientation has emerged as the decisive factor in this (continental) differentiation. This is especially evident in the choice of socialist or capitalist socio-economic orientation . . . Consequently, the trend toward forming different, relatively small political alliances and groups of both neighboring and non-neighboring countries is gaining strength in Africa.[27]

Although radical states and scholars have begun to challenge established aspects and interests, the latter have not been unresponsive in defending more orthodox policies and paradigms, for the reconsiderations provoked by the shocks of the last decade have generated their own responses.

BEYOND CONTRADICTIONS

Radical critiques combined with continuing difficulties symbolised by the Ethiopian famine have generated a range of revisionist responses located within the modernisation and realist *problématiques*, some of which treat new rather than old issues — for example, economics rather than politics or institutions — but in an orthodox manner. One of the more sophisticated of these is Robert Bates' anticipatory monograph on Africa's agricultural decline: *Markets and States in Tropical Africa*. An explicitly non-materialist exercise in political economy, *Markets and States* seeks to explain the food crisis — post-1980 a major concern of African(ist) scholars and planners — by reference to policies and politics rather than production and contradiction.[28] Like other non-Marxists, Bates takes such relations out of historical and social context. Instead of treating alienation and tensions resulting from production, he

> seeks to document the manner in which the governments have intervened in this market to transfer resources from the producers of cash crops to other sectors of society; the state itself; the new industrialists and manufacturers; and the bureaucracies . . .[29]

There is no sense here of class struggle or informal sector, of foreign relations or external transitions, all of which are central to the food-commodity nexus let alone to Basic Needs, national security or national interests; Bates is overly statecentric despite the palpable decline in the state nexus. Agricultural production in Africa as elsewhere involves class and fractional conflict, negotiations with external consumers and producers, and cycles in the global economy: 'intervention' is never disinterested nor discrete, as is apparent in any consideration of the growing 'parallel' economy with its official protectors. Rather, it is but one part of the process of social relations and the structure of social history. So although it is just possible still to describe and explain Africa's agricultural problems and politics in benign terms as Bates does, this lacks a certain plausibility, particularly given the recurrence of Ethiopian, Sahelian and other droughts and the generally catastrophic state of the continent's food sector:

> The agricultural policies of the nations of Africa confer benefits on highly concentrated and organized groupings. They spread costs over the masses of the unorganized. They have helped to evoke the self-interested assent of powerful interests to the formation of a new political order, and have provoked little organized resistance. In this way, they have helped to generate a political equilibrium.[30]

Such an idealised image of Africa projected by Bates — the 'golden age' of equilibrium — is not only ahistoric and uncritical; it is now also inaccurate — there *have* been a series of peasant revolts and circumventions — and misleading — the 'equilibrium' is as elusive as ever and decay now more likely than development. In short, Bates' assumption that development is a function of 'the capacity for autonomous choice on the part of local actors, both public and private'[31] is naive if not nonsense: history and position, let alone capitalism and colonialism, circumscribe and constrain any purpurted 'autonomous choice'. Yet this perspective has been dominant within the non-materialist political economy mode, a straight derivative of the modernisation-development-ethnicity nexus.[32]

Ironically, post-dependence neo-Marxist scholars reinforce the preference of Bates *et al*. for a national rather than international level of analysis whilst rejecting his espousal of a non-materialist perspective. So Ronald Munck's concept 'dependent reproduction'[33] is a partial reaction 'Against a general emphasis on the "external" factors causing underdevelopment; this current stresses the "internal" factors and in particular the relationships and struggles between social classes'.[34] By seeking a new balance between dependence and dialectic, and in drawing on the intricate Latin American debate, Munck can not only proceed to distinguish among peripheral social formations, he can also lay the basis for a reinterpretation of diplomacy; a purpose he may not identify or recognise himself but which scholars concerned with the social bases of foreign policy would appreciate.

A somewhat contrary trend, apparent particularly in studies of the never-ending Middle East 'crisis', is to concentrate on religious, especially Islamic, values rather than on political economy. Whilst the return to Islamic fundamentalism is an issue throughout that region, stretching over to Indonesia and Malaysia as well as down to Nigeria and Uganda, its independent impact on foreign policies has been quite limited: somewhat salient in Iran or Libya, much less so in Egypt and Morocco. A timely collection by Adeed Dawisha, on *Islam in Foreign Policy*[35] has a will-of-the-wisp quality to it. Islam can legitimise and rationalise but in few cases is it the primary factor despite any appearances to the contrary. Arab African states have always been schizophrenic between Arabia and Africa, compounded by Middle Eastern, European and global connections; the link which Bill Zartman attributes to Morocco[36] or the circles which many suggest for Egypt. In his own essay on Egypt in the Dawisha volume, Dessouki asserts that 'the experience of modern Muslim states shows that there is no specific foreign policy orientation that can be identified as Islamic'.[37] Compatible with his other work on Arab foreign policy, Dessouki argues that religion is instrumental not fundamental:

> Islam has primarily been a capability and a resource to Egypt's foreign policy. Both Abd al-Nasir and Sadat used Islam as an instrument. Islam was more of a rationale or vindication for policy choices, rather than a motivation or a constraint.[38]

The real pressures came from internal dissent — which has increasingly been clothed in fundamentalist garb — and external conditions — the unyielding global political economy. Islam provides some ideological touchstones not bureaucratic checklists: it does not undermine, and indeed may serve to reinforce, extant political economy.

Religious fervour correlates with social cycles rather than causes them; its diminution as a foreign policy variable is welcome on a number of levels.

BEYOND IDEOLOGY

Current changes in the global economy and in peripheral formations have generated novel social and survival structures — as well as foreign relations — as reflected in the debate about alternative development strategies. The issues of dominant fractions, political coalitions and policy directions come together over questions of African capitalism and of socialism in Africa, which may themselves coincide with distinctions between Third and Fourth World states, respectively.[39] If neo-Marxists like Bill Warren and Colin Leys are preoccupied by the former, then old-style structuralists of the Africa Institute remain committed to the latter. Eschewing troublesome notions of non-capitalist path or national democracy, and based on the near-classic cases of Angola, Benin, Ethiopia, and Tanzania, 'The Institute of African Studies of the USSR Academy of Science has calculated that the zone of socialist orientation in Africa and Asia comprises over 12 million square kilometers and about 150 million people'![40]

However, such 'socialism', let alone development, by decree (let alone by domino) in Africa has hardly brought about a proletarian, let alone a productive, revolution. Indeed, as Bates and others have indicated, under pressure from both social forces and international organisations — and not just the 'devilish' World Bank[41] and IMF — many of the supposedly 'socialist' states have moderated if not reversed their strategies over the last decade: increased producer prices, privatisation of parastatals, investment incentives, currency devaluations, and so on. The imperatives of such retreats are two-fold: the 'national interest' of economic revival and BHN satisfaction and the 'class project' of personal and fractional security and continuity, the ultimate redefinition of 'security' in an unstable and unimportant continent. These come together in more pragmatic programmes of the Bank's structural adjustment and Fund's conditionality as well as USAID's Economic Incentive Program, thus serving to undermine Africa's own preferred directions and priorities as expressed in the genesis of and revision to *The Lagos Plan of Action*[42]; hence the ironies of Arica's mid-1985 economic summit right in the middle of Ethopia's famine.

But such calculating ploys will not all be sustainable in the mid-term because of the marginalisation of African economies and proletariats and the scarcity of external interest and investment. Hence the overly stark alternative visions of either self-reliance or anarchy — along with intermediate types about to be proposed — recognising that these polar types are never likely to be completely realised in practice, but only to be abstracted as idealised goals. Nevertheless, their identification can serve to clarify alternative development directions, political positions and alternative futures. And Arlinghaus adds a crucial dimension to Africa's own formulation of self-reliance by including strategic as well as economic, political, psychological and cultural forms.[43]

BEYOND SCENARIOS

If the underlying goal of foreign policy is to ameliorate antagonistic contradictions, then that of development strategy is to avoid unattractive futures. The 'historical trends' scenario identified by the UN Economic Commission for Africa (ECA) at its recent silver jubilee celebrations projects an unattractive and unpromising mid-term for the continent — an absence of either security, growth or development — hence the desirability of transcending such troubled times through the adoption of an alternative 'willed future'.[44] The espousal of 'self-reliance', especially when broadened to include explicitly strategic factors, offers some prospect to embattled and devalued regimes of containing some internal and external contradictions including those of informal self-reliance, in a period of contraction and marginalisation: one way to respond positively to the challenges of the new division of labour. If such a reorientation is necessary in terms of policy it is even more so in terms of analysis. Ironically, some African international institutions, particularly the UN's regional organisation, the ECA, have been more innovative and progressive in this context than many African 'international relations' scholars, as befits the successor to ECLA's status as vanguard regional organisation.[45]

The new genre of African political economy points to the salience of distinctions between periods, between states and between social forces. As modes of production have evolved so have their social relations and formations. Hence the need for a new 'comparative politics' which treats political economy and focuses on changing class constellations: the succession of regimes and class coalitions. Such a framework already exists for Latin American studies with the sophisticated comparative critique and context advanced by Munck in *Politics and Dependence in the Third World*. In going beyond both orthodox *dependencia* and dialectics, he attempts to capture the essence of 'late capitalism' in which the 'bourgeois revolution' was despite stereotypes of that continent 'neither classically democratic, nor fascist, nor communist revolutionary,'[46] Rather, he proposes a 'periodization of capitalist development in Latin America'[47] centred on 'three main state forms: the oligarchic, populist and military' which share a common 'Latin' orientation: the 'bureaucratic-authoritarian' state.[48]

Such an approach with its emphasis on corporatism would clearly have implications for foreign relations as both analysis and practice in the late 20th century: the external links of bureaucratic authoritarian states with their domestic inter-class and fractional disputes. As African political economies also become more distinctive and 'corporatist', so we might expect their foreign policies to diverge: the external aspects of regimes dominated by some mixture of bureaucratic, technocratic and militaristic indigenous fractions. In particular, if the dichotomies suggested in the new wave of literature are salient, we might expect the divergence to intensify between African capitalist and African corporatist regimes.

African capitalism remains a controversial notion for both the modernisation —why 'capitalism'? — and materialism — why 'African'? — perspectives. It builds upon the state and class distinctions already identified within (semi-) peripheral social formations and suggests that in the Third World, at least, indigenous national fractions may yet achieve a dominance over other bourgeois forces, particularly those advancing bureaucratic and comprador interests. The former would be undermined by the privatisation preferences of the World Bank, while the latter would be discarded by international capital concerned more with reindustrialisation at home than by global reach abroad; that is, outside of the Fourth World, the established bureaucratic bourgeoisie may be an endangered species. In short, the prevailing direction within the problématique of the new international division of labour contains positive elements for the reinforcement of African capitalism: one possible, albeit perverse and non-socialist, form of self-reliance.

African corporatism, by contrast, is most likely to emerge in those Fourth World states in decline: the response of bureaucratic and military fractions to economic contraction and political tension. In such cases, capital, whether national or international, will be disinterested as the periphery is further marginalised, abandoning ex-neo-colonies to their hapless fate, except when occasional strategic (for instance, US bases in Somalia) or diplomatic (for example, recognition of Western Sahara) imperatives dictate otherwise. This is particularly so for the myriad island and enclave states long since discarded as their utility declined with shifts in merchant capital.[49] Such peripheral states will, alas, be most vulnerable to aberration (for instance, Nguema's Equatorial Guinea and Bokassa's Central African Empire) and anarchy (for example, the disintegration of Chad, Sudan or Uganda). By contrast, the relatively expansive capitalisms of Cote d'lvoire and Nigeria in West Africa or Kenya and Zimbabwe in Eastern Africa will attract further investment, assistance and migrants, even if to increasingly unequal economies. Growth at least perpetuates false hopes; decline serves only to smash them. Yet out of decay can emerge a renaissance as well as anarchy, particularly if informal economies have sustained and redirected communities in the interim.

Thus, the African continent is apparently faced with a stormy future, yet one which will continue to command some analytic, diplomatic and strategic attention.[50] The region with the most states, particularly that with the most impoverished states, cannot be completely dismissed, in either academic or economic terms, even if it is increasingly marginal. Furthermore, the decay and pathos, juxtaposed with occasional elements of optimism and expansion, will continue to demand attention and explanation.[51] African(ist)s may at times appear as vultures picking over decaying carcasses. But vultures can only exist in such a fashion, and the cadaver may yet revive depending on the degrees of decay, faith and fortune: a second chance in a post-neo-colonial, post-industrial world in which indigenous self-reliance[52] is an imperative rather than a preference? Marginalisation means minimal intervention, structural or strategic; an occasion for social and intellectual creativity which will go beyond orthodox focii on coups and crises and draw attention to and determination from structural conditions and contradictions, as illustrated by the authentic and non-dogmatic Dakar statement of May 1986 'For Democracy, For Development, For Unity':

> Africa today is caught up in a convergence of crises in all sectors of economic, political, social and cultural life . . .
>
> Everything is interrelated. The causes of Africa's economic problems themselves and the solutions they require cannot be pinpointed by purely economic analysis and therapy . . . the strategy

needed for the recovery and salvation of our continent must be deployed in three fundamental, interdependent areas: democracy, development and unity.[53]

NOTES

1. This review essay originally appeared in *Journal of Modern African Studies* 24(3) (September 1986) 489–508.
2. Bahgat Korany, 'Foreign Policy in the Third World: an introduction', *International Political Science Review* 5 (1984), 7.
3. (Boulder: Westview, and New York: NOK, 1977).
4. (London: Macmillan, 1984), (London: Longman, 1981) and (New Haven: Yale University Press, 1984).
5. See '70th birthday tribute to Basil Davidson', *Third World Book Review* 1 (3) (1985) 6–13.
6. See David F. Luke and Timothy M. Shaw, 'Introduction: continental crisis and the significance of the *Lagos Plan of Action*' in their collection on *Continental Crisis: the Lagos Plan of Action and Africa's Future* (Washington: University Press of America, 1984) 1–9.
7. For one attempt to relate these intellectual and evolutionary interactions among scholarly studies and organisations see Timothy M. Shaw, *Towards a Political Economy for Africa: the dialectics of dependence* (London: Macmillan, 1985), especially 104–08.
8. See Ali E. Hillal Dessouki and Bahgat Korany, 'A literature survey and a framework for analyses', 'The global system and Arab foreign policies: the primacy of constraints' and 'Foreign policy process in the Arab world: a comparative perspective' in their *Foreign Policies of Arab States*,(Boulder: Westview, 1984) 5–39, 323–31.
9. Dessouki and Korany, 'A literature survey and a framework for analysis', 2.
10. Dessouki and Korany, 'Foreign policy process in the Arab world', 329. One of them has since offered one comparative collection in response to the suggestion: Bahgat Korany (ed.), *How Foreign Policy Decisions are Made in the Third World: A Comparative Analysis* (Boulder: Westview, 1986).
11. Cf. the pioneering yet *dependentiste* collection by Petter Nore and Terisa Turner (eds), *Oil and Class Struggle* (London: Zed Press, 1980).
12. See Peter Evans' comparative conceptualisation based on the Brazilian case: *Dependent Development: the Alliance of Multinational, State and Local Capital in Brazil* (Princeton: Princeton University Press, 1979) 11 and 313.
13. See Bahgat Korany, 'Third Worldism and Pragmatic Radicalism: the Foreign Policy of Algeria' and 'Defending the Faith: the Foreign Policy of Saudi Arabia' in Korany and Dessouki *et al.*, *Foreign Policies of Arab States*, 103 and 277. On similar instances in the Nigerian case see Timothy M. Shaw and Olajide Aluko (eds), *Nigerian Foreign*

Policy: Alternative Perceptions and Projections (London: Macmillan and New York: St. Martin's Press, 1983), especially 26, 77–92 and 108–09.

14. See, for example, Arthur Gavshon, *Crisis in Africa: Battleground of East and West* (Harmondsworth: Pelican, 1981); cf. the rather ahistoric and static collection for the Council on Foreign Relations by William J. Foltz and Henry S. Bienen (eds), *Arms and the African: Military influences on Africa's International Relations* (New Haven: Yale University Press, 1985).
15. In addition to his personal monograph on *Military Development in Africa* (Boulder: Westview, 1984) Arlinghaus has recently edited *Arms for Africa: Military Assistance and Foreign Policy in the Developing World* (Lexington: Lexington Books, 1983) and *African Security Issues: Sovereignty, Stability and Solidarity* (Boulder: Westview, 1984). And he has just coedited with Pauline H. Baker *African Armies: Evolution and Capabilities* (Boulder: Westview, 1985).
16. Military as 'political modernisers' and 'nation builders', militarism becoming rampant, disarmament producing development, and new conventional weapons revolutionising military development (Arlinghaus, *Military Development in Africa*, 7–15).
17. William G. Thom, 'Sub-Saharan Africa's Changing Military Environment', *Armed Forces and Society*, 11(Autumn 1984) 55.
18. But see the radical strategic studies for Africa by Robin Luckham and Diwit Bekele, 'Foreign Powers and Militarism in the Horn of Africa', *Review of African Political Economy*, 30 (September 1984) 9–20 and 31 (December 1984) 7–28.
19. Bahgat Korany, 'The take-off of Third World studies? The case of foreign policy', *World Politics*, 35 (April 1983) 487.
20. Anatoly Gromyko *et al.*, *African Countries' Foreign Policy,* (Moscow: Progress, 1983) 197.
21. Ibid, 75.
22. Freund, *The Making of Contemporary Africa*, 14–15.
23. See Timothy M. Shaw, 'Non-Alignment and the New International Economic Order' in Herb Addo (ed.), *Transforming the World Economy? Nine Critical Essays on the New International Economic Order* (London: Hodder & Stoughton, 1984, for United Nations University) 138–62.
24. See Adebayo Adedeji and Timothy M. Shaw (eds), *Economic Crisis in Africa: African Perspectives on Development Problems and Potentials* (Boulder: Lynne Rienner, 1985).
25. Gromyko *et al.*, *African Countries' Foreign Policy*, 198.
26. Ibid, 169.
27. Ibid, 76.
28. See my attempt to focus on economy rather than ecology and informal rather than formal sector in 'Towards a political economy of the African crisis: diplomacy, debates and dialectics' in Michael Glantz (ed) *Drought and Hunger in Africa: denying famine a future* (Cambridge: Cambridge University Press, 1986) 127–47.

29. Robert H. Bates, *Markets and States in Tropical Africa: the political bases of agricultural policies* (Berkeley: University of California Press, 1981) 12.
30. Ibid, 129.
31. Ibid, 8.
32. For contemporary work within this neo-behavioural, non-structural mode see Donald Rothchild and Robert L. Curry, *Scarcity, Choice and Public Policy in Middle Africa* (Berkeley: University of California Press, 1978) and Donald Rothchild and Victor A. Olorunsola (eds), *State versus Ethnic Claims: African Policy Dilemmas* (Boulder: Westview Press, 1983).
33. See Ronaldo Munck, *Politics and Dependency in the Third World: the case of Latin America* (London: Zed Press, 1984) 31.
34. Ibid, 12.
35. (Cambridge: Cambridge University Press for Royal Institute of International Affairs, 1983).
36. See I. William Zartman, 'Explaining the nearly inexplicable: the absence of Islam in Moroccan foreign policy' in ibid., 97–111.
37. Ali E. Hillal Dessouki, 'The limits of instrumentalism: Islam in Egypt's foreign policy', in ibid., 85.
38. Ibid., 85.
39. See Timothy M. Shaw, 'The future of the Fourth World: choices of and constraints on the very poor in the 1980s' in Dennis Pirages and Christine Sylvester (eds), *The Transformation of the Global Political Economy* (London: Macmillan, 1989).
40. Gromyko *et al.*, *African Countries' Foreign Policies*, 51.
41. See the trio of IBRD reports on and responses to the African crisis, from the didactic 'Berg report' to a consensual 'programme': *Accelerated Development in Sub-Saharan Africa: an Agenda for Action* (1981), *Sub-Saharan Africa: Progress Report on Development Prospects and Programs* (1983), and *Toward Sustained Development in Sub-Saharan Africa: a Joint Program of Action* (1984).
42. See Adedeji and Shaw (eds), *Economic Crisis in Africa*, Robert S. Browne and Robert J. Cummings (eds), *The Lagos Plan of Action vs the Berg Report: contemporary issues in African Economic Development* (Washington: Howard University, 1984. Monograph in African Studies); and Timothy M. Shaw (ed.), *Alternative Futures for Africa* (Boulder: Westview Press, 1982).
43. See Arlinghaus, *Military Development in Africa*, 83–92. See also Celestine Bassey, 'Collective Amnesia or Perpetual Debate? The African Security Agenda' in Luke and Shaw (eds), *Continental Crisis*, 103–30.
44. See *ECA and Africa's Development 1983–2008: a preliminary perspective study* (Addis Ababa: ECA, April 1983), *passim*, especially 2 and 93–103.
45. See Shaw, *Towards a Political Economy for Africa*, 105–06.
46. Munck, *Politics and Dependence in the Third World*, 64.
47. Ibid, 353.

48. Ibid, 358. For a very promising attempt to supply such a nuanced perspective to African cases see Paul M. Lubeck (ed.), *The African Bourgeoisie: development in Nigeria, Kenya and Ivory Coast* (Boulder: Lynne Rienner, 1986).
49. See Robin Cohen (ed.), *African Islands and Enclaves* (Beverly Hills: Sage, 1983).
50. See, for example, new yet orthodox texts by Richard Hodder-Williams, *An Introduction to the Politics of Tropical Africa* (London: Allen & Unwin, 1984) and William Tordoff, *Government and Politics in Africa* (Bloomington: Indiana University Press, 1984).
51. For preliminary attempts to do so see, from contrary perspectives: Richard Sandbrook, *The Politics of Basic Needs: Urban Aspects of Assaulting Poverty in Africa* (Toronto: University of Toronto Press, 1982); Claude Ake, *A Political Economy of Africa* (London: Longman, 1981); and Jerker Carlsson (ed.), *Recession in Africa* (Uppsala: Scandinavian Institute of African Studies, 1983).
52. On the importance of the informal sector see Naomi Chazan and Donald Rothchild (eds), *The Reordering of the State in Africa* (Boulder: Westview, 1988) and Naomi Chazan and Timothy M. Shaw (eds), *Coping with Africa's Food Crisis:* (Boulder: Lynne Rienner, 1988).
53. See 'For democracy, for development, for unity. Declaration on Africa' *IFDA Dossier* 54 (July/August 1986), 40 and 41.

Index